Berlitz®

Italian BUSINESS PHRASE BOOK

Easy to use features

Handy thematic colour coding

•

Quick reference pronunciation guide — opposite page

•

Country factfile – inside back cover

•

Question and multiple response indicators throughout

How best to use this Phrase Book

This business phrase book has been designed to provide the handiest reference source to suit your business needs — whether you're on a trip to Italy, entertaining a Italian-speaking visitor, or corresponding by telephone, fax or letter with a Italian-speaking business partner.

- Consult the **Contents** pages (3-4) to locate the section you need. Separate, descriptive contents lists are included at the beginning of each chapter, to help you find your way around.
- Your fastest look-up is via the **English-Italian dictionary** (pp. 125-160), which contains over 2,500 essential business terms. For help in translating Italian documents, use the **Italian-English dictionary** (pp.161-191).
- For more technical terminology, consult **Industries and professions** (pp. 97-124). This section contains specific terms for use in 12 major business fields.
- Practical guidelines and the essential phrases for telephoning and introducing yourself and your company are provided in the section on **Making contact** (pp. 5-32).
- For more complex business situations, consult **Communication skills** (pp. 33-64). Sequenced phrases provide a progressive framework for developing meetings and negotiations successfully.
- For day-to-day business transactions, **Company departments** (pp. 65-96) provides the essential terms and model phrases for dealing effectively with your Italian-speaking counterpart.

Note: where applicable, feminine forms appear in parentheses, e.g. **ocupado (-a)**: feminine adjective ***ocupada***. With nouns, the appropriate feminine article should be substituted, e.g. **il direttore (-trice)**: feminine noun ***la direttrice***.

First edition 1996 Printed in Spain

CONTENTS

Projects and performance 56

Company departments 65

Industries and professions 97

English-Italian business dictionary 126

Italian–English business dictionary 161

Regional map of Italy 192

Acknowledgements

This material was developed in association with Nick Brieger and Jeremy Comfort of York Associates, and JOHN GREEN TEFL TAPES; business dictionaries were compiled by Peter Collin Publishing Ltd; our thanks also to Able Translations Ltd – a division of Berlitz International Inc. and Oxford Brookes Language Services for their help in the preparation of this book.

Making Contact

BUSINESS COMMUNICATION

On the Telephone

Formality is important: use titles and surnames, not first names – unless you know your Italian contact very well.

answering machine	**la segreteria telefonica**
code	**il codice**
conference call	**la teleconferenza**
direct line	**la linea diretta**
engaged/busy	**impegnato (-a)/occupato (-a)**
extension	**l'interno** *m*
get through	**passare**
international call	**la telefonata internazionale**
local call	**la telefonata locale**
switchboard	**il centralino**
telephone (n)/(v)	**il telefono/telefonare**
telephone directory	**l'elenco** *m* **telefonico**

Identifying yourself

● Hallo, ... Co./Inc. here.	● **... SpA, buongiorno.**
◗ Good morning/afternoon.	◗ **Buongiorno.**
◗ My name is ...	◗ **Il mio nome è/Mi chiamo ...**
◗ This is ... here.	◗ **Qui parla ...**

Asking to speak to someone

In Italian, the article precedes the title when referring to someone, though not when addressing them directly; for example, you'd ask to speak to **il signor Rossi**, but would greet him "**Signor Rossi!**"

INTRODUCTIONS, see page 23

Could I speak to ... please?	**Potrei parlare con il/la ... per favore?**
Could you put me through to ... please?	**Potrebbe passarmi il/la... per favore?**
Can I have extension 351 please?	**Posso parlare con l'interno 351, per favore?**
Could I speak to someone who deals with ...?	**Potrei parlare con qualcuno che si occupa di ...?**
◗ Who's calling?	**◗ Chi parla?, Chi lo/la desidera?**
◗ Could you tell me what it's about?	**◗ Potrebbe dirmi di che cosa si tratta?**
◗ Can I help you?	**◗ Posso esserle di aiuto?**
◗ Who would you like to speak to?	**◗ Con chi desidera parlare?**
◗ Speaking	**◗ Pronto/Si, sono io.**

Giving the reason for the call

It's in connection with ...	**È a proposito di ...**
It's about ...	**Riguarda ...**
I'm calling about ...	**Chiamo per ...**
I'm phoning to tell you ...	**Telefono per dirle che ...**
The reason I'm calling is ...	**Il motivo della mia chiamata è ...**

Making excuses

I'm afraid ______ is...	**Mi spiace il/la ______ ...**
not available.	**è impegnato (-a).**
in a meeting.	**è in riunione.**
with a customer at the moment.	**in questo momento è impegnato (-a) con un cliente.**
I'm sorry but ______ ...	**Spiacente ma il/la ______ ...**
is on holiday/vacation.	**è in vacanza.**
is not in the office.	**è fuori ufficio.**
is on the other line at present.	**è impegnato (-a) sull'altra linea.**
is no longer with the company.	**non lavora più in questa società.**
I'm afraid his line's engaged/ busy.	**Mi spiace ma il suo interno è occupato.**
Do you want to hold?	**Vuole attendere?**
Can I pass you to his ... assistant/colleague/ replacemen	**Posso passarle il suo/la sua ... assistente/collega/ sostituto(-a)**

INTRODUCING THE COMPANY, see pages 28 & 45

Taking a message

Would you like to leave a message?	**Desidera lasciare un messaggio?**
May I take a message?	**Vuole lasciare un messaggio?**
Can I take your name and number?	**Può lasciare il suo nome e il suo numero di telefono?**
Can I get him to call you back?	**Posso dirgli di richiamarla?**

Leaving a message

Could you give him a message?	**Potrebbe lasciargli un messaggio?**
Could you ask her to call me back? The number is ...	**Potrebbe dirle di richiamarmi? Il numero è ...**
Could you tell her I'll call back later?	**Potrebbe dirle che la richiamerò più tardi?**

Showing you understand

I see.	**Capisco.**
I understand.	**Ho capito.**
Right/Fine/Okay.	**D'accordo/Bene/Ok.**

Communication problems

Could you repeat that?	**Potrebbe ripetere, per favore?**
I'm sorry, I didn't catch your name.	**Mi spiace ma non ho afferrato bene il suo nome.**
● Could you spell that please?	**● Mi può dire come si scrive?**
◗ R-A-I-T.	**◗ R come Roma, A come Ancona, I come Imola, T come Torino.**
Could you speak a little slower/louder?	**Potrebbe parlare un po' più lentamente/forte?**
Let me just repeat that ...	**Mi lasci ripetere ...**

Ending the call

Thanks very much for your help.	**Molte grazie per il suo aiuto.**
I look forward ...	**Mi auguro di ...**
to seeing you soon.	**vederla presto.**
hearing from you soon.	**sentirla presto.**
Speak to you soon.	**A risentirci presto.**
Good-bye/Bye.	**Arrivederci/Ciao.**
Thanks for calling.	**Grazie per la telefonata.**

TELEPHONE ALPHABET, TELEPHONE NUMBERS, see page 18

Correspondence

Italian business letters tend to be brief and concise.

The Preliminaries

Bruno Graziano Srl *importatore • esportatore*

Vs/Rif: PR/AB
Ns/Rif: MF/104

Spett. Ditta Bertolino S.r.l.
Via Della Casa 3
Torino

Alla cortese attenzione del
Dott. Pinco Pallino

Padova 11 Agosto, 199_

OGGETTO: Vs ordine No. 1857

Spettabile (abbreviated to **Spett.**) **ditta** should precede the name of Italian companies when addressing them in letters and on envelopes.

Since the Italian postal service is not the most reliable, you may find faxing more successful.

Vinitalia S.p.A. ***Messagio del Fax***

A: Worldwide Wines Ltd
c.a.: Sig. Marco Molino
Fax N.: +44 01234 683445
Da: Pietro Garavelli
Fax N.: +39 01987 654321
N. pagine: 1
Data: 23 marzo 199_

The greeting

A greeting is only included in Italian letters if the correspondent is known personally. The equivalent of the impersonal 'Dear Sir(s)' is not used.

Dear Mr/Director Albi	**Egregio Direttor/Signor Albi**
Dear Mrs Bianchi	**Egregia Signora Bianchi**

Dear Professor Rossi	**Gentile Professor Rossi**

Note that **Direttore** and **Professore** drop the 'e' before a surname.

The start

Thank you for your letter of ______ (*date*), ...	**Grazie per la sua lettera del ______ ...**
I have received your letter of ______ (*date*), ...	**Ho ricevuto la sua lettera del ______ ...**
asking if/about ...	**con la quale chiede se/ riguardante ...**
enclosing ...	**con allegati ...**
in which you asked ...	**con la quale ci chiede ...**

Explaining the purpose

We are writing to enquire/ inquire about/whether ...	**Scriviamo per informarci ariguardo a/se ...**
I am writing in connection with ...	**Scrivo a proposito di ...**
In response to ...	**In risposta a ...**
With reference to ...	**Con riferimento a ...**
Further to ...	**Facendo seguito a ...**
With regard to ...	**Al riguardo di ...**

Requesting

We would be very grateful if you could ...	**Vi saremmo molto grati se poteste ...**
I would be much obliged if you could ...	**Vi sarei riconoscente se poteste ...**
We would appreciate it if you could ...	**Gradiremmo molto se poteste ...**
Please could you ... (*informal*)	**Potreste ...**

Giving information or replying to a request for information

Positive

Please find enclosed ...	**Alleghiamo alla presente ...**
We are happy to enclose ...	**Siamo lieti di allegare ...**
We wish to inform you that ...	**Desideriamo informarvi che ...**
We are pleased to inform you that ...	**Abbiamo il piacere di informarvi che ...**

Negative

We regret to inform you that ...	**Ci spiace informarvi che ...**
We are sorry to tell you that ...	**Siamo spiacenti di comunicarvi che ...**

Thanking

I am much obliged to you for sending me ...	**Vi sono molto riconoscente per avermi inviato ...**
I am grateful to you for ...	**Vi sono grato per ...**
We are much obliged to you for	**Vi siamo molto riconoscenti per ...**
Thank you for ... (*informal*)	**Grazie per ...**

Apologizing

We were extremely sorry to hear about the problem.	**Siamo estremamente spiacenti di aver appreso il vostro problema.**
We regret that this problem has happened.	**Ci spiace che questo imprevisto sia accaduto.**
We apologise for ...	**Ci scusiamo per ...**

Linking ideas

The following linking words show the relationship between your sentences and can make your letter easier to read.

Cause	
therefore	**perciò/per tanto**
so/consequently	**quindi/di conseguenza**
Comparison	
similarly/in the same way	**analogamente/nello stesso modo**
Contrast	
however/nevertheless	**tuttavia/ciò nonostante**
Addition	
in addition	**inoltre/anche**
also/too	**anche**
Equivalence	
in other words/that means	**in altri termini/vale a dire**

Inclusion	
for example/e.g.	**per esempio/p.e.**
such as/as follows	**cioè/come segue**
Highlight	
in particular/especially	**in particolare/specialmente**
mainly	**soprattutto**
Generalization	
usually/normally/as a rule	**di solito/generalmente/di norma**
Stating the obvious	
obviously/naturally	**ovviamente/logicamente**
of course	**naturalmente**
Summary	
in summary/to sum up	**riassumendo/per riassumere**
overall	**complessivamente**
in brief/short	**in breve/in poche parole**
Conclusion	
in conclusion/finally/lastly	**in conclusione/infine/da ultimo**

The closing

Please don't hesitate to contact if you need any further information.	**Non esitate a contattarci qualora aveste bisogno di ulteriori informazioni.**
We look forward to meeting/ hearing from you.	**Ci auguriamo di incontrarvi/ sentirvi presto.**
We look forward to receiving the proposal/your order/your reply.	**Restiamo in attesa della vostra proposta/del vostro ordine/di una vostra risposta.**

The farewell

Yours sincerely	**Cordialmente**
With best wishes	**Con i migliori auguri**
With best regards	**Cordiali saluti**

The enclosures

Encl.	**All. (allegato)**

The number of enclosures is usually included; eg. **All. 4**.

ARRANGING APPOINTMENTS

appointment	**l'appuntamento** *m*
calendar	**il calendario**
date	**la data**
diary	**l'agenda** *f*
meeting	**la riunione**
schedule	**il programma**
timetable	**l'orario** *m*

Opening

You may remember, ...	**Ricorderà probabilmente che ...**
we met at ...	**ci siamo incontrati ...**
... suggested I contact you.	**... mi ha suggerito di contattarla.**
I feel we should get together.	**Credo che dovremmo incontrarci.**
Mr/Mrs .... said he/she would like to talk about ...	**Il Signor .../La Signora ... ha detto che gradirebbe parlare di ...**
I'd like to tell you about ...	**Gradirei parlarle a proposito di ...**
I'd like to arrange a meeting.	**Gradirei organizzare una riunione.**
Let's fix a date.	**Fissiamo una data.**
Could we meet?	**Possiamo incontrarci?**
● Could you tell me what it's about?	● **Potrebbe dirmi di che cosa si tratta?**
● Why do want to see Mr. Rossi?	● **Per quale motivo vorrebbe vedere il Sig. Rossi?**
◗ I'd like to discuss ...	◗ **Gradirei discutere di ...**
◗ We need to talk about ...	◗ **Dobbiamo parlare di ...**

Arranging a time

Could you manage next week?	**Potrebbe andare bene la settimana prossima?**
What about Friday afternoon?	**Che ne dice di venerdì pomeriggio?**
Would Monday suit you?	**Le andrebbe bene lunedì?**
Shall we say 2 o'clock?	**Diciamo alle 2?**
◗ I'm afraid I can't manage Friday.	◗ **Mi spiace ma venerdì non posso.**
◗ Next week is out.	◗ **La prossima settimana non è possibile/non va bene.**
◗ Can you make the following week?	◗ **Va bene la settimana prossima?**

DATES, see page 15/TIME, see page 16

▸ Tuesday would suit me better. ▸ **Per me sarebbe meglio martedì.**
▸ 4 o'clock would be fine. ▸ **Alle 4 andrebbe bene.**

Duration

It'll have to be short. I've got another meeting at 5. **Dovrà essere breve. Ho un'altra riunione alle 17.**
It won't take more than an hour. **Non dovrebbe durare più di un ora.**

Place

Where do you suggest? **Dove suggerisce?**
I'll come to your office. **Verrò nel suo ufficio.**
Shall we meet in my office? **Ci incontriamo nel mio ufficio?**

Directions

Can you give me some directions? **Può indicarmi la strada?**
Will you be coming by car? **Verrà in macchina?**
I would take a taxi from the airport. **Prenderei un taxi dall'aeroporto.**
I'll fax you a map. **Le manderò una piantina via fax.**
Just ask for me at reception. **Basta chiedere di me all'entrata.**
My office is on the fifth floor (*US* sixth floor). **Il mio ufficio è al quinto piano.**

Ending

Let me just confirm that. Friday 24th, 3:30 at your office. **Glielo confermo. Venerdì 24, alle 15:30 nel suo ufficio.**
I look forward to seeing you then. **Allora l'aspetto.**
See you next Friday. **Ci vediamo venerdì prossimo.**

En route

Where can I get a taxi? **Dove posso prendere un taxi?**
Could you take me to ...? **Potrebbe portarmi ...?**
Could you tell me how to get to ...? **Potrebbe indicarmi la strada per ...?**
Where can I park? **Dove posso parcheggiare?**
▸ Straight ahead. ▸ **Sempre diritto.**
▸ Turn left/right. ▸ **Giri a sinistra/destra.**
▸ You'll see it on your right/left. ▸ **Lo troverà alla sua destra/ sinistra.**

TRAVELLING AROUND, see page 19

Arriving

My name's ...	**Il mio nome è ...**
I've got an appointment with ...	**Ho un appuntamento con ...**
◗ Please take a seat.	**◗ Prego si accomodi.**
◗ Mr ... will see you now.	**◗ Il Signor ... La riceverà subito.**
◗ She'll be with you shortly.	**◗ Sarà da Lei tra poco.**

Cancelling an appointment

Unfortunately, I'll have to cancel our meeting on ...	**Purtroppo, devo disdire la riunione del ...**
I'll be unable to make the meeting.	**Mi sarà impossibile tenere la riunione.**
Can we fix a new time? How about ...?	**Possiamo fissare un'altra ora? Che ne dice delle ...?**
◗ I'll check.	**◗ Controllerò.**
◗ I'm afraid that's not possible.	**◗ Mi spiace ma non è possibile.**

Months

January	**gennaio**
February	**febbraio**
March	**marzo**
April	**aprile**
May	**maggio**
June	**giugno**
July	**luglio**
August	**agosto**
September	**settembre**
October	**ottobre**
November	**novembre**
December	**dicembre**

Date

● What is the date today?	**● Che data è oggi?**
◗ It's the 1st January.	**◗ È il primo/1° gennaio.**
on September 7	**il sette/7 settembre**
in May	**a maggio**
from June to August	**da giugno ad agosto**
at the beginning of October	**all'inizio di/ai primi di ottobre**
in the middle of March	**a metà (di) marzo**
at the end of June	**alla fine di giugno**

Seasons

in spring	**in primavera**
in summer	**in/d'estate**
in autumn/fall	**in autumno**
in winter	**in/d'inverno**

Years

1996	**millenovecentonovantasei**
1998	**il millenovecentonovantotto**
2001	**il duemilauno**
in 2010	**nel duemiladieci**

Days

Monday	**lunedì**
Tuesday	**martedì**
Wednesday	**mercoledì**
Thursday	**giovedì**
Friday	**venerdì**
Saturday	**sabato**
Sunday	**domenica**

today	**oggi**
tomorrow	**domani**
the day after tomorrow	**dopodomani**
yesterday	**ieri**
the day before yesterday	**ieri l'altro**
the day before	**il giorno prima**
this Wednesday	**questo mercoledì**
next Friday	**venerdì prossimo**
a week on/from Tuesday	**martedì della settimana prossima**
by Thursday	**entro giovedì**
on Saturday	**sabato**
every Monday/on Mondays	**tutti i lunedì/di lunedì**
in 5 days' time	**fra cinque giorni**
last/next month	**il mese scorso/prossimo**
for 3 days	**per tre giorni**

Time of day

early morning	**al mattino presto**
morning	**in mattinata**

NUMBERS, see page 17

midday	**a mezzogiorno**
lunchtime	**all'ora di pranzo**
before lunch	**prima di pranzo**
after lunch	**dopo pranzo**
afternoon	**nel pomeriggio**
late afternoon	**nel tardo pomeriggio**
evening	**di sera**

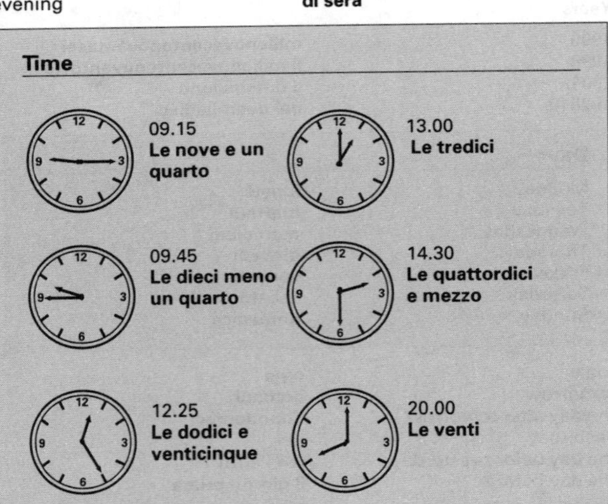

● What time does it start/end?	● **A che ora inizia/finisce?**
◗ at 9:00 am.	◗ **alle nove della mattina**
◗ by 3 o'clock	◗ **per le quindici**
● How long will it last?	● **Quanto durerà?**
◗ for 10 minutes	◗ **da dieci 10 minuti**
◗ from ... up to ...	◗ **dalle ... alle ...**
about ...	**circa verso le ...**
... exactly	**le ... esattamente/ precise**
... at the latest	**le ... al massimo**

Numbers

0	**zero**
1	**uno**
2	**due**
3	**tre**
4	**quattro**
5	**cinque**
6	**sei**
7	**sette**
8	**otto**
9	**nove**
10	**dieci**
11	**undici**
12	**dodici**
13	**tredici**
14	**quattordici**
15	**quindici**
16	**sedici**
17	**diciassette**
18	**diciotto**
19	**diciannove**
20	**venti**
21	**ventuno**
22	**ventidue**
30	**trenta**
40	**quaranta**
50	**cinquanta**
60	**sessanta**
70	**settanta**
80	**ottanta**
90	**novanta**
100	**cento**
110	**centodieci**
200	**duecento**
300	**trecento**
400	**quattrocento**
500	**cinquecento**
600	**seicento**
700	**settecento**
800	**ottocento**
900	**novecento**
1000	**mille**
1100	**millecento**
1200	**milleduecento**
2000	**duemila**
5000	**cinquemila**
10.000	**diecimila**
50.000	**cinquantamila**
100.000	**centomila**
1.000.000	**un milione**

Ordinal numbers

first (1st)	**primo (1°)**
second (2nd)	**secondo (2°)**
third (3rd)	**terzo (3°)**
fourth	**quarto**
fifth	**quinto**
sixth	**sesto**
seventh	**settimo**
eighth	**ottavo**
ninth	**nono**
tenth	**decimo**
hundredth	**centesimo**
millionth	**milionesimo**

Fractions etc.

a half	**un mezzo**
a quarter	**un quarto**
one third	**un terzo**
four fifths	**quattro quinti**
three point four (3.4)	**tre virgola quattro (3,4)**
once/twice/three times	**una volta/due volte/tre volte**

Telephone numbers

Telephone numbers are usually read in pairs.

00 44 - 60 96 12 extension 210	**zero zero quattro quattro, sessanta novantasei tredici interno duecentodieci**

Money

10,523.50 Lira	**Lire diecimilacinquecentoventitre e cinquanta (L.10.523,50)**
$10 per unit	**dieci dollari l'uno**
profits have doubled trebled/halved	**gli utili sono stati raddoppiati triplicati/dimezzati**

Measurements

1.2 metres/meters	**un metro e venti (1,2 m)**
500 litres/liters	**cinquecento litri**
in the region of ⅞ths	**nell'ordine di sette ottavi**
between 50 and 60 percent	**tra il cinquanta e il sessanta percento**
30-40,000	**trenta-quarantamila**
sales have dropped/risen by 30,000 units	**le vendite sono diminuite/ aumentate di trentamila unità**

Reference numbers

3580-16-22	**tremilacinquecentoottanta tratto sedici tratto ventidue**
254/DG	**duecentocinquantaquattro sbarra DG**

Alphabet pronunciation – Telephone alphabet

A ah	**Ancona**	I ee	**Imola**	R **erray**	**Roma**
B bee	**Bari**	J ee **loonga**		S **ehssay**	**Sassari**
C chee	**Catania**	K **kappah**		T tee	**Torino**
D dee	**Domo-dossola**	L ellay	**Livorno**	U oo	**Udine**
E ay	**Empoli**	M **emmay**	**Milano**	V vee	**Venezia**
F **effay**	**Firenze**	N **ennay**	**Napoli**	W vee **doappeeah**	
G jee	**Genova**	O o	**Otranto**	X eeks	
H **akkah**	**Hotel**	P pee	**Palermo**	Y ee **graykah**	
		Q koo	**Quarto**	Z **dzaytah**	

TRAVELLING AROUND

Travel by plane

Is there a flight to ...?	**C'è un volo per ...?**
When does it leave/take off?	**A che ora parte/decolla?**
When does it arrive/land?	**A che ora arriva/atterra?**
What time do I have to check in?	**A che ora devo fare il check-in?**

Booking and changing flights

ticket	**il biglietto**
single/one-way	**di sola andata**
business class	**business class**
I'd like to book a return/round-trip flight to...	**Vorrei prenotare un volo di andata e ritorno per ...**
I'd like to cancel/change my reservation on flight number ...	**Vorrei cancellare la mia prenotazione per il volo numero ...**

Travel by train

platform	**il binario**
ticket office	**la biglietteria**
ticket reservation	**la prenotazione**
timetable	**l'orario** *m*

Enquiring about rail travel

When is the next train to...?	**Quando c'è il prossimo treno per ...?**
What's the fare to...?	**Qual è la tariffa per ...?**
Do I have to change?	**Devo cambiare?**
When does it arrive at ...?	**Quando arriva a ...?**
Which platform does the train leave from/arrive at?	**Da quale binario parte/arriva il treno?**

Buying a ticket

I'd like a ... ticket to ______	**Vorrei un biglietto ... per ______**
single/one-way	**di andata**
return/round trip	**di andata e ritorno**
first-class	**di prima classe**
I'd like to reserve a seat.	**Vorrei fare una prenotazione.**

On the train

buffet/restaurant car	**il vagone ristoro/ristorante**
couchette/sleeping car	**il vagone cuccette/letto**
first-class compartment	**lo scompartimento di prima classe**
Is this the right train to...?	**È questo il treno che va ...?**
Is this seat taken?	**È occupato questo posto?**
I think that's my seat.	**Credo che sia il mio posto.**

Travel by taxi

Could you get me a taxi?	**Potrebbe chiamarmi un taxi?**
Where is the taxi rank/stand?	**Dov'è il posteggio dei taxi?**
Take me to ...	**Mi porti ...**
the Trade Fair	**alla Fiera Campionaria**
this address	**a questo indirizzo**
Please stop here.	**Si fermi qui, per favore.**
Could you wait for me?	**Mi può aspettare?**
I'll be back in 10 minutes?	**Sarò di ritorno fra 10 minuti.**
How much do I owe you?	**Quanto le devo?**
Keep the change.	**Tenga pure il resto.**

Travel by car

Car hire/rental

I'd like to hire/rent a car.	**Vorrei noleggiare una macchina.**
medium-sized	**media**
automatic	**con cambio automatico**
with air-conditioning	**con aria condizionata**
Is mileage included?	**Il chilometraggio è compreso?**
I'd like to leave the car in ...	**Vorrei lasciare la macchina a ...**
How much is the deposit?	**Quant'è la cauzione?**
I'd like full insurance.	**Vorrei un'assicurazione globale.**

At the petrol/gas station

Could you fill it up, please?	**Può farmi il pieno, per favore.**
Give me ... litres/liters, please.	**Mi dia ... litri, per favore.**
petrol/gasoline	**la benzina**
regular/premium/unleaded	**normale/super/senza piombo**

Garage–Breaking down

My car's broken down.	**La mia macchina ha avuto un guasto.**
May I use your phone?	**Posso usare il suo telefono?**
My car won't start.	**La mia macchina non parte.**
The battery is dead.	**La batteria è scarica.**
I've run out of petrol.	**Sono rimasto senza benzina.**
I've got a flat tyre/tire.	**Ho uno pneumatico a terra.**
There's something wrong with the ...	**C'è qualcosa che non va con ...**
carburettor/carburetor	**il carburatore**
windscreen/windshield wipers	**i tergicristallo**
Please check the ...	**Per cortesia mi controlli ...**
battery	**la batteria**
brakes	**i freni**
spare tyre/tire	**la ruota di scorta**
tyre/tire pressure	**la pressione dei pneumatici**

Accidents

Where's the nearest telephone?	**Dov'è il telefono più vicino?**
Where's the nearest garage?	**Dov'è l'officina meccanica più vicina?**
Could you call an ambulance?	**Potrebbe chiamare un' ambulanza?**
Here's my driving licence/ driver's license.	**Ecco la mia patente (di guida).**
What's your name and address?	**Può darmi il suo nome e il suo indirizzo?**
What's your insurance company.	**Qual è la sua compagnia di assicurazioni?**

Directions

Go straight ahead.	**Vada sempre diritto.**
It's on the left/right.	**È sulla sinistra/destra.**
opposite/behind ...	**di fronte/dietro a ...**
next to/after ...	**di fianco a/dopo ...**
Turn left at the ...	**Giri a sinistra al ...**
next corner	**prossimo isolato**
traffic lights	**semaforo**
Take the A3.	**Prenda la A3.**
You have to go back to ...	**Deve tornare indietro fino a ...**

Accommodation

Booking a room

I'd like a single room for two nights.	**Vorrei una camera singola per due notti.**
From ... to ...	**Dal ... al ...**
single room	**camera singola**
double room	**camera doppia**
twin-bedded room	**camera a due letti**
family room	**camera con letto aggiuntivo**
with bath/shower	**con bagno/doccia**
I'd like a room with a shower.	**Vorrei una camera con doccia.**
It must be quiet.	**Deve essere tranquilla.**
I'll be arriving late.	**Arriverò tardi.**
How much does it cost?	**Quanto costa?**
Do you accept credit cards?	**Accettate carte di credito?**

Registering at a hotel

● My name's ...	**● Il mio nome è ...**
● I've got a reservation for two nights.	**● Ho una prenotazione per due notti.**
◗ Could you fill in this form?	**◗ Compili questo modulo per favore.**
◗ How will you be paying?	**◗ Come pagherà?**
◗ May I see your credit card?	**◗ Posso vedere la sua carta di credito?**

Complaining

Could I have a quieter room?	**Potrei avere una camera più tranquilla.**
My room's too small/noisy.	**La mia camera è troppo piccola/rumorosa.**

Checking out

May I have the bill please?	**Posso avere il conto per favore?**
I'm leaving early in the morning so could you have the bill ready?	**Può prepararmi il conto dato che domattina parto presto?**
There's a mistake in this bill.	**C'è un errore nel conto.**
Can you order a taxi please?	**Mi potrebbe chiamare un taxi per favore?**

DATES, see page 15

INTRODUCTIONS

Italians always shake hands on meeting and taking leave, even with business colleagues seen every day.

Greetings

Good morning/afternoon.	**Buon giorno.**
Good evening.	**Buona sera.**
How do you do?	**Piacere di conoscerla.**
Pleased to meet you.	**Lieto (-a) di conoscerla.**
Here's my card	**Ecco il mio biglietto**

Introducing yourself

My name's ...	**Il mio nome è ...**
I'm ...	**Sono ...**
Please call me ...	**La prego mi chiami pure ...**
Everybody calls me ...	**Tutti mi chiamano ...**

Responding

How do you do? I'm ...	**Piacere. Sono ...**
Pleased to meet you too. Mine's ...	**Piacere mio. Il mio nome è ...**
Nice to meet you too.	**Sono lieto (-a) anch'io.**

Introducing others

When introducing someone, use **il signor** (Mr) or **la signora** (Mrs/Ms) before the surname, followed by their title or position, if known. Note that **Dottore** can apply to any graduate, not just a medical doctor.

May I introduce you to ...	**Posso presentarle ...?**
Have you two met?	**Vi siete già conosciuti prima?**
This is ...	**Questo è ...**
Mr. Rossi, director of marketing	**il Signor Rossi, Direttore del marketing**
Mrs. Bianchi, sales manager	**la Signora Bianchi, Direttor delle vendite**
my colleague, Mr. Peters	**il mio collega, il Signor Peters**

Everyday greetings

● How are you?	**● Come sta?**
◗ Fine, and you?	**◗ Bene, e Lei?**

◗ Not so bad.	◗ **Non c'è male.**
◗ Could be worse.	◗ **Potrebbe andare peggio.**

Presenting your job

● What do you do?	● **Di che cosa si occupa?**
● What line are you in?	● **In quale settore lavora?**
◗ I'm a ...	◗ **Sono ...**
secretary	**segretario (-a)**
an engineer	**ingegnere**
an accountant	**ragioniere**
◗ I work in ...	◗ **Lavoro presso ...**
an insurance company	**una compagnia di assicurazioni**
a school	**una scuola**
◗ I work for ...	◗ **Lavoro per ...**
IBM/the local newspaper	**l'IBM/il giornale locale**
a pharmaceutical company	**una società farmaceutica**
◗ I'm on the ... side.	◗ **Sono nel campo ...**
technical/commercial	**tecnico/commerciale**
administrative	**amministrativo**
◗ I'm in ...	◗ **Mi occupo di ...**
marketing	**marketing**
sales/finance	**vendite/finanze**
◗ I'm self-employed/ retired	◗ **Sono un(a) libero (-a) professionista/pensionato (-a).**

Origins

● Where do you come from?	● **Da dove viene?**
● Where are you from?	● **Di dove è?**
● Where do you live?	● **Dove abita?**

◗ I come from ...	*I'm ...*	◗ **Vengo ...**	***Sono ...***
Belgium	*Belgian*	**dal Belgio**	***belga***
Britain	*British*	**dalla Gran Bretagna**	***inglese/ britannico (-a)***
Canada	*Canadian*	**dal Canada**	***canadese***
England	*English*	**dall'Inghilterra**	***inglese***
France	*French*	**dalla Francia**	***francese***
Germany	*German*	**dalla Germania**	***tedesco (-a)***
Ireland	*Irish*	**dall'Irlanda**	***irlandese***
Scotland	*Scottish*	**dalla Scozia**	***scozzese***
Switzerland	*Swiss*	**dalla Svizzera**	***svizzero (-a)***
United States	*American*	**dagli Stati Uniti**	***americano (-a)***
Wales	*Welsh*	**dal Galles**	***gallese***

COMPANY POSITIONS, see page 28

Socializing

For after-hours socializing in Italy, it is much more common to be invited to a restaurant than to someone's home. Punctuality varies from region to region. 15 minutes late may be acceptable in the south, but even 5 minutes would be frowned upon in the north.

Arriving

● How was your trip?	● **Com'è andato il suo viaggio?**
● How was the journey?	● **Com'è andato il viaggio?**
◗ Not bad.	◗ **Abbastanza bene.**
◗ No problems.	◗ **Senza problemi.**
◗ Rather long.	◗ **Piuttosto lungo.**
● When did you arrive?	● **Quando è arrivato (-a)?**
● When did you get in?	● **Quando è arrivato (-a)?**
● Did you ... take the train/fly? come by car?	● **Ha preso ... il treno/l'aereo? in macchina?**
◗ I came by car/I drove.	◗ **Sono venuto (-a) in macchina./Ho guidato io.**
◗ I took the last flight.	◗ **Ho preso l'ultimo volo.**

Leaving

● I'm leaving tomorrow.	● **Riparto domani.**
◗ What time does your plane leave?	◗ **A che ora parte il suo aereo?**
◗ When do you have to check in?	◗ **Quando deve fare il check-in?**
Could you book a taxi for me?	**Mi può prenotare un taxi?**
I need a taxi to take me to the airport.	**Ho bisogno di un taxi per andare all'aeroporto.**
How long do you think it will take?	**Quanto impiegherò ad arrivare?**

Accommodation

● How's your hotel?	● **Com'è il suo albergo?**
◗ Yes, it's fine.	◗ **Sì, va bene.**
◗ It's OK.	◗ **È ottimo.**
◗ It's a bit noisy.	◗ **È un pò rumoroso.**

Weather

● What was the weather like when you left?	● **Come era il tempo quando è partito (-a)?**

TRAVELLING AROUND, see page 19/ACCOMMODATION, see page 22

◗ Much the same as here.	◗ **Quasi come qui.**
◗ Very sunny.	◗ **Molto soleggiato.**
◗ Lovely and warm.	◗ **Bello e caldo.**
◗ Dreadful.	◗ **Terribile.**
◗ Cold for the time of year.	◗ **Freddo per questa stagione.**
What a lovely day!	**Che bella giornata!**
What awful weather!	**Che tempo orribile!**
What's the weather forecast?	**Quali sono le previsioni del tempo?**

Family

● Are you married?	● **È sposato (-a)?**
◗ Yes, my wife is ...	◗ **Sì, mia moglie è ...**
◗ My husband is ...	**Mio marito è ...**
◗ No, I'm single.	◗ **No, sono celibe/nubile.**
I'm divorced.	◗ **Sono divorziato (-a).**
● Have you got any children?	● **Ha figli?**
◗ Yes, two boys and a girl.	◗ **Sì, due maschi e una femmina.**
one daughter/three sons	**una femmina/tre maschi**
● How old are they?	● **Quanti anni hanno?**
◗ They're ten and twelve.	◗ **Hanno dieci e dodici anni.**
◗ The oldest/youngest is ...	◗ **Il più grande/piccolo ha ...**
◗ Oh, they've left home.	◗ **Vivono da soli.**

Interests

● What do you do at/on the weekends?	● **Cosa fa nel fine settimana?**
● Are you interested in sports?	● **Le piace lo sport?**
● Do you play any sports?	● **Pratica qualche sport?**
◗ I play football/golf/tennis.	◗ **Gioco a calcio/golf/tennis.**
◗ I don't play but I watch ...	◗ **Non gioco ma guardo ...**
◗ I go ... fishing/swimming/walking	◗ **Vado ... a pesca/in piscina/a piedi**

Invitations

● Would you like to come to/for dinner?	● **Verrebbe a cena?**
◗ I'd love to./I'd like that very much.	◗ **Mi piacerebbe./Con molto piacere.**
◗ I'd love to but ...	◗ **Mi piacerebbe ma ...**

◗ I'm afraid I can't.	◗ **Mi spiace ma non posso.**
◗ I've got another engagement.	◗ **Ho un altro impegno.**
● Could you manage next Tuesday?	● **È libero (-a) martedì prossimo?**
◗ Tuesday would be fine.	◗ **Martedì va benissimo.**
● How about a drink after work?	● **Che ne dice di andare a bere qualcosa dopo il lavoro?**
◗ Good idea.	◗ **Ottima idea.**
● Let me buy you a drink.	● **Posso offrirle qualcosa da bere?**
◗ That's very kind of you.	◗ **Molto gentile, grazie.**

Dining out

Arriving & ordering

We've booked a table for four.	**Abbiamo prenotato un tavolo per quattro.**
Could we sit by the window, please?	**Possiamo sederci vicino alla finestra?**
Are you having a starter/dessert?	**Prende un antipasto/dessert?**
I'd recommend the fish.	**Le consiglierei il pesce.**
What are you going to have?	**Che cosa prende?**
I think I'll have the beef.	**Penso che prenderò della carne di manzo.**
Could you tell me what ... is?	**Mi può dire che cos'è ...?**

Commenting

The fish is delicious.	**Il pesce è squisito.**
Are you enjoying the beef?	**Le piace il manzo che ha preso?**
Thank you for a lovely meal.	**Grazie per il pasto squisito.**

Paying

Could I have the bill?	**Il conto, per favore.**
Do you accept ... credit card?	**Accettate la carta di credito ...?**
Is the service included?	**Il servizio è compreso?**

Saying goodbye

I'm afraid we must go now.	**Mi spiace ma ora dobbiamo andare.**
I look forward to seeing you again soon/next year.	**Mi auguro di rivederla presto/il prossimo anno.**
Good-bye/Bye.	**Arrivederci/Ciao.**

Introducing the company

Sectors

Heavy Industry	**l'industria pesante**
Manufacturing	**l'industria manufatturiera**
Services	**i servizi**

Types of company

company	**la società**
firm	**la ditta, l'azienda *f*, l'impresa *f***
sole trader	**l'imprenditore (-trice) in proprio**
partnership	**il partnership, la società**
limited company	**la società a responsabilità limitata (S.R.L.)**
public limited company	**la società per azioni (S.P.A.)**
cooperative	**la società accomandita semplice (S.A.S.)**
state company	**l'impresa *f* a partecipazione statale**
private company	**la società privata**

Parts of company

Head Office/Headquarters	**la sede centrale il direzione generale**
Parent company	**la casa madre**
Holding company	**la società finanziaria**
Subsidiary	**la consociata**
Business Unit	**l'unità *f* operativa**
Branch	**la filiale**
Sales Office	**l'ufficio *m* commerciale**
Division	**la divisione**
Department	**il servizio**
Section	**la sezione**

Position in a company

Companies are generally hierarchical, especially the larger ones. Status is considered important in all Italian companies.

Board of Directors	**il consiglio di amministrazione**
Chairman *(public representative of the company)*	**il/la presidente**

PERSONNEL, see page 86

Managing Director/CEO *(head of board of directors)*	**l'amministratore (-trice) delegato (-a)**
Vice President	**il/la vice presidente**
Director	**il/la consigliere (-a) di amministrazione, il Direttore (-trice)**
Manager	**il/la dirigente**
Supervisor	**l'ispettore (-trice) sorvegliante, il capo intermedio**
Assistant	**l'assistente** *m*
Shop floor worker	**le maestranze** *f*
Office staff	**personale impiegatizio** *m*

People in a company

headcount	**la forza lavoro**
staff	**gli impiegati**
personnel	**il personale**
management	**la direzione, l'amministrazione** *f*
workers	**gli operai**

People around the company

suppliers	**i fornitori**
customers	**i clienti**
clients	**il cliente**
agents	**gli agenti**
distributors	**i distributori**
dealers	**i concessionari**

Location

We're based in ...	**La nostra sede è ...**
Our head office is located in ...	**La nostra sede centrale si trova a ...**
We have branches throughout the world.	**Abbiamo filiali in tutto il mondo.**

Activity

We're in the telecommunications field.	**Siamo nel campo delle telecomunicazioni.**
We're a leading company in ...	**Siamo una società leader nel settore ...**
There are three major business units.	**Ci sono tre unità operative principali.**

Size

There are four partners in the firm.	**La società ha 4 partner/soci.**
We employ 20,000 people.	**Gli addetti sono 20.000.**
We have 20,000 employees.	**Abbiamo 20.000 dipendenti.**
We have an annual sales/ turnover of $250 million.	**Il fatturato è di $250 milioni.**
Annual profits are in the region of $25 million.	**Gli utili annuali sono di circa $25 milioni.**

Career development

I started as a foreman on the shop floor.	**Ho iniziato come caposquadra in officina.**
I got promoted to plant manager.	**Sono stato (-a) promosso (-a) a direttore (-trice) impianto (-a).**
I was recently appointed Production Director.	**Sono stato (-a) nominato (-a) recentemente Direttore (-trice) di produzione.**
I'm due to retire next year.	**Andrò in pensione il prossimo anno.**
I've stayed with the same company.	**Sono rimasto (-a) nella stessa azienda.**
I've worked for ... since 1988/ for 20 years.	**Ho lavorato per ... dal 1988/ per 20 anni.**
I joined the company 20 years ago.	**Sono entrato (-a) in azienda 20 anni fa.**
I've changed jobs often.	**Ho cambiato spesso lavoro.**

Company history

The company was founded in 1884.	**L'azienda è stata fondata nel 1884.**
We set up the company in 1982.	**Abbiamo costituito la società nel 1982.**
The company was first registered in 1982.	**L'azienda è stata registrata nel 1982.**
It went public 2 years ago.	**E' quotata in borsa da 2 anni.**
The company was taken over by Blaskins.	**La società è stata rilevata dalla Blaskins.**
Later we merged with ...	**Successivamente vi è stata la fusione con ...**

NUMBERS, see page 17/DATES, see page 15

Introducing the product

product line	**la linea di prodotti**
product attributes	**gli attributi del prodotto**
product features	**le caratteristiche del prodotto**
product benefits/advantages	**l'utilità *f* del prodotto i vantaggi**
Our main product is ...	**Il nostro prodotto principale è ...**
We have two major product lines:	**Abbiamo due linee principali di prodotti ...**
It is designed to ...	**È stato progettato per ...**
Its main application is in the ... industry.	**La sua principale applicazione è nel campo dell'industria ...**

Life & service

after sales/customer service	**post vendita/servizo clienti**
maintenance	**la manutenzione**
repairs	**le riparazioni**
replacement	**la sostituzione**
It will last at least ten years.	**Durerà almeno dieci anni.**
You won't have to replace it before ten years.	**Non dovrà sostituirlo per almeno dieci anni.**
It should be regularly serviced.	**Deve essere sottoposto a manutenzione programmata.**
We have a 24-hour help desk.	**Forniamo un servizio assistenza 24 ore su 24.**
Any repairs will be carried out on site.	**Tutte le riparazioni saranno eseguite sul posto.**

Delivery

You can expect delivery within 2 weeks.	**Consegna prevista entro 2 settimane.**
The earliest delivery will be next month.	**Le prime consegne avverranno il prossimo mese.**
The delivery may be delayed by 24 hours.	**La consegna potrebbe essere rinviata di 24 ore.**

Price

low/cheap	**basso (-a)/conveniente**
medium/reasonable	**medio (-a)/ragionevole**
high/expensive	**alto (-a)/caro (-a)**
We can offer you a 15% discount.	**Possiamo concedere uno sconto del 15%.**

CUSTOMER SERVICE, see page 66/PRODUCTS, see page 82

Touring the premises

office building	**il palazzo uffici**
plant/factory	**lo stabilimento/la fabbrica**

Offices

board room	**la sala consiglio**
canteen/company restaurant	**la mensa/il ristorante aziendale**
corridor	**il corridoio**
floors	**i piani**
lift	**l'ascensore** *m*
meeting room	**la sala riunioni**
open-plan design	**la configurazione 'spazi aperti'**

Office furniture & equipment

desk	**la scrivania**
fax machine	**il fax**
filing cabinet	**l'archivio** *m*
PC	**il PC**
photocopier	**la fotocopiatrice**
printer	**la stampante**
work station	**il posto di lavoro**

Plant layout

components	**i componenti**
despatch/dispatch area	**il settore spedizioni**
factory floor	**l'officina** *f*
machine room	**il reparto macchine**
paint shop	**la verniciatura**
raw materials	**le materie prime**

Showing visitors around

I'm pleased to welcome you to ...	**Sono lieto (-a) di darvi il benvenuto a ...**
Welcome to ...	**Benvenuti a ...**
Please come this way.	**Prego da questa parte.**
Follow me.	**Seguitemi.**
Be careful!	**Fate attenzione!**
Mind/Watch your head!	**Attenti alla testa!**
Over there, you can see ...	**Da quella parte, potete vedere ...**
Are there any questions?	**Ci sono domande?**

Communication Skills

BUSINESS PRESENTATIONS

Check-list

To help you organize your presentation, it is useful to plan it around the following stages:

1. The introduction	❑	**1. The introduction**
2. The overview	❑	**2. The overview**
3. The main part	❑	**3. The main part**
4. The summary	❑	**4. The summary**
5. The ending	❑	**5. The ending**
6. Questions and answers	❑	**6. Questions and answers**

1. The introduction

Good morning/afternoon, ladies and gentlemen/colleagues.	**Buon giorno/Buona sera, signore e signori/colleghi.**
My name is ...	**Il mio nome è/Mi chiamo ...**
I work for Rossomon as Marketing Director.	**Sono il direttore del Marketing della Rossomon.**
I am the Personnel Director at Rossomon.	**Sono il capo del personale della Rossomon.**

INTRODUCTIONS, see page 23/COMPANY POSITIONS, see page 28

In this talk, I'd like to ...	**In questo intervento, vorrei ...**
describe the main activities of our company.	**descrivere le principali attività della nostra società.**
present our product range.	**presentare la nostra gamma di prodotti.**
explain the production processes at our plant.	**spiegare i processi produttivi nel nostro stabilimento.**

2. The overview

I've divided my talk into 4 main parts.	**Ho suddiviso il mio intervento in 4 parti principali.**
My presentation is split into 4 major sections.	**La presentazione è suddivisa in 4 sezioni principali.**
In the description, I aim to cover the 4 key processes.	**Nella descrizione, intendo trattare i 4 processi chiave.**
Firstly, we'll look at ...	**In primo luogo, vedremo ...**
Secondly, I'm going to talk about ...	**In secondo luogo, parlerò di ...**
After that, I'll tell you about ...	**Successivamente, vi darò notizie su ...**

The order of points

First(ly)	**In primo luogo**
Second(ly)	**In secondo luogo**
Third(ly)	**In terzo luogo**
Fourth(ly)	**In quarto luogo**
After that	**Poi**
Next	**Successivamente**
Finally	**Infine**

3. The main part

Now let's look at the first point.	**Vediamo ora il primo punto.**
Now I'd like to start the first part.	**Vorrei ora iniziare la prima parte.**

Ending a point

That's all about ...	**Questo è tutto su ...**

NUMBERS, see page 17

That's all I want to say about the first point.	**Questo è tutto quello che dovevo dire sul primo punto.**
That brings me to the end of the first part.	**Questo mi porta alla conclusione della prima parte.**

Moving on to the next point

Next let's look at ...	**Vediamo ora ...**
Now I'd like to move on to the next point.	**Vorrei ora passare al prossimo punto.**
So now I'd like to talk about ...	**Quindi vorrei ora parlare di ...**

Visual aids

As you can see on the transparency, ...	**Come potete vedere sui lucidi ...**
You can see the relevant information ...	**Potete vedere le informazioni pertinenti ...**
on the screen	**sullo schermo**
on the monitor	**sul monitor**
on the transparency	**sul lucido**
in the illustration	**sull'illustrazione**
in the drawing	**sul disegno**
from the model	**dal modello**
from the plan	**dal progetto**

The relevant figures are shown ...
I valori pertinenti sono rappresentati ...

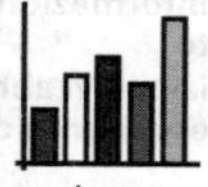

on the pie/bar chart	by a solid/broken/dotted line
con il diagramma a torta/ l'istogramma *m*	**con una linea continua/ tratteggiata/punteggiata**

The shaded boxes ...	**I riquadri ombreggiati ...**
The unshaded circles ...	**I cerchi non ombreggiati ...**
The blue triangles ...	**I triangoli azzurri ...**
The red rectangles ...	**I rettangoli rossi ...**
show the major activities.	**rappresentano le principali attività.**

COLOURS/COLORS, see page 36

Colours/Colors

black	**nero (-a)**	light blue	**azzurro (-a)**
blue	**blu**	orange	**arancio**
brown	**marrone**	pink	**rosa**
dark ...	**... scuro (-a)**	purple	**viola**
golden	**dorato (-a)**	red	**rosso (-a)**
green	**verde**	silver	**argentato (-a)**
grey/gray	**grigio (-a)**	white	**bianco (-a)**
light ...	**... chiaro (-a)**	yellow	**giallo (-a)**

4. The summary

Well, that brings me to the end of my final point. — **Bene, questo mi porta alla conclusione del punto finale.**

That concludes the main part of my talk. — **Con questo ho concluso la parte principale del mio intervento.**

So now, I'd just like to summarize the main points. — **Vorrei ora riassumere semplicemente i punti principali.**

In brief, we have looked at ... — **In sintesi, abbiamo visto ...**

5. The ending

That's all I have to say for now. — **Al momento ritengo di non aver altro da aggiungere.**

I hope that ... — **Mi auguro che ...**
- the presentation has given you all the relevant information for your needs. — **la presentazione vi abbia fornito tutte le informazioni che cercavate.**
- the description has provided you with a clear picture of our activities. — **la descrizione vi abbia fornito un quadro esauriente delle nostre attività.**

6. Questions and answers

Are there any questions? — **Ci sono domande?**

Your question, please. — **La sua domanda, prego.**
Any more questions? — **Ci sono altre domande?**
Does that answer your question? — **Ho risposto alla sua domanda?**
If there are no more questions, I'd like to thank you for your attention. — **Se non ci sono altre domande, vorrei ringraziarvi per la vostra attenzione.**

MEETINGS, CONFERENCES AND TRADE FAIRS

Preparing for the meeting

a chairperson	**un presidente**
the participants	**i partecipanti**
an agenda	**un ordine del giorno**
a secretary	**un segretario (-a)**
the minutes	**i verbali**

The agenda

point	**il punto**
item	**la voce**
AOB (any other business)	**Altre ed eventuali**
to prepare	**preparare**
to draft	**redigere**
to circulate	**distribuire**

The time and place

I'd like to call a meeting to discuss ...	**Vorrei indire una riunione per discutere ...**
I'd like to fix a time and place for the meeting.	**Vorrei fissare l'ora e il luogo della riunione.**
Does Monday at ... o'clock suit you?	**Va bene per voi lunedì alle ...?**
We are planning to meet in my office/the meeting room.	**Pensiamo di riunirci nel mio ufficio/nella sala riunioni.**

Preparing the agenda

I've prepared an outline agenda.	**Ho preparato uno schema dell'ordine del giorno.**
Could you look through it, please?	**Può esaminarlo per favore?**
Could you add any points you'd like to discuss?	**Ci sono altri punti da aggiungere che vorrebbe discutere?**
Could I ask you to lead item 2 on staff training?	**Potrebbe seguire lei il punto 2 sulla formazione del personale?**
I've finalized the agenda.	**L'ordine del giorno è pronto.**
You'll receive all the papers tomorrow.	**Riceverà tutti i documenti domani.**

ARRANGING APPOINTMENTS, see page 12/TIME, see page 16

The Chairperson's role

Opening the meeting

Good morning/afternoon, ladies and gentlemen/colleagues.	**Buon giorno/Buona sera, signore e signori/colleghi.**
If we are all here ... let's start./shall we start?	**Se ci siamo tutti, ... iniziamo./possiamo iniziare?**
First of all I'd like to introduce ...	**Prima di tutto vorrei presentarvi ...**
Would you like to say a few words about yourselves?	**Volete parlare brevemente di voi?**
Have you all got a copy of the agenda?	**Avete tutti una copia dell'ordine del giorno?**
The objective/purpose/aim/target of this meeting is to ...	**L'obiettivo/La finalità/Lo scopo/Il fine di questa riunione è ...**
Now let's look at the agenda in detail.	**Vediamo ora in dettaglio l'ordine del giorno.**
As you can see there are four main points/items.	**Come potete vedere ci sono quattro punti/voci principali.**
I think we will need about 30 minutes for point 1, 20 minutes for point 2, ...	**Penso che occorrano circa 30 minuti per il primo punto, 20 minuti per il secondo punto, ...**
We will break for coffee/lunch at ...	**Faremo una pausa per il caffè/pranzo alle ...**
We aim to finish at ... o'clock.	**Abbiamo intenzione di finire alle ...**
Is that OK for everybody?	**Va bene per tutti?**

Moving to points on the agenda

Let's look at the first point.	**Vediamo ora il primo punto.**
I'd like to start with item one.	**Vorrei iniziare con la prima voce.**
OK, Marianne, over to you.	**Bene Marianna, può iniziare.**
I believe you're going to lead this one.	**Penso tocchi a lei gestire questo punto.**
Can I ask you to present the background information?	**Può illustrare i precedenti?**
Right. Let's move on to the next point.	**Bene. Passiamo al punto successivo.**

NUMBERS, see page 17/TIME, see page 16

Pietro, would you like to introduce the next point?	**Pietro, vuole presentare il punto successivo?**
OK, on to item 2.	**Bene, ora passiamo alla voce 2.**

Keeping the meeting on track

Inviting contributions

What's your opinion on this, Liz.	**Qual'è la sua opinione, Liz?**
Guido, we haven't heard from you yet.	**Guido, non abbiamo ancora sentito la sua voce.**
Would you like to add anything, Giancarlo?	**Vuole aggiungere qualcosa, Giancarlo?**

Stopping people talking

We can't all speak at once. Mario first, then Liz, then Guido.	**Non possiamo parlare tutti insieme. Prima Mario, poi Liz, e infine Guido.**
One at a time, please!	**Uno per volta, per piacere!**
Well, thank you, Giancarlo. I think that's clear now. Could we have some other opinions?	**Bene, grazie, Giancarlo. Penso che sia chiaro adesso. Possiamo sentire altre opinioni?**

Dealing with problems of comprehension

I'm sorry. I didn't hear what you said. Would you mind repeating it, please?	**Mi spiace ma non ho sentito che cosa ha detto. Potrebbe ripeterlo, per favore?**
I'm sorry. I don't quite follow you.	**Mi spiace ma proprio non la seguo.**
Could you go over that again, please.	**Potrebbe spiegarsi meglio, per favore?**
What exactly do you mean by ...?	**Che cosa intende esattamente con ...?**

Preventing irrelevance

I'm afraid that's outside the scope of this meeting.	**Temo che ciò esuli dall'argomento di questa riunione.**
We're beginning to lose sight of the main point.	**Stiamo perdendo di vista il punto principale.**

Keep to the point, please.	**Si attenga all'argomento, per favore.**
We're running short of time.	**Ci rimane poco tempo.**
Please be brief.	**Siate brevi, per favore.**

Paraphrasing

So what you're saying is ...	**Quindi sta dicendo che ...**
In other words ...	**In altre parole ...**
So you mean ...	**Dunque secondo lei ...**

Controlling decision-making

I'd like to (formally) propose that ...	**Vorrei proporre (formalmente) che ...**
Can we take a vote on that proposal?	**Possiamo votare su quella proposta?**
All those in favour/favor. Right. All those against. Right, thank you.	**Tutti quelli a favore. Bene. Tutti quelli contro. Bene, grazie.**
So that motion has been accepted/rejected by 4 votes to 3.	**Quindi la mozione è stata accettata/respinta con 4 voti contro 3.**

Summarizing & minuting/recording

To sum up then, ...	**Per riassumere quindi, ...**
So far we have agreed that ...	**Finora siamo d'accordo che ...**
Could you minute/record that, please?	**Può metterlo a verbale, per favore?**
Have you minuted/recorded that?	**Lo ha messo a verbale?**

Concluding a point on the agenda

So, on point one we have agreed that ...	**Quindi, sul punto uno siamo d'accordo che ...**
we have accepted the figures.	**abbiamo accettato i dati.**
That leaves two follow-up tasks.	**Questo ci lascia due compiti da portare a termine.**
Diego, could you prepare some information for the next meeting?	**Diego, può preparare qualche informazione per la prossima riunione?**

Guido, when could we have the results of your survey?	**Guido, quando potremo avere i risultati dell'indagine?**
Well, I think that covers everything on that point.	**Bene, penso che con ciò abbiamo trattato esaurientemente quel punto.**

Closing the meeting

Right. That just about covers everything.	**Bene. Abbiamo trattato praticamente tutti gli argomenti.**
So, the next meeting will be on ... (*date*) at ... (*time*)	**La prossima riunione si terrà il ... alle ...**
I'll circulate the minutes of this meeting in the next few days.	**Distribuirò una copia del verbale di questa riunione nei prossimi giorni.**
Thanks for your participation.	**Grazie per la vostra partecipazione.**
Right, I declare the meeting closed.	**Bene, dichiaro chiusa la riunione.**

The Participants' role

Getting the chair's attention

(Mister/Madam) chairman.	**(Signor/Signora) presidente.**
Excuse me for interrupting.	**Mi scusi per l'interruzione.**
May I come in here?	**Posso entrare?**
I'd like to comment on that.	**Vorrei fare un commento in proposito.**

Giving opinions

strongly

I'm convinced/sure/positive that ...	**Sono convinto (-a)/sicuro (-a)/ certo (-a) che ...**
I strongly believe that ...	**Sono fortemente convinto (-a) che ...**
I definitely/certainly think that ...	**Ritengo assolutamente/ sicuramente che ...**

neutrally

I think/consider that ...	**Penso/Considero che ...**
As I see it, ...	**Secondo me, ...**
From my point of view ...	**Dal mio punto di vista ...**

weakly

I'm inclined to think that ...	**Sono propenso (-a) a pensare che ...**
I tend to think that ...	**Tendo a pensare che ...**

Making recommendations

Shall we hear the figures now?	**Può darci i dati, ora?**
Let's discuss the results first.	**Prima discutiamo i risultati.**
I suggest we postpone the decision till the next meeting.	**Suggerisco di rinviare la decisione alla prossima riunione.**

Agreeing or disagreeing with others

Full agreement

I totally agree with you.	**Sono perfettamente d'accordo con lei.**
I'm in total agreement with you on that point.	**Sono perfettamente d'accordo con lei su quel punto.**
I'm all in favour/favor of that proposal.	**Sono totalmente favorevole a quella proposta.**

Partial agreement

Up to a point, I agree with you, but ...	**Fino a un certo punto, sono d'accordo con lei, ma ...**
Of course, on the other hand ...	**Naturalmente, d'altra parte ...**
You could/may be right, but ...	**Può/Potrebbe avere ragione, ma ...**

Disagreement

I don't agree with you on that point.	**Non sono d'accordo con lei su quel punto.**
I can't accept that proposal.	**Non posso accettare quella proposta.**
I disagree totally.	**Non sono assolutamente d'accordo.**

Conferences

congress	**il congresso**
symposium	**il simposio**
seminar	**il seminario**
convention	**il convegno**
to attend	**intervenire**
to participate	**partecipare**
to take part in	**prender parte**
chairperson	**il presidente**
participant	**il/la partecipante**
delegate	**il delegato (-a)**
speaker	**il relatore (-trice)**
keynote speaker	**il relatore (-trice) introduttivo (-a)**
presenter	**il presentatore (-trice)**

Introducing the speaker

It gives me great pleasure to introduce Dr Stefano Gerardi.	**È con grande piacere che vi presento il Dott. Stefano Gerardi.**
I am very pleased to present Professor Marina Scaiola.	**Sono molto lieto di presentarvi la Professoressa Marina Scaiola.**
He is going to present the findings of his latest research.	**Presenterà i risultati dell'ultima indagine.**
She will deliver a paper entitled 'Management 2000'.	**Illustrerà un documento intitolato 'Management 2000'.**

Research and findings

findings	**i rilevamenti**
results	**i risultati**
conclusions	**le conclusioni**
outcome	**l'esito** *m*

Addressing the audience

Ladies and gentlemen	**Signore e signori**
Dear colleagues	**Cari colleghi**
It gives me great pleasure to address you today on ...	**È con grande piacere che oggi mi rivolgo a voi ...**
I should also like to thank ... for sponsoring me.	**Vorrei anche ringraziare ... per avermi sponsorizzato.**

INTRODUCTIONS, see page 23

Thanking the speaker & inviting questions

I should like to thank Dr Stefano Gerardi for his most interesting talk.	**Vorrei ringraziare il Dott. Stefano Gerardi per il suo interessantissimo intervento.**
Dr Gerardi's talk touched many important issues.	**Il discorso del Dott. Gerardi ha toccato molti argomenti importanti.**
So now, there will be an opportunity for questions.	**Siamo così giunti al momento delle domande.**
Are there any questions or comments?	**Ci sono domande o commenti?**
Yes, your question, please.	**Sì, la sua domanda prego.**

Concluding the talk

I'm afraid that I will have to interrupt this interesting discussion.	**Mi dispiace di dover interrompere questa interessante discussione.**
I'd like, once again, to thank Professor Scaiola.	**Vorrei ringraziare, ancora una volta, la Professoressa Scaiola.**
It is now time to move on to the next speaker.	**Passiamo ora all'oratore successivo.**
We have scheduled a lunch break/coffee break until ...	**Abbiamo previsto una pausa per il pranzo/caffè fino alle ...**
The next talk will start at ... o'clock.	**Il prossimo intervento inizierà alle ...**

Concluding the conference

It has been a very interesting conference.	**È stato un convegno molto interessante.**
We have heard a range of stimulating presentations.	**Abbiamo ascoltato una serie di presentazioni molto stimolanti.**
It has been ...	**È stato (-a) ...**
inspiring	**ispiratore (-trice)**
intriguing	**intrigante**
provocative	**provocatorio (-a)**
Finally, we look forward to seeing you all again next year in Miami.	**Per concludere ci auguriamo di riverdervi tutti il prossimo anno a Miami.**

QUESTIONS & ANSWERS, see page 36

Exhibitions and Trade Fairs

The Exhibitor's role

Introducing yourself and your company

Good morning/afternoon. My name's ...	**Buon giorno. Mi chiamo ...**
Here's my card.	**Ecco il mio bigliettino.**
Do you know our company?	**Conosce la nostra società?**
I'm sure you know our organization.	**Sono sicuro (-a) che conosce la nostra azienda.**
We make/provide ...	**Produciamo/Forniamo ...**
We are the largest company in our field.	**Siamo l'azienda più grande nel nostro settore.**

Finding out about your visitor

What do you do?	**Di che cosa si occupa?**
Who do you work for?	**Per chi lavora?**
What do they do?	**Che attività svolge la sua azienda?**
Would you like some information about our products/services?	**Posso fornirle informazioni sui nostri prodotti/servizi?**
Any specific product/service?	**Qualche prodotto/servizio in particolare?**
What exactly would you like to know?	**Che cosa vorrebbe sapere esattamente?**

Giving information to the visitor

We have a number of products which can ...	**Abbiamo numerosi prodotti che possono ...**
For your needs, I would recommend ...	**Per le vostre esigenze, raccomanderei ...**
This product/service ...	**Questo prodotto/servizio ...**
is just right for your needs.	**è proprio quello che vi serve.**
exactly covers your needs.	**risponde esattamente alle vostre esigenze.**
could be the answer.	**potrebbe essere la soluzione.**
may be able to solve your problem.	**potrebbe risolvere il vostro problema.**

GREETINGS, see page 23/INTRODUCING THE COMPANY, see page 28

I'm afraid we don't make anything like that.	**Mi spiace ma non produciamo niente di simile.**
I'm sorry but we can't provide that service.	**Sfortunatamente non siamo in grado di fornire quel servizio.**
Please take a copy of our brochure/leaflet/prospectus.	**Prenda pure una copia del nostro opuscolo/depliant/prospetto.**
It contains all the product information.	**Contiene tutte le informazioni sui prodotti.**

Planning follow-up action

Would you like …	**Gradirebbe …**
someone to visit your company?	**che qualcuno visitasse la sua società?**
us to prepare a quotation?	**che preparassimo un preventivo?**
to discuss this over lunch/ dinner/a coffee?	**discutere questo argomento a pranzo/a cena/mentre prendiamo un caffè?**
to return to the stand/booth later?	**ritornare allo stand più tardi?**
a demonstration of the equipment?	**una dimostrazione dell'attrezzatura?**
We'd be delighted to …	**Saremmo lieti di …**
visit your company	**visitare la vostra azienda.**
prepare a quotation	**preparare un'offerta.**
discuss this later	**discutere su questo argomento più tardi.**

Saying goodbye

We'll be in touch with you next week/month.	**Ci metteremo in contatto con voi la prossima settimana/il prossimo mese.**
Good-bye.	**Arrivederci.**

The Visitor's role

Explaining your areas of interest

I am interested in …	**Sono interessato (-a) a …**
I would like to know more about …	**Gradirei maggiori informazioni su …**

INTRODUCING THE PRODUCT, see page 31

Questioning the exhibitor

Could you explain exactly ...	**Potrebbe spiegarmi esattamente ...**
what this product does?	**a che cosa serve questo prodotto?**
how this machine works?	**come funziona questa macchina?**
where this service is provided?	**dove fornite questo servizio?**
if this service is available here?	**se questo servizio è disponibile qui?**

Planning follow-up action

I/We would like ...	**Gradirei/Gradiremmo ...**
someone to visit our company.	**che qualcuno visitasse la nostra società.**
to have a quotation.	**ricevere un preventivo.**
to discuss this further.	**discutere ulteriormente questo argomento.**
to see a demonstration.	**assistere ad una dimostrazione.**
I look forward to hearing from you.	**Mi auguro di sentirla presto.**

Communication difficulties

Could you speak ...	**Potrebbe parlare ...**
a bit slower, please?	**un po' più lentamente, per favore?**
a bit louder, please?	**un po' più forte, per favore?**
I'm sorry ...	**Scusi, ...**
could you repeat that, please?	**potrebbe ripetere, per favore?**
what exactly do you mean by ...?	**potrebbe ripeterlo, per favore?**
Could you explain that, please?	**Mi puo' spiegare, per favore?**

Showing understanding

I see.	**Capisco.**
I understand.	**Comprendo.**
Yes, I've got that now.	**Sì, adesso ho capito.**
Yes, that's clear now.	**Sì, adesso è chiaro.**

NEGOTIATIONS

Check-list

To help you prepare your negotiation, it is useful to plan it around the following stages:

1. Creating the right environment	❑	**1. Creazione dell'ambiente adatto**
2. Defining the issues	❑	**2. Definizione degli argomenti**
3. Establishing opening positions	❑	**3. Definizione dei punti iniziali**
4. Handling the offer and counter-offer	❑	**4. Gestione dell'offerta e contro offerta**
5. Testing the other side's case	❑	**5. Valutazione degli argomenti della controparte**
6. Strengthening your case	❑	**6. Sostenimento della propria posizione**
7. Handling stalemate	❑	**7. Gestione di una posizione di stallo**
8. Clinching the deal	❑	**8. Conclusione della trattativa**
9. Getting it in writing	❑	**9. Conferma scritta**
10. The legal aspects	❑	**10. Aspetti legali**

The processes

to negotiate	**trattare**
to bargain	**contrattare**
to discuss	**discutere**
to persuade	**persuadere**
to compromise	**venire a un compromesso**
to make a deal	**concludere un affare**
to strike a bargain	**condurre in porto una contrattazione**
to reach agreement	**raggiungere un accordo**
to draft a contract	**redigere un contratto**
to sign the contract	**firmare il contratto**

to implement the agreement	**attuare l'accordo**
to break the contract	**rompere il contratto**

The subject of negotiation

price	**il prezzo**
delivery and terms	**la consegna e termini**
payment and credit	**il pagamento e credito**
discount	**lo sconto**
licences/licenses	**le licenze**
warranties and guarantees	**le garanzie**
penalties	**la penalità**
legal jurisdiction	**il foro competente**

1. Creating the right environment

For key phrases for introducing yourself and making small talk, see Section 1 Making Contact: Introductions and Socializing.

2. Defining the issues

Stating the agenda

OK. Shall we start?	**Bene. Cominciamo?**
Our position is as follows:	**La nostra posizione è questa:**
We would like to buy ...	**Vorremmo acquistare ...**
We are interested in selling ...	**Ci interessa la vendita di ...**
We need to reach agreement about ...	**Dobbiamo raggiungere un accordo su ...**
We are eager to make a decision about ...	**Vorremmo veramente prendere una decisione su ...**
The aim/purpose/target/ objective of this negotiation is to solve the problem over ...	**Il fine/Lo scopo/L'obiettivo/ L'intento di questa trattativa è la soluzione del problema relativo a ...**

Clarifying the agenda

So, if we understand you correctly, you want to sell ...	**Quindi, se abbiamo ben capito, voi vorreste vendere ...**

INTRODUCTIONS, see page 23/SOCIALIZING, see page 25

So, are we right in thinking that you would like us to sell ...?	**Quindi, abbiamo capito bene che vorreste che noi vendessimo ...?**
We fully understand your views/position ...	**Comprendiamo benissimo il vostro punto di vista ...**
but what would you actually like us to do?	**ma che cosa vorreste che facessimo in realtà?**
but what precisely are you offering?	**ma che cosa offrite esattamente?**

3. Establishing opening positions

Price

In your proposal ...	**Nella vostra proposta ...**
your asking price is ...	**il prezzo di offerta è di ...**
you have set the price at ...	**avete fissato il prezzo a ...**
We are willing to pay ...	**Siamo disposti a pagare ...**
Our initial offer is ...	**La nostra offerta iniziale è di ...**

Delivery and terms

In addition, we/you can deliver the goods on 25th July.	**Inoltre, possiamo/potete consegnare la merce il 25 luglio.**
we can supply the products by 25th July.	**possiamo fornirvi i prodotti entro il 25 luglio.**
Our position is that we need the goods by 20th July.	**La nostra posizione è che abbiamo bisogno della merce entro il 20 luglio.**
Can you arrange delivery to our site by truck?	**Potete disporre per la consegna con autotrasporto alla nostra sede?**
However, you expect us to provide transport and insurance.	**Tuttavia, prevedete che da parte nostra si provveda al trasporto e all'assicurazione.**
However, you do not agree to pay for ...	**Tuttavia, non siete d'accordo a pagare per ...**

Payment and credit

We expect payment by bank transfer ...	**Prevediamo pagamento tramite bonifico bancario ...**
within 60 days.	**entro 60 giorni.**
90 days after invoice.	**90 giorni dalla data della fattura.**

PAYMENT, see page 77/DISTRIBUTION, see page 71

Our normal payment terms are by letter of credit. — **I nostri pagamenti avvengono di norma con lettera di credito.**

Do you accept our payment terms? — **Accettate le nostre condizioni di pagamento?**

We do not normally pay ... — **Di norma non paghiamo ...**
in cash — **in contanti**
by bank transfer — **con bonifico bancario**

Discount

However, we can offer an initial discount of 5%. — **Possiamo tuttavia concedere uno sconto iniziale del 5%.**

But we are prepared to reduce the total price by 5%. — **Siamo disposti tuttavia a ridurre il prezzo totale del 5%.**

What discount can you offer? — **Che sconto potete concedere?**

Licences/Licenses

What licence/license can you offer? — **Che tipo di licenza potete concedere?**

We are prepared to offer a licence/license to sell the product. — **Siamo disposti a concedere una licenza per la vendita del prodotto.**

We cannot grant a licence/license to manufacture the product. — **Non possiamo concedere una licenza per la fabbricazione del prodotto.**

The licence/license will initially be limited to 5 years. — **La licenza avrà una validità iniziale di 5 anni.**

Warranties and guarantees

What warranties and guarantees do you offer? — **Quali garanzie fornite?**

We warrant the goods for a period of 5 years. — **Le nostre merci sono garantite per 5 anni.**

We cover all parts and labour/labor for 1 year. — **Accordiamo una garanzia di 1 anno (ricambi e manodopera).**

You must return the goods. — **Le merci devono essere restituite.**

In that case, ... — **In tal caso, ...**
we will replace the goods. — **la merce sarà sostituita.**
we will repair the equipment free of charge. — **l'apparecchiatura sarà riparata gratuitamente.**

PRICING, see page 84/DATES, see page 14

We cannot guarantee the goods against ...	**La garanzia non interviene in caso di ...**
breakdown	**danneggiamenti accidentali**
normal wear and tear	**usura normale**

Penalties

What happens if anything goes wrong?	**Cosa accade in caso di imprevisti?**
What compensation will you ...? pay if ...?	**Quale indennizzo prevedete se**
We will claim compensation if ...	**Pretenderemo l'indennizzo in caso di ...**
you don't deliver on time.	**ritardata consegna.**
the goods are delayed.	**arrivo ritardato delle merci.**
the equipment breaks down.	**danneggiamenti delle apparecchiature.**

Legal jurisdiction

What happens if there is a dispute?	**Che cosa accade in caso di controversia?**
Any disputes will be settled according to Italian law.	**Eventuali controversie saranno definite secondo la legislazione italiana.**
We resolve any disagreements by arbitration.	**Risolviamo eventuali divergenze con arbitrato.**

4. Handling the offer and counter-offer

Positive

That's great.	**Ottimo (-a).**
(That's a) good/excellent/great idea.	**È una buona/eccellente/ottima idea.**
We accept/agree.	**Accettiamo./Siamo d'accordo.**
We can accept your payment/ delivery/discount terms.	**Possiamo accettare le vostre condizioni di pagamento/ consegna/sconto.**
We are in agreement over penalty clauses.	**Siamo d'accordo sulle clausole penali.**

LEGAL DEPARTMENT, see page 78/CONTRACT LAW, see page 122

Partial

Yes, but ...	**Va bene, ma ...**
We're on the right track.	**Siamo sulla strada giusta.**
We're getting there.	**Ci siamo quasi.**

Negative

That's out of the question.	**È fuori discussione.**
We can't accept that.	**Non possiamo accettarlo.**
We don't agree to that.	**Non siamo d'accordo.**
We are not in agreement over compensation clauses.	**Non siamo d'accordo sulle clausole di indennizzo.**

5. Testing the other side's case

Have you given us all the relevant facts?	**Ci avete illustrato tutti i fatti pertinenti?**
On what are those figures based?	**Su che cosa si basano quei dati?**
We have heard that ...	**Ci risulta che ...**
your normal prices are ...	**i vostri prezzi ordinari sono ...**
normal delivery terms are ...	**le vostre condizioni di consegna sono ...**
We don't follow the logic of your argument.	**Non seguiamo la logica del vostro ragionamento.**
If your normal prices are ..., then we expect ...	**Se i vostri prezzi ordinari sono ..., allora ci attendiamo che ...**
Could you explain how you got to those figures?	**Potreste chiarire come avete ottenuto quei dati?**

6. Strengthening your case

If we accept ...	**Se accettiamo ...**
your prices, then we will have to raise our prices.	**i vostri prezzi, dovremo poi aumentare i nostri.**
That will not be good for our business.	**Non è un elemento positivo per la nostra azienda.**
If you can reduce your price by ..., then we will ...	**Se potete ridurre il vostro prezzo di ..., allora potremo ...**

GIVING OPINIONS, see page 41

If you are prepared to speed up delivery by ..., then we will ...	**Se siete disposti ad accelerare la consegna di ..., allora potremo ...**
If you are willing to reconsider your payment terms, then we will ...	**Se siete disposti a riconsiderare le vostre condizioni di pagamento, potremo ...**
look at prices for our next contract.	**rivedere i prezzi per il prossimo contratto.**

7. Handling stalemate

We are very far apart on this issue.	**Le nostre posizioni sono molto lontane su questo argomento.**
Our positions are very different on the question of ...	**Le nostre posizioni divergono notevolmente su ...**
I don't think we can resolve this matter now.	**Non penso che la questione possa essere risolta adesso.**
Let's see where we agree ...	**Vediamo quali sono i punti sui quali siamo d'accordo ...**
Shall we summarise the points of agreement ...	**Possiamo riassumere i punti su cui siamo d'accordo ...**
and then take a short break.	**e poi fare una breve pausa.**
and then adjourn till this afternoon.	**e poi aggiornarci al pomeriggio.**
So far, we've agreed on the following points: ...	**Finora, siamo d'accordo sui seguenti punti: ...**
We disagree on ...	**Non siamo d'accordo su ...**
So we'll come back to those issues after the break.	**Torneremo quindi su quegli argomenti dopo la pausa.**

8. Clinching the deal

We have covered a lot of ground in this meeting.	**Abbiamo fatto molta strada in questa riunione.**
We cannot change our offer.	**Non possiamo modificare la nostra offerta.**
This is our final offer.	**Questa è la nostra offerta definitiva.**

We have/have not reached agreement on ...	**Abbiamo/Non abbiamo raggiunto un accordo su ...**
You have accepted our terms on ...	**Avete accettato le nostre condizioni relative a ...**
You cannot accept our terms on ...	**Non potete accettare le nostre condizioni relative a ...**
Let me go over all the details again.	**Lasciatemi rivedere ancora tutti i dettagli.**
Have I covered everything?	**Ho trattato tutti gli argomenti?**
Do you agree?	**Siete d'accordo?**
Do you accept these terms?	**Accettate queste condizioni?**

9. Getting it in writing

I will draft an outline agreement.	**Redigerò una bozza dell'accordo di massima.**
Can you prepare a draft contract?	**Può preparare una bozza del contratto?**
I will send the agreement to you for your comments.	**Vi invierò copia dell'accordo per eventuali commenti.**
Please send the draft contract to me for our comments.	**Gradirei ricevere la bozza del contratto per eventuali commenti.**
After the contract/agreement has been signed, we can ...	**Dopo la firma del contratto/dell'accordo possiamo ...**
make the goods.	**fabbricare la merce.**
deliver the equipment.	**fornire l'attrezzatura.**

10. The legal aspects

contract	**il contratto**
parties to the contract	**le parti del contratto**
to sign a contract	**firmare un contratto**
signatories to the contract	**i firmatari del contratto**
scope of the contract	**la finalità del contratto**
terms of the contract	**i termini contrattuali**
clauses of the contract	**le clausole de contrattuali**
breach of contract	**l'inadempimento *m* di un contratto**

CONTRACT LAW, see page 122/LEGAL JURISDICTION, see page 52

PROJECTS AND PERFORMANCE

Check-list

To help you manage your project better, it is useful to plan it around the following stages or milestones:

1. Defining objectives	❑	**1. Definizione degli obiettivi**
2. Prioritizing and sequencing activities	❑	**2. Definizione delle priorità e della successione delle attività**
3. Allocating resources	❑	**3. Assegnazione delle risorse**
4. Evaluating performance	❑	**4. Valutazione delle prestazioni**
5. Project completion	❑	**5. Completamento del progetto**

Project types

Company reorganisation	**la riorganizzazione aziendale**
Company restructuring	**la ristrutturazione aziendale**
Automation project	**il progetto di automazione**
Cost control project	**il progetto controllo costi**
Manpower planning project	**il progetto pianificazione manodopera**
Quality project	**il progetto qualità**
Research project	**il progetto ricerca**
Installation project	**il progetto installazione**
Construction project	**il progetto costruzione**
Product launch	**il lancio del prodotto**

The project team

The team consists of a ...	**Il gruppo è costituito da ...**
We have appointed a ...	**Abbiamo nominato ...**
project leader	**capo del progetto**
project supervisor	**supervisore** ***m/f*** **del progetto**
project manager	**responsabile** ***m/f*** **del progetto**
project assistant	**assistente** ***m/f*** **del progetto**
project secretary	**segretario** ***m/f*** **del progetto**

1. Defining objectives

What exactly do we want to achieve?	**Che cosa vogliamo ottenere esattamente?**
How exactly are we going to achieve it?	**In che modo pensiamo di ottenerlo?**
Is this project really necessary?	**Questo progetto è veramente necessario?**
The objectives/goals/ targets of this project are to ...	**Lo scopo/Gli obiettivi/ Gli intenti di questo progetto sono ...**
In this project, we ...	**Con questo progetto, ...**
aim to ...	**miriamo a ...**
plan to ...	**programmiamo di ...**
mean to ...	**intendiamo ...**
propose to ...	**proponiamo di ...**
intend to ...	**vogliamo ...**
reorganize the company	**riorganizzare l'azienda**
increase output	**incrementare l'efficienza**
introduce new equipment	**introdurre nuove attrezzature**
launch an updated product	**lanciare un prodotto d'avanguardia**

2. Prioritizing and sequencing activities

The stages

The project consists of 10 phases.	**Il progetto prevede 10 fasi.**
The project will be divided into 10 stages/activities.	**Il progetto sarà diviso in 10 fasi/ attività.**
At the end of each stage, there is a milestone.	**Alla fine di ogni fase, è previsto un obiettivo parziale.**
The phases and milestones are shown on this project schedule.	**Le fasi e gli obiettivi parziali sono indicati su questo programma.**
You can see the phases ...	**Potete notare le fasi ...**
on the critical path analysis	**sull'analisi critica dei vari punti**
on the flowchart	**sul diagramma di flusso**
on the Gantt chart	**sul diagramma Gantt**

VISUAL AIDS, see page 35

Questions about the schedule

When are we due to start the project?	**Quando dobbiamo iniziare il progetto?**
When will the first stage be finished?	**Quando sarà ultimata la prima fase?**
How long will the first activity take?	**Quanto tempo richiederà la prima attività?**
When do we plan to complete the whole project?	**Quando pensiamo di ultimare l'intero progetto?**

Details about the schedule

The first stage will start on 25th July.	**La prima fase inizierà il 25 luglio.**
We will begin this activity on 25th July.	**Inizieremo questa attività il 25 luglio.**
This phase will take 3 weeks.	**Questa fase richieder à 3 settimane.**
This stage will last until 4th August.	**Questa fase durerà fino al 4 agosto.**
The next stage will be to ...	**La prossima fase sarà ...**
The whole project must be completed by 15th April.	**L'intero progetto deve essere ultimato entro il 15 aprile.**

Prioritising

The most important activity is ...	**L'attività più importante è ...**
The most critical activity is ...	**L'attività più critica è ...**
The key stages are ...	**Le fasi chiave sono ...**
The major stages are ...	**Le fasi principali sono ...**

Project activities

collecting the data	**la raccolta dati**
interpreting the data	**l'intepretazione *f* dati**
researching the market	**la ricerca di mercato**
designing the prototype	**la progettazione prototipo**
testing the prototype	**il collaudo prototipo**
selecting the subcontractors	**la scelta subappaltatori**
recruiting the workforce	**il reclutamento forza lavoro**
subcontracting the manufacture of components	**il subappalto fabbricazione componenti**

DATES, see page 14

producing the equipment	**la produzione attrezzatura**
choosing an advertising agency	**la scelta agenzia pubblicitaria**
agreeing the promotion	**l'accordo *m* sulla promozione**
finalizing the launch date	**la scelta della data di lancio**
building the foundations	**la costruzione delle fondazioni**
installing the equipment	**l'installazione *f* dei mezzi di lavoro**
starting up the plant	**l'avviamento impianto**
handing over the plant	**la consegna impianto**

3. Allocating resources

Forecasting

I am sure/convinced that ... we will need more time.	**Sono certo (-a)/convinto (-a) che ... ci servirà più tempo.**
It is likely that ... we will need more money.	**È probabile che ... ci occorra altro denaro.**
We may ... need more people.	**Potremmo ... aver bisogno di più personale.**
We are unlikely to ... need more equipment.	**È improbabile che ... ci occorrano altre attrezzature.**
We definitely/certainly won't ... need more materials.	**Sicuramente/Certamente non ... avremo bisogno di altri materiali.**

Time

How much time will we need?	**Quanto tempo ci occorrerà?**
How long do we have for the first stage?	**Quanto tempo abbiamo per la prima fase?**
We will need ... more/less time than budgeted.	**Ci occorrerà ... più/meno tempo rispetto a quello previsto.**
a longer time for stage 1.	**più tempo per la prima fase.**
a shorter time for stage 2.	**meno tempo per la seconda fase.**
another 3 days for stage 3.	**altri 3 giorni per la terza fase.**
We need to complete this phase in spring/summer/autumn (fall)/ winter.	**Dobbiamo ultimare questa fase entro la primavera/l'estate/ l'autunno/l'inverno.**

FINANCE DEPARTMENT, see page 73

Budget

How much will it cost?	**Quanto costerà?**
What is the budget?	**Qual'è il budget?**
We will need more money than allocated.	**Ci occorrerà più denaro di quanto stanziato.**
It will cost more than budgeted.	**Costerà più di quanto previsto dal budget.**
We forecast it will cost another 15 million lira.	**Prevediamo che occorreranno altri 15.000.000 di lire.**

People

How many people do we need?	**Quante persone ci occorrono?**
How many people do we need to employ?	**Quante persone dobbiamo assumere?**
We don't have enough people.	**Non abbiamo abbastanza personale.**
Should we use our people or can we subcontract some of the work out?	**Dobbiamo utilizzare il nostro personale o possiamo subappaltare parte del lavoro?**
We will need to employ/hire some extra ...	**Avremo bisogno di assumere altri ...**
operators	**operatori** *mpl*
technicians	**tecnici** *mpl*
workers	**operai** *mpl*
We plan to subcontract some of the work out.	**Prevediamo subappaltare parte del lavoro.**

Responsibilities

The project leader has overall responsibility for ...	**Il capo progetto ha la responsabilità totale di ...**
The project supervisor is in charge of ...	**Il supervisore progetto ha l'incarico di ...**
The project manager will take care of ...	**Il direttore del progetto si occuperà di ...**
The project assistant is responsible for ...	**L'assistente progetto ha la responsabilità di ...**
The project secretary will support/assist the project leader.	**Il segretario progetto aiuterà/ assisterà il capo progetto.**

COMPANY POSITIONS, see page 28

financial questions	**questioni finanziere**
personnel matters	**questioni relative al personale**
day-to-day administration	**amministrazione giornaliera**
accommodation on site	**sistemazione in sede**
contracts with suppliers	**contratti con i fornitori**
dealing with contractors	**relazioni con gli appaltatori**
buying in materials	**acquisto di scorte materiale**
organizing transport	**organizzazione del trasporto**

Materials

What materials do we need?	**Che materiali ci occorrono?**
Do we have the necessary equipment?	**Disponiamo dell'attrezzatura necessaria?**
We don't have enough materials/equipment.	**Non abbiamo sufficienti materiali/attrezzature.**
We can produce the materials in-house.	**Possiamo produrre materiali all'interno.**
We need to buy in the materials.	**Dobbiamo acquistare scorte di materiale.**
What equipment do we need to hire/lease/buy?	**Quale tipo di attrezzatura dobbiamo noleggiare/prendere in leasing/acquistare?**

4. Evaluating performance

The project

How is the project going?	**Come procede il progetto?**
The project is on target.	**Il progetto procede come previsto.**
We are ahead of schedule.	**Siamo in anticipo rispetto al programma.**
We are behind schedule.	**Siamo in ritardo rispetto al programma.**
The costs are as forecast.	**I costi rispettano le previsioni.**
The costs are running above/below budget.	**I costi tendono ad essere superiori/inferiori al budget.**
We have had a cost overrun.	**Abbiamo avuto un'eccedenza di costi.**

We are facing some difficulties/ problems with ...	**Incontriamo alcune difficoltà/ alcuni problemi con ...**
the timing of the project.	**il tempi del progetto.**
the financing of the project.	**il finanziamento del progetto.**
the manpower for the project.	**la manodopera per il progetto.**
the equipment for the project.	**l'apparecchiatura del progetto.**
We can't ...	**Non possiamo ...**
recruit the right workers.	**reclutare gli operai adatti.**
We need to review the situation.	**Dobbiamo rivedere la situazione.**
We need to look again at ...	**Dobbiamo analizzare di nuovo ...**
the schedule.	**il programma.**
the budgets.	**il budget.**
our manpower needs.	**le esigenze in fatto di manodopera.**
our material requirements.	**il fabbisogno di materiale.**
We must control costs.	**Dobbiamo controllare i costi.**
We need to ...	**Dobbiamo ...**
lay off some of the workers.	**licenziare alcuni operai.**
fire the supervisor.	**licenziare il supervisore.**

Personal qualities

The project leader is ...	**Il capo progetto è ...**
efficient	**efficiente**
effective	**efficace**
hard-working	**laborioso (-a)**
competent	**competente**
conscientious	**scrupoloso (-a)**
The project supervisor is ...	**Il supervisore del progetto è ...**
logical	**logico (-a)**
methodical	**metodico (-a)**
analytical	**analitico (-a)**
rational	**razionale**
calm	**calmo (-a)**
inflexible	**inflessibile**
The project manager is ...	**Il direttore del progetto è ...**
practical	**pratico (-a)**
energetic	**energico (-a)**
dynamic	**dinamico (-a)**
single-minded	**orientato (-a) allo scopo**
good at negotiating	**bravo (-a) nelle trattative**

The project designer is ...	**Il progettista è ...**
creative	**creativo (-a)**
imaginative	**fantasioso (-a)**
unorthodox	**non ortodosso (-a)**
impractical	**non pratico (-a)**
good at brainstorming	**abile nelle idee**
The project assistant is ...	**L'assistente del progetto è ...**
sympathetic	**comprensivo (-a)**
perceptive	**intuitivo (-a)**
communicative	**comunicativo (-a)**
good at developing team relationships	**abile nel promuovere relazioni di gruppo**

Business trends

to increase/to raise	**maggiorare/aumentare**
to put up/to step up	**alzare/incrementare**
We have increased the budget for stage one.	***Abbiamo maggiorato il budget per la prima fase.***
an increase/a rise	**una maggiorazione/un aumento**
We have to budget for an increase in the cost of materials.	***Dobbiamo preventivare una maggiorazione del costo dei materiali.***
to decrease/to cut	**diminuire/tagliare**
to reduce	**ridurre**
We have decreased the budget for phase two.	***Abbiamo diminuito il budget per la secondo fase.***
to fall/to drop	**abbattere/cadere**
to go down/to slump,	**scendere/crollare**

dramatic(ally)	**drammatico (drammaticamente)**
vast(ly)	**ampio (-amente)**
huge(ly)	**smisurato (-amente)**
enormous(ly)	**enorme(mente)**
substantial (ly)	**sostanziale (-mente)**
considerable (considerably)	**considerevole (-mente)**
significant(ly)	**significativo (-amente)**
moderate(ly)	**moderato (-amente)**
slightly	**leggero (-mente)**
a little	**di poco**

a fall/a drop — **un abbattimento/una caduta**
a cut/a reduction — **un taglio/una riduzione**
a collapse/a slump — **un collasso/un crollo**
We estimate there will be a decrease in the cost of materials. — ***Prevediamo che vi sarà una diminuzione del costo del materiale.***

to hold ... stable — **mantenere ... stabile**
to maintain ... at the same level — **mantenere ... allo stesso livello**
We have kept costs constant during the project. — ***Abbiamo mantenuto i costi costanti durante il progetto.***

to remain constant — **rimanere costante**
to stay stable — **restare stabile**

5. Project completion

We have finished the project. — **Abbiamo completato il progetto.**

The project is complete. — **Il progetto è ultimato.**
The plant is operational. — **L'impianto è operativo.**
The product is ready for launch. — **Il prodotto è pronto per il lancio.**

We are ready to ... — **Siamo pronti a ...**
start up the new equipment. — **mettere in esercizio le nuove attrezzature.**

We have managed to ... — **Siamo riusciti a ...**
increase output. — **aumetare la produzione.**

Congratulations. We have completed the project successfully. — **Complimenti. Il progetto è stato ultimato con successo.**

Well done. You have achieved your aim/goal/target/objective. — **Perfetto. Avete raggiunto lo scopo/il traguardo/il fine/l'obiettivo.**

I'd like to thank the project team for their ... — **Vorrei ringraziare il gruppo di questo progetto per ...**
hard work during the project — **il lavoro assiduo durante il progetto**
commitment — **l'impegno**
dedication — **la dedizione**
collaboration — **la collaborazione**
participation — **la partecipazione**

Company Departments

ADMINISTRATION

Administrative staff

administrator — **l'amministratore (-trice)**
clerk — **l'impiegato (-a)**
office manager — **il vice-capoufficio**
personal assistant — **l'assistente personale** *m/f*
she's the personal assistant to the Managing Director/CEO — ***lei è l'assistente personale dell'amministratore delegato***
secretary — **il segretario (-a)**
typist — **il dattilografo (-a)**

Information organization

archive — **l'archivio** *m*
we keep the old records in the archives — ***conserviamo i documenti negli archivi***
file (n)/(v) — **l'archivio** *m* **archiviare**
have you filed that letter? — ***hai/ha archiviato quella lettera?***
filing cabinet — **il casellario**
photocopier — **la fotocopiatrice**
sort (v) — **classificare**

CUSTOMER SERVICE

agent — l'agente *m/f*
he acts as agent for us in Australia — ***lui è il nostro agente in Australia***
busy — **occupato (-a)**
cater for/serve — **soddisfare le esigenze di**
we cater for/serve a wide range of customers — ***noi soddisfiamo le esigenze di una clientela alquanto vasta***
custom — **la clientela**
customer — **il/la cliente**
customize — **personalizzare**
all our products are customized — ***tutti i nostri prodotti sono personalizzati***
deal (v) — **negoziare, trattare**
delay (n) — **il ritardo**
we're sorry for the delay — ***ci scusiamo per il ritardo***
demand (n) — **la domanda, la richiesta**
we can't keep up with demand — ***non siamo in grado di far fronte alla domanda***
discontinue — **fuori produzione**
I'm afraid this line has been discontinued — ***sono spiacente di comunicare che questa linea di prodotti non è più in produzione***
exchange (n)/(v) — **lo scambio/scambiare**
exempt (adj) — **esente**
these products are VAT/sales tax exempt — ***questi prodotti sono esenti da IVA***
export (n)/(v) — **l'esportazione** *f*/**esportare**
fetch/pick up — **evadere un ordine**
we'll fetch/pick up the order this afternoon — ***evaderemo l'ordine oggi pomeriggio***
file (n) — **l'archivio** *m*
we keep all our customers on file — ***noi abbiamo un archivio di tutti i nostri clienti***
customer file — **l'archivio clienti**
handle (v) — **commerciare in**
import (n)/(v) — **l'importazione** *f*/**importare**
install — **installare**
when would you like the equipment installed? — ***quando desidera che le installiamo l'attrezzatura?***

DISTRIBUTION, see page 71

item	**l'articolo** *m*
the order consisted of four items	***l'ordine comprendeva quattro articoli***
off-season	**fuori stagione**
paperwork	**le pratiche**
there's a lot of paperwork to do	***ci sono molte pratiche da svolgere***
part-exchange	**lo scambio di articoli**
quality	**la qualità**
run out of	**esaurire un articolo**
I'm afraid we've run out of those items	***siamo spiacenti ma quegli articoli sono esauriti***
scarce	**raro (-a), scarso (-a), insufficiente**
schedule (n)/(v)	**programma** *m***/programmare**
we've scheduled delivery for the end of the month	***la consegna è in programma per la fine del mese***
service (n)	**l'assistenza** *f*
the service is slow	***il servizio di assistenza è alquanto lento***
after-sales service	**assistenza post-vendita**
service industry	**industria** *f* **di servizi**
tariff	**la tariffa**
triplicate	**triplice copia**
the order form needs filling out in triplicate	***il modulo d'ordine deve essere compilato in triplice copia***

Negotiating

bargain (n)/(v)	**il contratto, l'affare** *m***/ contrattare**
barter	**lo scambio**
conditions of sale	**le condizioni di vendita**
our conditions of sale are printed on the back of the invoice	***le nostre condizioni di vendita sono riportate sul retro della fattura***
haggle	**mercanteggiare, discutere sul prezzo**
negotiate	**condurre una trattativa**
negotiable	**trattabile**
these terms are not negotiable	***questi termini non sono trattabili***

NEGOTIATIONS, see page 48

negotiation	**la trattativa**
reach agreement	**raggiungere un accordo**

Complaints

blame (v)	**incolpare, attribuire la responsabilità a**
claim (n)	**la rivendicazione, il reclamo, la richiesta di risarcimento**
the customer has made a claim for damages	***il cliente ha presentato una richiesta di risarcimento danni***
compensate	**compensare**
damage (n)	**il danno**
the accident caused a lot of damage	***l'incidente ha causato molti danni***
damages	**i danni**
fault (n)	**il difetto, l'anomalia *f*, l'avaria *f***
guarantee (n)	**la garanzia**
the guarantee lasts 3 years	***la garanzia ha una durata di tre anni***
hazard	**il rischio**
insure	**assicurare**
insurance claim	**la richiesta di indennizzo assicurativo**
insurance cover	**la copertura assicurativa**
insurance policy	**la polizza assicurativa**
does your policy cover this claim?	***la sua polizza assicurativa copre il seguente indennizzo?***
overdue	**scaduto (-a), in ritardo**
the delivery is overdue	***il termine di consegna è scaduto***
repair (v)	**riparare**
spoil	**rovinare, subire danni**
the goods were spoiled in transit	***le merci hanno subito danni durante il trasporto***

Payment

credit	**il credito**
credit note	**la nota di accredito**
hire purchase	**vendita *f* con pagamento rateale**

ON THE TELEPHONE, see page 5/PAYMENT, see also page 76

invoice (n)/(v)	**la fattura/fatturare**
you'll be invoiced at the end of the month	***riceverete la fattura a fine mese***
lease (n)/(v)	**la locazione/dare in locazione, affittare**
outright purchase	**acquisto** *m* **in contanti**
over-charged	**addebito (-a) superiore alla somma concordata**
overpay	**pagare più del dovuto**
you've overpaid so we'll send you a credit note	***la cifra da voi versata è superiore a quella dovuta e pertanto vi invieremo una nota di accredito***
pay (v)	**pagare**
pay by cheque/check	**pagare con assegno**
pay in cash	**pagare in contanti**
payable	**pagabile**
this invoice is payable in 30 days	***la fattura è pagabile a 30 giorni***
payment	**il pagamento**
we demand payment in advance	***esigiamo il pagamento anticipato***
prepaid	**prepagato (-a)**
please enclose a prepaid envelope	***si prega di allegare una busta con affrancatura prepagata***
rebate	**uno sconto**
settle	**saldare**
could you settle the bill in advance?	***potreste saldare il conto in anticipo?***
statement	**l'estratto** *m* **conto**
we will send you a monthly statement	***vi invieremo un estratto conto mensile***

Orders

acknowledge	**accusare ricevuta**
the order was acknowledged on 30 June	***la ricevuta dell'ordine è stata registrata in data 30 giugno***
acknowledgment	**accusa** *f* **di ricevuta**
available	**disponibile**
availability	**la disponibilità**

bring forward/move up	**anticipare**
we'd like to bring forward/ move up the delivery date	***desidereremmo anticipare la data di consegna***
bulk	**all'ingrosso, di grandi quantità**
we offer 10% discount for bulk orders	***applichiamo uno sconto del 10% su ordinativi di grandi quantità***
cancel	**cancellare, annullare**
cancellation	**la cancellazione, l'annullamento** *m*
confirm	**confermare**
could you please confirm your order in writing?	***potreste inviarci una conferma scritta del vostro ordine?***
notify	**informare, avvisare, notificare**
we'll notify you of any delay	***vi informeremo di eventuali ritardi***
offer (n)/(v)	**l'offerta/offrire**
order	**l'ordine** *m*
fulfil an order	***evadere un ordine***
on order	**sull'ordine**
we've got 25 on order	***ne abbiamo ordinato 25***
back order	**ordine arretrato**
place an order	**ordinare, inoltrare un ordine**
are you ready to place an order?	***siete pronti ad inoltrarci un ordine?***
postpone	**posticipare**
quote (v)	**quotare, sottoporre un'offerta**
could you quote us for 500 units?	***potreste sottoporci un'offerta per 500 unità?***
quotation	**l'offerta** *f*, **la quotazione**
how long is your quotation valid for?	***quando scade la vostra offerta?***
ready	**pronto (-a)**
receive	**ricevere**
receipt	**la ricevuta**
could you let me have a receipt?	***potrebbe farmi avere una ricevuta?***
reorder	**riordinare**
repeat order (n)	**l'ordine** *m* **ripetuto**
shortage	**la carenza**
there's a severe shortage of stock	***abbiamo una grave carenza di scorte a magazzino***
in stock/out of stock	**a magazzino/esaurito (-a)**

DISTRIBUTION

by boat/ferry/ship — **per battello/traghetto/nave**

by post/special delivery/airmail — **per posta/posta celere/posta aerea**

by truck/van/train — **per autocarro/furgone/treno**

cargo — **il carico**

carriage/freight — **il trasporto**

the price includes carriage — ***il prezzo è comprensivo di trasporto***

cif (cost, insurance, freight) — **c.i.f.**

crate — **la cassa da imballaggio**

deliver — **consegnare**

delivery — **la consegna**

delivery note — **la bolla di consegna**

there should be a delivery note with the invoice — ***alla fattura dovrà essere allegata una bolla di consegna***

delivery time — **il termine di consegna**

28 days delivery time — ***consegna a 28 giorni***

depot — **il deposito, il magazzino**

dispatch (v) — **spedire**

distribute — **distribuire**

duty — **il dazio, l'imposta** *f*

enclose — **allegare**

please find enclosed our price list — ***vi inviamo in allegato il nostro listino prezzi***

envelope — **la busta**

f.o.b. (free on board) — **f.o.b**

forward (v) — **spedire, inviare**

could you forward the goods to the distributor? — ***potreste inviare le merci al distributore?***

freight — **il nolo**

in transit — **durante il trasporto**

the order was lost in transit — ***le merci sono state smarrite durante il trasporto***

lading, bill of — **la polizza di carico**

load (v) — **caricare**

the goods were loaded onto the trucks — ***le merci sono state caricate sugli autocarri***

mail (n)/(v) — **posta** *f* **/spedire**

pack (v)	**imballare**
package	**l'imballo** *m*
pallet	**il pallet**
ship (v)	**spedire via mare**
have you shipped the goods?	***avete spedito la merce via mare?***
shipment	**la spedizione**
unload	**scaricare**

Channels

branch	**la filiale, la succursale**
there is a branch in every major town	***esiste una filiale in tutte le maggiori città***
bottleneck	**la strozzatura, l'ostacolo** *m*
chain	**la catena**
this store is part of a chain	***questo negozio fa parte di una catena***
channel	**il canale**
our main distribution channel is via the wholesaler to the retailer	***il nostro principale canale di distribuzione è rappresentato dalla vendita al dettaglio tramite i grossisti***
consignment	**la partita di merce**
we're expecting a consignment later today	***attendiamo una partita di merce più tardi in giornata***
dealer	**il concessionario**
department store	**il grande magazzino**
direct export	**l'esportazione** *f* **diretta**
franchise (n)	**la franchigia**
middleman	**l'intermediario** *m*
network	**la rete**
we're building a dealer network	***stiamo costituendo una rete di concessionari***
quota	**la quota, l'aliquota** *f*
retail (n)	**la vendita al dettaglio**
retail outlet	**il punto di vendita**
retailer	**il dettagliante**
scarce	**scarso (-a), insufficiente**
storage	**l'immagazzinamento** *m*
tariff	**la tariffa**
warehouse	**il magazzino**
wholesale	**vendita** *f* **all'ingrosso**

FINANCE

accounts — **gli estratti conto**
the monthly accounts show all the figures — ***le cifre sono riportate negli estratti conto mensili***
accountancy — **la contabilità**
accountant — **il ragioniere (-a), il/la contabile**
acquire — **acquisire, acquistare**
acquisition — **l'acquisizione *f***
advance (n)/(v) — **l'anticipo *m*, l'acconto *m*/dare un acconto**

backdate — **retrodatare**
the cheque/check was backdated — ***l'assegno era retrodatato***
black, in the — **in attivo**
books, keep the — **tenere la contabilità**
borrow — **prendere in prestito**
break even (v) — **essere in pareggio**
break-even point — **il punto di pareggio**
we've reached the break-even point — ***abbiamo raggiunto il punto di pareggio***
budget (n)/(v) — **il budget, il bilancio preventivo/preventivare**
we've budgeted for a loss — ***abbiamo preventivato una perdita***

capital — **il capitale**
cash — **il denaro contante**
petty cash — **piccola cassa *f***
cheque/check — **l'assegno *m***
cost — **il costo**
fixed/variable/running — **fisso/variabile/corrente**
credit (n) — **il credito**
currency — **la valuta, la divisa**
debt — **il debito**
debtor — **il debitore (-trice)**
deduct — **dedurre, detrarre**
defer — **differire**
the taxation can be deferred until next year — ***l'imposta può essere differita fino al prossimo anno***
due — **scaduto (-a), maturato (-a)**
earn — **guadagnare**

BANKING, see page 116

earnings — **i guadagni, i profitti, gli utili**
annual earnings exceeded our forecast — ***i guadagni annuis sono stati superiori alle nostre previsioni***
finance (n)/(v) — **finanza** *f*/**finanziare**
they are willing to finance the project — ***sono disponibili a finanziare il progetto***
funds — **i fondi, gli stanziamenti**
income — **il reddito**
interest — **l'interesse** *m*
interest rate — **il tasso d'interesse**
interest rates were cut by ½% — ***i tassi d'interesse sono stati ridotti dello 0,5%***
lend — **prestare**
lender — **il prestatore (-trice)**
loan — **il mutuo, il prestito**
overdraw — **andare in rosso**
overdraft — **lo scoperto di conto**
our overdraft facility is L.100m — ***la nostra elasticità di cassa è di 100 milioni di lire***
owe — **essere debitore (-trice)**
profit (n) — **il profitto**
profitable — **remunerativo (-a), redditizio (-a)**
profitability — **la redditività**
rate — **il tasso, l'aliquota** *f*
recover — **ricuperare, reintegrare**
red, in the — **in rosso, in passivo**
save (v) — **risparmiare**
savings — **i risparmi**
subsidize — **sovvenzionare**
subsidy — **la sovvenzione, il sussidio**

Investment

base rate — **il tasso base**
terms are 2% above base rate — ***le condizioni sono superiori del 2% rispetto al tasso base***
bond — **l'obbligazione** *f*, **il titolo a reddito fisso**
broker — **il broker, il mediatore (-trice)**
our broker advised us to sell our shares — ***il nostro broker ci ha consigliato di vendere le nostre azioni***

FINANCIAL PROBLEMS, see page 80

dealer	**l'operatore (-trice) commerciale, l'operatore (-trice) di borsa**
debenture	**l'obbligazione** *f*
dividend	**il dividendo**
they announced the same dividend as last year	***hanno annunciato che il dividendo sarà uguale a quello dello scorso anno***
earnings per share	**il reddito per azione**
equity	**il capitale/patrimonio netto**
gross yield	**il rendimento lordo**
invest	**investire**
investment	**l'investimento** *m*
portfolio	**il portafoglio**
you should have some oil shares in your portfolio	***nel tuo portafoglio dovresti inserire alcune azioni di società petrolifere***
premium	**il premio**
securities	**i titoli, i valori mobiliari**
the securities market can be very volatile	***il mercato mobiliare (dei titoli) è soggetto a notevoli variazioni***
share/stock	**l'azione** *f*, **il titolo azionario**
shareholder/stockholder	**l'azionista** *m/f*

Financial statements

asset	**l'attività** *f*
current assets	**le attività correnti, le disponibilità**
fixed assets	**le attività fisse, le immobilizzazioni**
intangible assets	**le attività immateriali**
audit (n)	**la revisione contabile, la revisione dei conti**
annual audit	**la revisione contabile annuale**
auditor	**il revisore dei conti**
balance sheet	**il bilancio patrimoniale**
the balance sheet looks very sound	***il bilancio patrimoniale appare estremamente positivo***
cash flow	**il flusso di cassa**
debit	**il debito**
current liabilities	**le passività correnti**

depreciate	**deprezzare, ammortizzare**
these assets are depreciated over 3 years	***il periodo di ammortamento di queste attività è di 3 anni***
depreciation	**il deprezzamento, l'ammortamento** *m*
expenditure	**la spesa**
expenses	**le spese**
gearing	**il rapporto d'indebitamento**
goodwill	**l'avviamento** *m*
goodwill is included under intangible assets	***l'avviamento è compreso tra le attività immateriali***
gross (adj)	**lordo (-a)**
gross margin	**il margine lordo**
gross profit	**l'utile** *m* **lordo**
half-yearly results	**i risultati semestrali**
inventory	**l'inventario** *m*
ledger	**il libro mastro**
sales/purchase ledger	**il libro mastro delle vendite/ degli acquisti**
liabilities	**le passività, il passivo**
margin	**il margine**
overheads	**i costi comuni, le spese generali**
our overheads are too high	***i nostri costi comuni sono troppo elevati***
profit and loss account/ income statement	**il conto profitti e perdite, il conto economico**
quarterly	**trimestralmente**
reserves	**le riserve**
results	**i risultati**
retained earnings	**gli utili non distribuiti, il capitale di risparmio**
return	**il rendimento**
return on investment	**il rendimento degli investimenti**
turnover/sales	**il giro d'affari**
annual turnover/sales has doubled over 5 years	***il giro d'affari annuo in cinque anni è stato raddoppiato***
working capital	**il capitale netto di esercizio**
write-off (n)/(v)	**lo storno/stornare**
this asset has now been written off	***quest'attività adesso è stata stornata***

PAYMENT, see also page 76

Payment

bad debt	**il credito inesigibile**
this invoice has been posted as a bad debt	***questa fattura è stata inserita tra i crediti inesigibili***
bank draft/check	**l'assegno circolare *m*, la cambiale bancaria**
bank statement	**il rendiconto bancario**
blank cheque/check	**l'assegno *m* in bianco**
bounced cheque/check	**l'assegno *m* scoperto**
convert (v)	**convertire**
credit limit	**il castelletto, il limite di credito**
credit rating	**la posizione finanziaria, la posizione creditizia**
direct debit	**il debito diretto**
demand (n)	**la domanda**
discount	**lo sconto**
invoice (n)/(v)	**la fattura/fatturare**
letter of credit	**la lettera di credito**
we will pay by letter of credit	***pagheremo con lettera di credito***
outstanding	**insoluto (-a), in arretrato, scoperto (-a)**
L.10m is still outstanding	***l'insoluto ammonta ancora a 10 milioni di lire***

Tax

capital gains tax	**l'imposta *f* sui redditi di capitale**
corporation tax	**l'imposta *f* sulle società**
declare	**dichiarare**
income tax	**l'imposta *f* sul reddito**
taxable	**imponibile**
is this purchase taxable?	***questo acquisto è soggetto ad imponibile?***
tax allowance	**la detrazione d'imposta**
tax deductible	**la dichiarazione delle tasse**
tax evasion	**l'evasione *f* fiscale**
tax loophole	**la scappatoia fiscale**
tax relief	**la detrazione d'imposta, la detrazione fiscale**
you can get tax relief	***ha diritto alla detrazione d'imposta***
value added tax *(sales tax)*	**l'imposta *f* sul valore aggiunto (IVA)**

LEGAL

abide by	**attenersi, tener fede a**
abuse (n)/(v)	**l'abuso *m*/abusare**
abuse of power	**l'abuso di potere**
appeal (n)/(v)	**l'appello *m*/ricorrere in appello**
arbitrate	**sottoporre ad arbitrato**
arbitration	**l'arbitrato *m***
the dispute has gone to arbitration	***la controversia è stata sottoposta ad arbitrato***
bequest (n)	**un legato, un lascito**
the property was left to her as a bequest	***la proprietà le è stata donata mediante lascito***
bond (n)	**il vincolo, la cauzione**
break the law	**infrangere la legge**
case	**la causa, il processo, il caso giudiziario**
case law	**la giurisprudenza**
civil law	**il diritto civile**
claim (n)/(v)	**la rivendicazione, il diritto/ rivendicare, vantare**
they have a claim	***essi rivendicano un diritto***
claimant	**il/la ricorrente**
conflict (n)	**il conflitto**
conflict of interest	**il conflitto di interessi**
copyright	**il diritto d'autore**
court	**la corte, il tribunale**
go to court	**intentare una causa**
we're going to court	***intentiamo una causa***
damages	**i danni**
fee	**l'onorario *m***
fraud	**la frode**
illegal	**illegale**
indemnify	**indennizzare, risarcire**
indemnity	**l'indennità *f*, il risarcimento**
infringe copyright	**violare il diritto d'autore**
infringement	**la violazione**
irrevocable letter of credit	**la lettera di credito irrevocabile**
judicial	**giudiziario (-a), giudiziale**

CONTRACT LAW, see page 12/EMPLOYMENT LAW, see page 123

jurisdiction	**la giurisdizione**
this contract comes under British jurisdiction	***il contratto è soggetto alla giurisdizione inglese***
law	**la legge**
within/outside the law	**nella legge/fuori legge**
against the law	**contro la legge**
legal	**legale**
legal department	**la sezione legale**
liability	**la responsabilità**
limited liability	**la responsabilità limitata**
litigant	**la parte in causa**
loophole, tax	**la scappatoia fiscale**
misconduct	**l'infrazione** *f*
professional misconduct	**infrazione dell'etica professionale**
party	**la parte**
third party	**i terzi** *pl*
patent	**il brevetto**
file a patent application	**compilare una richiesta di brevetto**
penalty	**la penalità, la multa**
penalty clause	**la clausola penale**
the contract included a penalty clause for late completion	***una clausola del contratto prevedeva una penale per ritardato adempimento***
pledge (n)	**il pegno, la garanzia**
precedent	**il precedente**
there is no precedent for this decision	***non esistono precedenti in materia***
quorum	**il quorum**
settlement	**la definizione**
settle out of court	**la definizione in via extragiudiziale**
sue	**citare in giudizio**
we can sue them for non-payment	***possiamo citarli per inadempienza di pagamento***
suit	**l'istanza** *f*, **il procedimento civile**
trademark	**il marchio di fabbrica**
tribunal	**il tribunale**
unjust	**ingiusto, iniquo**

unlawful	**illegale**
waive	**rinunciare**
the company decided to waive its usual fee in this case	***in questo caso la società ha deciso di rinunciare al suo consueto onorario***

People

actuary	**l'attuario** *m*
advocate	**l'avvocato** *m*, **il difensore**
attorney/barrister	**il procuratore (-trice), l'avvocato** *m*
bailiff/sheriff	**l'ufficiale** *m* **giudiziario**
lawyer	**l'avvocato** *m*
legal advisor	**l'avvocato** *m* **tributarista, il patrocinatore (-trice) legale**
notary	**il notaio**
solicitor	**il procuratore (-trice) legale**

Financial problems

bankrupt	**fallito (-a)**
to go bankrupt	**fare fallimento, fallire**
bankruptcy	**il fallimento**
debt	**il debito**
foreclose	**precludere un diritto di riscatto/ un diritto ipotecario**
the bank foreclosed on the property	***la banca ha precluso il diritto ipotecario sulla proprietà***
foreclosure	**la preclusione, la decadenza dal diritto ipotecario**
insolvent	**insolvente**
insolvency	**l'insolvenza** *f*
liquidate	**liquidare**
liquidation	**la liquidazione**
the company has gone into liquidation	***la società è stata posta in liquidazione***
liquidator	**il liquidatore (-trice)**
receiver	**il curatore (-trice), l'amministratore (-trice) giudiziale** *m*
a receiver has been appointed to sell off the assets	***per la vendita delle attività è stato nominato un curatore***
receivership	**l'amministrazione** *f* **controllata**

MARKETING

capture *(market share)* **conquistare**
client **il/la cliente**
compete **competere, essere in concorrenza**
competition **la concorrenza**
competitor **il/la concorrente**
competitive **concorrenziale, competitivo (-a)**
  competitive pricing ***prezzi competitivi***
domestic market **il mercato interno**
down-market **economico (-a)**
end-user **l'utente *m/f* finale, il consumatore (-trice) finale**
  we sell direct to the end-user ***vendiamo direttamente ai consumatori finali***
exhibit (v) **esporre**
exhibition **la mostra**
flop (n) **il fiasco, il fallimento**
  the launch was a complete flop ***il lancio fu un fiasco completo***
forecast (v) **prevedere**
  we forecast that we will become market leader next year ***prevediamo di insediarci ai vertici del mercato entro il prossimo anno***
goodwill **l'avviamento *m***
logo **il logo**
market (n) **il mercato**
market leader **il leader di mercato**
market niche **l'area *f* di mercato**
  they have found a profitable market niche ***hanno individuato una redditizia area di mercato***
market penetration **la penetrazione nel mercato**
market segmentation **la segmentazione del mercato**
market share **la quota di mercato**
mass-market **il mercato di massa**
outlet **il punto di vendita**
resistance **la resistenza**
  there is some price resistance ***si registra una certa resistenza all'accettazione del prezzo***
saturate **saturare**
sector **il settore**

SALES DEPARTMENT, see page 96

segment — **il segmento**
share (n) — **la quota**
survey (n) — **l'indagine** *f*
target (n)/(v) — **l'obiettivo** *m***/designare come obiettivo**

up-market — **esclusivo (-a)**
it's an upmarket product aimed at the luxury sector — ***si tratta di un prodotto esclusivo destinato al settore dei beni di lusso***

Products

benefit (n) — **il beneficio, il vantaggio**
brand — **la marca**
brand leader — **il leader di marca**
brand loyalty — **la fedeltà alla marca**
brand loyalty will stop customers switching to generic products — ***la fedeltà alla marca interromperà il flusso di clienti rivolto ai prodotti generici***

by-product — **il sottoprodotto**
diversify — **diversificare**
flagship (adj) — **trainante**
a flagship product — **un prodotto trainante**
generic — **generico (-a)**
giveaway — **l'omaggio** *m*
goods — **le merci**
label — **l'etichetta** *f*
private label products are selling well — ***le vendite dei prodotti di etichetta privata vanno molto bene***
launch (n) — **il lancio di un prodotto**
life cycle — **il ciclo vitale**
positioning — **la collocazione**
product line/range — **la linea/la gamma di prodotti**
sell-by date — **la data di scadenza**
this product has passed its sell-by date — ***la data di scadenza di questo prodotto è già stata superata***
shelf-life — **la durata a magazzino**
tailor-made — **confezionato (-a) su misura**
trade mark — **il marchio di fabbrica**
white goods — **i beni di consumo durevoli**

INTRODUCING THE PRODUCT, see page 31

Advertising

advertise	**pubblicizzare, pubblicare una inserzione**
advertisement	**l'inserzione *f* pubblicitaria, l'annuncio *m* pubblicitario**
art director	**il direttore (-trice) artistico (-a)**
artwork	**il lavoro artistico**
audience	**il pubblico**
the ad has to reach a certain audience	***il messaggio pubblicitario è destinato ad un pubblico selezionato***
banner	**lo striscione, l'insegna *f***
body copy	**il testo (di un messaggio pubblicitario)**
brief (n)	**il trafiletto**
broadsheet	**il giornale di grande formato**
brochure	**l'opuscolo *m***
canvass	**effettuare un sondaggio**
we have canvassed a lot of potential customers	***abbiamo effettuato un sondaggio su numerosi potenziali clienti***
caption	**l'intestazione *f*, il titolo, la didascalia**
catalogue/catalog	**il catalogo**
this product is not included in our current catalogue/catalog	***questo prodotto non è riportato sul nostro attuale catalogo***
circular	**la circolare**
copy	**la copia**
endorse	**firmare**
endorsement	**la firma**
endorsement by a well-known actress will boost sales	***la firma di una nota attrice farà aumentare le vendite***
flier	**il volantino**
freesheet	**il volantino gratuito**
issue (n)	**la pubblicazione, l'edizione *f***
jingle	**il jingle**
the ad has a very catchy jingle	***il messaggio pubblicitario ha un jingle molto accattivante***
layout	**l'impaginazione *f***

magazine	**la rivista**
we'll reach our audience through magazines	***ci rivolgeremo al nostro pubblico mediante le riviste***
media	**i mezzi di comunicazione**
mass media	**la mass media, i mezzi di comunicazione di massa**
media coverage	**la copertura da parte dei mezzi di comunicazione**
outdoor advertising	**la pubblicità esterna**
we've designed some posters for outdoor advertising	***abbiamo realizzato alcuni manifesti per la pubblicità esterna***
pamphlet	**il manifestino, il volantino**
periodical	**il periodico**
poster	**il manifesto pubblicitario**
prospectus	**il prospetto, il programma**
the company issued a shareholder prospectus	***la società ha pubblicato un prospetto per gli azionisti***
publication	**la pubblicazione, il periodico, la rivista**
ratings	**gli indici di gradimento**
weekly TV ratings	***l'indice di gradimento settimanale dei programmi televisivi***
readership	**i lettori**
slogan	**lo slogan**
spot	**lo spot**
TV spot	**lo spot televisivo**
tabloid	**il tabloid**
viewer	**il telespettatore (-trice)**
voice-over	**la voce fuori campo**

Pricing

bargain (n)	**l'occasione *f*, l'affare *m***
ceiling	**il limite**
price ceiling	**il limite dei prezzi**
cut-price/cut-rate	**prezzo *m* scontato**
cut-price deals have reduced margins	***le occasioni a prezzi scontati hanno ridotto i margini***
discount (n)	**lo sconto**
elastic	**flessibile, elastico (-a)**

going rate	**il tasso corrente**
we should charge the going rate	***dovremmo applicare il tasso corrente***
gross margin	**il margine lordo**
inelastic	**inflessibile, rigido (-a)**
introductory offer	**l'offerta *f* promozionale**
knockdown/mask-down price	**il prezzo di liquidazione**
margin	**il margine**
mark up (v)/(n)	**aumentare/l'aumento *m*, il rialzo**
the retailer has marked up the price by 50%	***i venditori al dettaglio hanno aumentato i prezzi del 50%***
MRP (Manufacturer's Recommended Price)	**il prezzo consigliato dai costruttori**
overheads	**le spese comuni**
premium	**il premio**
rate	**il tasso**
refund (n)	**il rimborso**
retail price	**il prezzo al dettaglio**
retail price index	**l'indice *m* dei prezzi al dettaglio**
surcharge (n)	**il sovrapprezzo, il supplemento, la maggiorazione**
value (n)	**il valore**

Public relations

identity	**l'identità *f***
corporate identity	**l'identità aziendale**
image	**l'immagine *f***
corporate image	**l'immagine aziendale**
lobby (v)	**esercitare pressioni su, avere influenza su**
we are lobbying the Minister for/Secretary of Agriculture	***stiamo esercitando pressioni sul ministero dell'agricoltura***
press officer	**l'addetto *m* all'ufficio stampa**
press relations	**le relazioni/i rapporti con la stampa**
press release	**il comunicato stampa**
we have issued a press release	***abbiamo emesso un comunicato stampa***
sponsor (v)	**sponsorizzare**
sponsorship	**la sponsorizzazione**

PERSONNEL

absent	**assente**
absenteeism	**l'assenteismo** *m*
absenteeism has risen due to bad health	***l'assenteismo è aumentato per ragioni di salute***
canteen	**la mensa**
career	**la carriera**
conditions	**le condizioni**
working conditions	**le condizioni di lavoro**
conditions of employment	**le condizioni di assunzione**
core time	**l'orario** *m* **di presenza obbligatoria**
core time is between 10:00 and 15:00	***l'orario di presenza obbligatoria è dalle 10:00 alle 15:00***
employ	**assumere, impiegare**
employee	**il/la dipendente, l'impiegato (-a)**
employer	**il datore di lavoro**
equal opportunity	**la parità di condizioni, la uguale opportunità**
this company has an equal opportunities policy	***l'azienda persegue una politica di parità di condizioni***
flexitime	**l'orario** *m* **flessibile**
hire	**assumere**
human resources	**le risorse umane**
job centre/center	**l'ufficio** *m* **di collocamento**
job sharing	**la suddivisione del lavoro, l'attribuzione** *f* **dei compiti**
job satisfaction	**la soddisfazione tratta dal lavoro**
leader	**il leader, il capo**
leadership	**il comando, la direzione**
we are looking for leadership qualities	***cerchiamo personale con capacità di comando***
manpower	**la forza lavoro**
manpower planning	**la programmazione della forza lavoro**
position	**la posizione, la mansione**
punctuality	**la puntualità**
shift	**il turno di lavoro**
the first shift is from 06:00 to 14:00	***il primo turno è dalle 06:00 alle 14:00***
night shift	**il turno di notte**

shopfloor	**l'officina** *f*
shop steward	**il membro della commissione interna**
sick note	**il certificato di malattia**
trade union	**il sindacato**
vacation	**le ferie**
working hours	**le ore lavorative**
working hours are currently 37 per week	***le ore lavorative settimanali attualmente sono 37***
work load	**il carico di lavoro**

Types of jobs

blue-collar workers	**le maestranze**
board of directors	**il consiglio di amministrazione**
clerk	**l'impiegato (-a)**
management	**i quadri di gestione**
junior/middle/senior	**inferiori/intermedi/superiori**
manager	**il direttore (-trice)**
manual worker	**l'operaio (-a)**
skilled	**specializzato (-a)**
semi-skilled	**semispecializzato (-a)**
unskilled	**generico (-a)**
shift workers	**i turnisti**
staff	**il personale**
superior (n)	**il superiore**
his superior reports to the Managing Director/CEO	***il suo diretto superiore fa capo all'amministratore delegato***
white-collar workers	**gli impiegati**

Disputes

grievance	**la vertenza**
their grievances include low pay and long hours	***oggetto di questa vertenza sono anche l'aumento dei salari e la riduzione dell'orario di lavoro***
industrial action	**azione** *f* **industriale**
industrial relations	**relazioni** *f* **industriali**
industrial unrest	**le agitazioni nel settore industriale**

COMPANY POSITIONS, see page 28/EMPLOYMENT LAW, see page 123

picket (n)/(v)	**il picchetto/picchettare**
the factory was picketed during the strike	***durante lo sciopero sono stati effettuati picchetti***
strike (n)/(v)	**lo sciopero/scioperare**
work to rule	**lo sciopero bianco**

Recruitment

applicant	**l'aspirante *m/f* (ad un posto di lavoro)**
application form	**il modulo per la domanda di assunzione**
apply for a job	**richiedere l'assunzione**
appoint	**nominare**
candidate	**il candidato (-a)**
c.v. (curriculum vitae/resumé)	**il C.V. (curriculum vitae)**
experience (n)	**le esperienze *pl* lavorative**
fill (a position)	**ricoprire (un incarico)**
interview, to come for	**presentarsi ad un colloquio**
interviewee	**il candidato (-a)**
interviewer	**il selezionatore (-trice)**
job description	**la descrizione del lavoro**
qualifications	**le qualifiche**
qualified	**qualificato(-a)**
we're only interested in qualified personnel	***siamo interessati soltanto a personale qualificato***
well-qualified/unqualified	**ben qualificato (-a)/generico (-a)**
recruit (n)	**assumere**
recruitment	**l'assunzione *f***
reference	**le referenze *pl***
they followed up her references	***hanno esaminato le sue referenze***
select	**selezionare**
vacancy	**il posto vacante, l'impiego *m* disponibile**
I'm afraid we have no vacancies at present	***sono spiacente ma attualmente non assumiamo personale***

Leaving

dismissal	**il licenziamento**
fire (v) (on the spot)	**licenziare (in tronco)**
he was fired for stealing	***è stato licenziato per frode***

hand in one's notice	**dare le dimissioni**
lay-off (n)/(v)	**sospensione/sospendere per riduzione dell'attività produttività**
redundant/laid off	**in esubero**
2,000 workers will be made redundant/laid off	***2.000 lavoratori saranno in esubero***
resign	**dimettersi**
resignation	**la dimissione**
retire	**andare/mandare in pensione**
retirement	**il pensionamento**
he was offered early retirement	***gli è stato proposto il pensionamento anticipato***

Assessment

appraise/review	**valutare**
all the staff are appraised/reviewed annually	***tutto il personale è valutato annualmente***
appraisal/review	**la valutazione**
competence	**la competenza, la capacità, l'abilità** *f*
grade (n)	**il grado, il livello, la categoria**
perform	**eseguire, realizzare**
performance appraisal	**la valutazione delle prestazioni/dei risultati**
probation	**la prova, il periodo di prova**
he's on probation for 6 months	***è in prova per 6 mesi***

Training & development

apprentice	**l'apprendista** *m/f*
the company takes on 5 apprentices a year	***l'azienda assume cinque apprendisti all'anno***
apprenticeship	**l'apprendistato** *m*
course	**il corso**
facilitate	**facilitare**
the training should facilitate decision-making	***la formazione dovrebbe facilitare i processi decisionali***
mentor	**il formatore**
on-the-job training	**la formazione sul posto di lavoro**
promote	**promuovere**
progress (v)	**progredire, avanzare**

seminar	**il seminario**
we are organizing a seminar on leadership skills	***stiamo organizzando un seminario sulle capacità direzionali***
train (v)	**addestrare, formare**
training	**la formazione**
workshop	**il corso pratico**

Remuneration

benefit	**l'indennità** *f*
fringe benefit	**indennità accessoria**
company cars are a common fringe benefit	***le vetture di servizio sono un'indennità accessoria molto comune***
sickness benefit	**indennità di malattia**
collective bargaining	**la contrattazione collettiva**
compensate	**compensare**
deduction	**le trattenute**
my take-home pay after all deductions is very little	***la mia retribuzione al netto di tutte le trattenute è molto bassa***
incentive	**l'incentivo** *m*
income	**le entrate** *pl*
overtime	**gli straordinari**
you can make up the wage with overtime	***è possibile arrotondare il salario con del lavoro straordinario***
pay (n)	**il salario**
pay package	**il trattamento economico**
payroll	**il foglio paga**
pension	**il pensionamento**
perk	**la gratifica**
profit-sharing	**la compartecipazione agli utili**
the employees all benefit from a profit-sharing scheme	***tutti i dipendenti beneficiano di un piano di compartecipazione agli utili***
raise (n)/(v)	**l'aumento** *m*/**aumentare**
I just received a salary raise	***ho appena avuto un aumento di stipendio***
reward	**il compenso, il premio**
salary	**lo stipendio**
wage	**il salario**

COMPANY DEPARTMENTS

Personnel

PRODUCTION

Quality

accurate	**preciso (-a)**
accuracy	**la precisione**
assess	**valutare, stimare**
defect	**il difetto**
the defect was caused by a faulty machine	***il difetto è stato causato da una macchina difettosa***
evaluate	**valutare, stimare**
inspect	**esaminare**
ISO	**ISO**
quality assurance/control	**l'assicurazione *f* qualità**
quality circle	**il circolo della qualità**
the plant has set up quality circles	***nello stabilimento sono stati istituiti controlli della qualità***
reject (n)/(v)	**lo scarto/scartare**
reject rate	**il tasso di scarti**
scrap (n)	**il rottame**
zero defect	**zero difetti**
we are aiming for zero defect production	***puntiamo a raggiungere una produzione con zero difetti***

Process

assemble	**montare**
assembly	**il montaggio**
assembly line	**la linea di montaggio**
the assembly line has been automated	***la linea di montaggio è stata automatizzata***
automate	**automatizzare**
automation	**l'automazione *f***
component	**il componente**
continuous process	**il processo a ciclo continuo**
convert	**trasformare, convertire**
efficiency	**l'efficienza *f***
efficient	**efficiente**
finished goods	**i prodotti finiti**
goods	**le merci, i prodotti**
intermittent production	**la produzione intermittente**
line assembly	**la catena di montaggio**

line worker	**l'operatore (-trice) di catena di montaggio**
off-the-shelf	**l'articolo *m* comune a magazzino**
produce (v)	**produrre**
production	**la produzione**

Planning

backlog	**l'accumulo *m***
there is a backlog of orders to deal with	***dobbiamo occuparci di un accumulo di ordini arretrati***
batch	**il lotto**
batch size	**la dimensione del lotto**
capacity	**la capacità**
we are working at full capacity	***operiamo al pieno delle nostre capacità***
critical path analysis	**l'analisi *f* del percorso critico**
cycle time	**il tempo del ciclo**
delivery cycle	**il ciclo di consegna**
downtime	**il fermo macchina**
machine downtime costs money	***i fermi macchina sono alquanto costosi***
flow rate	**la velocità di lavorazione**
idle	**inattivo (-a)**
we can't afford for the machines to be idle	***non possiamo permetterci di lasciare inattivi i macchinari***
job lot	**il lotto**
lead time	**il tempo di rifornimento**
the lead time is too long	***il tempo di rifornimento è eccessivamente lungo***
make-to-order	**produzione *f* a fronte di ordini**
make-to-stock	**produzione *f* per stock**
output	**la produzione**
productive	**produttivo (-a)**
productivity	**la produttività**
productivity levels have increased	***i livelli di produttività sono migliorati***
prototype	**il prototipo**
schedule	**il programma**
set-up time	**il tempo di avviamento**
slack (adj)	**inattivo (-a)**

throughput	**il volume**
work-in progress	**la lavorazione in corso**

Resources & stock

bill of materials	**la distinta base**
equip	**equipaggiare**
equipment	**l'attrezzatura** *f*
inventory	**l'inventario** *m*
just-in-time	**in un tempo stabilito**
machine	**la macchina**
machinery	**il macchinario**
MRP (Materials Requirements Planning)	**la programmazione richieste materiali**
materials handling	**la movimentazione materiali**
raw materials	**le materie prime**
stock (n)	**le scorte**
stock levels	**il livello delle scorte/giacenze**
in stock	**a magazzino/esaurito (-a)**
we have just one left in stock	***ne abbiamo solamente uno in magazzino***
out of stock	**lo stoccaggio**
stock control	**il controllo del livello delle scorte**
store (n)/(v)	**il magazzino/mettere in magazzino**
storage	**l'immagazzinaggio** *m*

Maintenance

breakdown	**il guasto, l'avaria** *f*
this machine has never broken down	***questa macchina non è mai stata fuori uso***
failure	**l'inconveniente** *m*
fault	**il difetto**
faulty	**difettoso (-a)**
maintain	**eseguire la manutenzione**
maintenance	**la manutenzione**
repair	**riparare**
reliable	**affidabile**
reliability	**l'affidabilità** *f*
shut-down (n)	**l'arresto** *m* **della produzione**
shut down (v)	**arrestare/interrompere la produzione**

PURCHASING

auction (n)	**l'asta *f***
buy	**acquistare**
buyer	**l'addetto *m* ufficio acquisti**
purchaser	**l'acquirente *m/f***
source	**la fonte di approvvigionamento**
you should have at least two sources	***dovresti avere almeno due fonti di approvvigionamento***
spend (n)/(v)	**la spesa/spendere**
total purchasing spend is over 1 million	***la spesa per gli acquisti ammonta complessivamente ad oltre 1 milione***
supply (v)	**fornire**
supplies	**le forniture**
we buy in supplies	***acquistiamo le forniture***
supplier	**il fornitore (-trice)**
vendor	**il venditore (-trice/-a)**

Functions

inventory management	**la gestione delle scorte**
inventory control	**il controllo del livello delle scorte**
logistics	**logistica *f***
materials management	**la gestione dei materiali**
vendor appraisal	**la valutazione del venditore**
the criteria for vendor appraisal include price, quality and delivery	***il criterio di valutazione dei venditori tiene conto dei prezzi, della qualità e della consegna***

Finance

bill	**la fattura**
billing	**la fatturazione**
we prefer quarterly billing	***preferiamo la fatturazione trimestrale***
currency	**la valuta**
weak/strong currency	**la valuta debole/forte**
currency fluctuations	**le variazioni della valuta**

Supply & demand

buyers'/sellers' market	**il mercato dell'acquirente/del venditore**

demand (n)	**la domanda**
under-demand	**la bassa domanda**
prices are low because of under-demand	***i prezzi sono contenuti a causa della bassa domanda***
over-demand	**l'eccesso *m* di domanda**
supply	**l'offerta *f***
under-supply	**la bassa offerta**
over-supply	**l'eccesso *m* di offerta**

Tendering process

accept	**accettare**
the offer was accepted	***l'offerta è stata accettata***
call (v) for tenders	**bandire gare d'appalto**
the call for tenders was published in the press	***il bando delle gare d'appalto è stato pubblicato sui giornali***
open/closed tender	**la gara d'appalto aperta/chiusa**
reject	**respingere**
submit a tender/an offer	**partecipare ad una gara d'appalto/presentare un'offerta**
tender specifications	**i capitolati delle gare d'appalto**
the tender specifications are very detailed	***i capitolati delle gare d'appalto sono molto dettagliati***
tender evaluation	**la valutazione offerte**

Documents

letter of intent	**la lettera d'intenti**
we sent the supplier a letter of intent	***abbiamo inviato una lettera d'intenti al fornitore***
purchase order	**l'ordine *m* d'acquisto**

Price negotiation

bottom-line	**il prezzo limite**
our bottom-line was L.300m	***il nostro prezzo limite era di 300 milioni di lire***
cut (n)	**la riduzione**
we forced a 10% price cut on all our suppliers	***abbiamo imposto una riduzione del 10% sui prezzi a tutti i nostri fornitori***
margin	**il margine**
target price	**il prezzo traguardo**

SALES

client	**il/la cliente**
customer	**l'acquirente** *m*
end-user	**il consumatore (-trice) finale**
give-away	**l'omaggio** *m*
we usually supply give-aways such as pens	***noi solitamente forniamo omaggi (penne, ecc.)***
prospect	**il/la cliente potenziale**
he's a good prospect	***è un buon cliente potenziale***
sales call	**visita a scopo di vendita**
I've got one more sales call to make	***mi rimane ancora una visita da fare***
sales conference	**la conferenza sulle vendite**
sales message	**il messaggio di vendita**
target	**l' obbiettivo** *m*, **traguardo**
we have a very ambitious sales target this year	***l'obbiettivo vendite di quest'anno è molto ambizioso***
sample	**il campione**

Selling people & organisation

field sales	**il commesso viaggiatore**
we've got a team of 3 field salespeople	***abbiamo un team composto da 3 commessi viaggiatori***
sales area	**l'area** *f* **di vendita**
the country is divided into four sales areas	***il paese è suddiviso in quattro aree di vendita***
sales assistant	**l'assistente** *m* **di vendita**
sales manager	**il vice direttore (-trice) delle vendite**
salesforce	**il personale addetto alle vendite**

Types of selling

door-to-door sales	**la vendita porta a porta**
direct sales	**la vendita diretta**
hard selling	**la vendita aggressiva**
hard selling doesn't work in this business	***la politica di vendita aggressiva non funziona in questo settore***
personal selling	**la vendita personale**
soft selling	**la vendita morbida**
telephone sales	**la vendita per telefono**

Industries and Professions

CONSTRUCTION

Materials used in construction

asphalt	**l'asfalto** *m*
brick	**il mattone**
red brick	**il mattone rosso**
cement	**il cemento**
clay	**l'argilla** *f*
concrete	**il calcestruzzo**
pre-fabricated concrete	**il calcestruzzo prefabbricato**
reinforced concrete	**il cemento armato**
glass	**il vetro**

frosted glass	**il vetro smerigliato**
plain glass	**il vetro semplice**
reinforced glass	**il vetro rinforzato**
safety glass	**il vetro di sicurezza**
gravel	**la ghiaia**
macadam	**il macadam**
masonry	**la muratura**
mortar	**la malta**
plastic	**la plastica**
slate	**l'ardesia** *f*
steel	**l'acciaio** *m*
steel girder	**la trave d'acciaio**
stone	**la pietra**
cobble stone	**il ciottolo**
tarmac	**il catrame**
tiles	**le piastrelle**
timber	**il legname**
uPVC	**il PVC**
wood	**il legno**
wooden beam	**la trave di legno**
wooden plank	**il rivestimento in legno**

Planning regulations in this area prohibit the use of prefabricated concrete. — ***I piani regolatori in questa zona vietano l'uso di calcestruzzo prefabbricato.***

Professions in construction

architect	**l'architetto** *m*
brick layer	**il muratore**
builder	**il costruttore (-trice)**
carpenter	**il carpentiere**
designer	**il/la progettista**
developer	**il lottizzatore (-trice)**
draughtsman	**il disegnatore (-trice)**
engineer	**l'ingegnere** *m*
civil	**civile**
sanitary	**sanitario**
structural	**strutturale**
glazier	**il vetraio**
joiner	**il falegname**
painter	**l'imbianchino** *m*
planner	**l'urbanista** *m/f*

PROPERTY, see page 110

plasterer	**l'intonacatore** *m*
plumber	**l'idraulico** *m*
surveyor	**il geometra**
quantity surveyor	**il misuratore**

Our on-site management team consists of an architect, responsible for drawing up the plan, a civil engineer and a surveyor.

Il nostro gruppo di gestione consiste di un architetto, responsabile della progettazione, un ingegnere civile e un geometra.

Processes in construction

to build	**costruire**
to chart	**fare un piano**
to construct	**edificare**
to cool	**raffreddare**
to demolish	**demolire**
to design	**progettare**
to dig	**scavare**
to draft	**abbozzare**
to draw	**disegnare**
to erect	**erigere**
to excavate	**scavare**
to heat	**riscaldare**
to install	**installare**
to maintain	**mantenere**
to measure	**misurare**
to plan	**pianificare**
to refurbish	**ristrutturare**
to renovate	**rimodernare**
to repair	**riparare**
to replace	**sostituire**
to scaffold	**innalzare un'impalcatura**
to sketch	**fare un bozzetto**
to ventilate	**ventilare**
to wire	**installare i fili per l'elettricità**

Our company specialises in refurbishing old houses: everything from designing the plans to carrying out the job.

La nostra azienda si specializza nella ristrutturazione di vecchie case; dalla progettazione alla realizzazione dei lavori.

ENGINEERING

Branches of engineering

architectural engineering	**l'ingegneria *f* architettonica**
chemical engineering	**l'ingegneria chimica**
civil engineering	**l'ingegneria civile**
drainage engineering	**l'ingegneria fognaria**
electrical engineering	**l'ingegneria elettrica**
electronic engineering	**l'ingegneria elettronica**
fire protection engineering	**l'ingegneria anti-incendio**
highway engineering	**l'ingegneria stradale**
hydraulic engineering	**l'ingegneria idraulica**
industrial engineering	**l'ingegneria industriale**
marine engineering	**l'ingegneria marina**
mechanical engineering	**l'ingegneria meccanica**
mining and metallurgical engineering	**l'ingegneria mineraria e metallurgica**
nuclear engineering	**l'ingegneria nucleare**
petroleum production engineering	**l'ingegneria petrolifera**
production engineering	**l'ingegneria di produzione**
railway engineering	**l'ingegneria ferroviaria**
safety engineering	**l'ingegneria della sicurezza**
sanitary engineering	**l'ingegneria sanitaria**
structural engineering	**l'ingegneria strutturale**
welding engineering	**l'ingegneria della saldatura**

We plan to call in a safety engineering company to advise us on improving standards.

Intendiamo chiedere ad un'azienda che si occupa di ingegneria per la sicurezza, di informarci sui metodi per migliorare il nostro livello di sicurezza.

Applications of engineering

boiler	**le caldaie**
boring	**le perforazioni**
bridge	**i ponti**
dye	**i coloranti**

electricity supply	**l'alimentazione *f* elettrica**
gas manufacture	**la produzione di gas**
hydraulics	**l'idraulica *f***
mining	**la mineraria**
paper manufacture	**la produzione di carta**
power generation	**la generazione di energia**
power transmission	**la trasmissione di energia**
printing	**la stampa**
shipbuilding	**la costruzione navale**

Equipment in engineering

boiler	**la caldaia**
crane	**la gru**
gas engine	**il motore a gas**
machine tools	**la macchina utensile**
pump	**la pompa**
turbine/engine	**la turbina**
steam turbine/engine	**la turbina a vapore**
water turbine/engine	**la turbina idraulica**

This boiler has an auxiliary safety valve to prevent a build-up of pressure.
Questa caldaia è dotata di una valvola di sicurezza aggiuntiva per evitare l'aumento di pressione.

Processes in treating metals

to anneal	**ricuocere**
to anodize	**anodizzare**
to electroplate	**trattare elettroliticamente**
to forge	**forgiare**
to found	**fondere**
to galvanize	**zincare**
to grind	**rettificare**
to harden	**indurire**
to mint	**coniare**
to plate	**placcare**
to roll	**filettare (con rulli)**
to temper	**rinvenire**
to terneplate	**piombare**
to tinplate	**stagnare**

FOOD AND CATERING

The meals

breakfast	**la colazione**
lunch	**il pranzo**
dinner	**la cena**
picnic	**la scampagnata**
snack	**la spuntino**

The elements of food

carbohydrates	**i carboidrati**
fats	**i grassi**
proteins	**le proteine**
vitamins	**le vitamine**
minerals	**i minerali**

Types of food

cereals	**i cereali**
dairy products	**i latticini**
drinks	**le bibite**
eggs	**le uova**
fats	**i grassi**
fish	**il pesce**
fruit	**la frutta**
game	**la cacciagione**
meat	**la carne**
nuts	**le noci**
organic food	**il nutrimento biologico**
pasta	**la pasta**
poultry	**il pollame**
preserves	**le conserve**
pulses/lentils	**i legumi**
sauce	**la salsa**
seafood	**i frutti di mare**
sweets	**i dolci**
vegetables	**la verdura**

We have changed the ingredients in many of our products, because of the danger to health caused by fats and sweets. — ***Abbiamo cambiato gli ingredienti in molti dei nostri prodotti dovuto al pericolo che corre la nostra salute per il consumo di grassi e dolci.***

DINING OUT, see page 27

Parts of a meal

aperitif	**l'aperitivo** *m*
starter/first course	**l'antipasto** *m*, **il primo**
soup	**la zuppa**
salad	**l'insalata** *f*
main course	**il secondo**
dessert	**il dolce**
cheese	**formaggio** *m*

Growing processes in food-making

to fatten	**ingrassare**
to fertilize	**concimare**
to germinate	**germogliare**
to grow	**crescere**
to harvest	**fare il raccolto**
to hatch	**covare**
to milk	**mungere**
to pick	**cogliere, raccogliere**
to plough/plow	**arare**
to propagate	**moltiplicare**
to rear	**allevare**
to slaughter	**macellare**
to sow	**seminare**
We guarantee that the animals have been organically reared and slaughtered in a humane way.	***Garantiamo che gli animali sono stati allevati con prodotti naturali e macellati senza sofferenza.***

Food preparation

to bake	**infornare**
to boil	**bollire**
to chop up	**tritare**
to cook	**cucinare**
to cure	**conservare salando**
to cut	**tagliare**
into pieces/slices	**a pezzi/a fette**
up	**a pezzetti**
to fry	**friggere**
to grill	**grigliare**
to heat	**scaldare**

to marinate	**marinare**
to melt	**sciogliere**
to pickle	**mettere sott'aceto**
to roast	**arrostire**
to salt	**salare**
to smoke	**affumicare**
to stew	**cuocere in umido**
to sweeten	**dolcificare**
to toast	**tostare**
We cut up the fruit into small pieces before we put it into cans.	***Tagliamo la frutta a pezzetti e poi la mettiamo nelle lattine.***

The business of catering

banquet hall	**la sala banchetti**
bar	**il bar**
buffet	**il buffet**
café/cafeteria	**il caffè, la caffetteria, il bar**
chef	**lo chef**
coffeeshop	**il posto di ristoro**
cook (n)	**il cuoco (-a)**
diner	**il/la commensale**
fast food	**la tavola calda**
feast	**il festino**
meal	**il pasto**
pub	**il pub**
refreshment	**il ristoro**
restaurant	**il ristoratore**
restaurateur	**il proprietario di un ristorante**
serve	**servire**
snack	**lo spuntino**
teahouse	**la sala da tè**
waiter	**il cameriere**
drinks waiter	**il sommelier**
waitress	**la cameriera**
The conference centre/center provides three main function rooms andis able to serve buffet meals for up to 300 delegates.	***Il centro convegni offre tre sale principali e il servizio di buffet fino a 300 coperti.***

INFORMATION TECHNOLOGY

Source of information

archive	**l'archivio** *m*
databank	**la banca dati, il centro dati**
database	**l'archivio computerizzato, il database**
file	**il file**
library	**la biblioteca**
The customer database contains the names and addresses of all our customers.	***Il database del cliente contiene i nomi e gli indirizzi di tutti i nostri clienti.***

The representation of information

digital data	**i dati numerici**
digitize	**digitalizzare, numerazione**
encipher	**cifrare**
image	**l'immagine** *m*
message	**il messaggio**
signal	**il segnale**
electric signal	**il segnale elettrico**
electromagnetic signal	**il segnale elettromagnetico**
transformation	**la trasformazione**
If you digitize data, you can store it in a digital form, i.e. as a series of 1s and 0s.	***Se digitate i dati, può memorizzarli in modo digitale, vale a dire una serie di 1 e 0.***

The storage of information

bit	**il bit**
byte	**il byte**
data	**i dati** *m/pl*
data recording	**la registrazione dei dati**
magnetic data recording	**la registrazione magnetica dei dati**
optical data recording	**la registrazione ottica dei dati**
disk	**il dischetto**
compact disk	**il compact disk (CD)**
floppy disk	**il disco floppy**
hard disk	**il disco fisso**

memory	**la memoria**
random access memory	**la memoria con accesso diretto**
read-only memory (ROM)	**la memoria a sola lettura (ROM)**
CD-ROM	**il CD-ROM**

The transmission and processing of information

amplifier	**l'amplificatore** *m*
computer	**il computer, il calcolatore elettronico**
computer system	**il sistema di elaborazione dati**
computer network	**la rete di calcolatori**
electrical impulses	**gli impulsi elettrici**
microphone	**il microfono**
radio communication systems	**i sistemi di radiocomunicazione**
radio transmitter	**il trasmettitore radio**
signal	**il segnale**
electronic signal	**il segnale elettronico**
electromagnetic signal	**il segnale elettromagnetico**
telephone	**il telefono**
telephone network	**la rete telefonica**
teletype network	**la rete telescrivente**
television	**la televisione**
The new Pentium® chip is at the heart of the system, processing huge amounts of data at incredible speeds.	***Il nuovo chip della Pentium® è al centro del sistema, esso è in grado di elaborare enormi quantità di dati a velocità incredibile.***

Processes

to convert	**convertire**
to degrade	**offrire una funzionalità ridotta**
to distort	**distorcere**
to receive	**ricevere**
to transmit	**trasmettere**
This equipment can convert the old analog signals into digital signals.	***Questa attrezzatura può convertire i vecchi segnali analogici in segnali digitali.***

TELECOMMUNICATIONS, see page 112

PHARMACEUTICALS AND CHEMICALS

Chemicals and life

alkaloids — **gli alcaloidi**
carbohydrates — **i carboidrati**
cholesterol — **il colesterolo**
coloration — **la colorazione**
drugs — **le medicine**
enzymes — **gli enzimi**
hormones — **l'ormone *m***
lipids — **i lipidi**
nucleic acids — **gli acidi nucleici**
  Deoxyribonucleic acid (DNA) — **l'acido *m* desossiribonucleico (ADN)**
  Ribonucleic acid (RNA) — **l'acido ribonucleico (ARN)**
peptides — **il peptide**
pigments — **il pigmento**
  chlorophyll — **la clorofilla**
  melanin — **la melanina**
proteins — **le proteine**
  amino acid — **l'aminoacido *m***
  glutamine — **la glutammina**
  gluten — **il glutine**
  keratin — **la cheratina**
  myoglobin — **la mioglobina**
steroids — **gli steroidi**
vitamins — **le vitamine**

As the lack of any hormone may cause a major deficiency, we now synthesize most of them artificially. — ***Siccome la mancanza di ormoni può provocare una deficienza grave, ne sintetizziamo adesso un gran numero.***

Body systems

autonomic nervous system — **il sistema nervoso autonomo**
cardiovascular system — **il sistema cardiovascolare**
central nervous system — **il sistema nervoso centrale**
digestive system — **l'apparato *m* digerente**
excretory system — **l'apparato *m* deferente**
histamine response system — **il sistema antistaminico**
immune response system — **il sistema immunitario**

reproductive system	**l'apparato *m* genitale**
skeletal muscle system	**l'apparato *m* scheletrico**

Our new digestive tablets help with the ingestion, digestion and absorption of food. — ***Le nostre nuove compresse servono per aiutare la digestione e l'assorbimento del cibo.***

Drugs

atropins	**l'atropina *f***
analgesics	**gli analgesici**
salicylic acid	**l'acido *m* salicilico**
anaesthetics	**gli anestetici**
chloroform	**il cloroformio**
cocaine	**la cocaina**
procaine	**la procaina**
antibiotics	**gli antibiotici**
penicillin	**la penicillina**
streptomycin	**la streptomicina**
antiseptics	**gli antisettici**
beta blockers	**il beta-bloccante**
chemotherapeutics	**i chemioterapeutici**
quinine	**la chinina**
sulfa drug	**il sulfamidico**
hallucinogens	**gli allucinogeni**
cannabis	**il cannabis**
hashish	**l'hascisc *m***
marijuana	**la marihuana**
mescaline	**la mescalina**
narcotics	**i narcotici**
heroin	**l'eroina *f***
methadone	**il metadone**
morphine	**la morfina**
opium	**l'oppio *m***
sedatives	**i sedativi**
barbiturates	**i barbiturici**
thalidomide	**la talidomide**
stimulants	**gli stimolanti**
amphetamine	**l'amfetamina *f***
caffeine	**la caffeinam**
tranquillizers	**i tranquillanti**
diazepam	**il diazepam**
others	**altri**

antacids	**l'antiacido** *m*
antihistamine	**l'antistaminico** *m*
diuretic	**il diuretico**
ephedrine	**l'efedrina** *f*
laxative	**il lassativo**

Some anaesthetics are used before or during surgery to depress the central nervous system.

Alcuni anestetici vengono usati prima dell'intervento chirurgico per addormentare il sistema nervoso centrale.

The drug business

ethical drugs	**i farmaci di impatto sociale (da vendersi solo dietro prescrizione medica)**
generic drugs	**i farmaci generici**
me-too products	**i farmaci di imitazione**
prescription drugs	**i farmaci che richiedono ricetta**
proprietary drugs	**le specialità farmaceutiche**
patent drugs	**i farmaci brevettati**
veterinary pharmaceuticals	**i farmaci ad uso veterinario**

Proprietary drugs are sold over the counter; ethical drugs may be obtained legally only with a prescription from an authorized health-care provider.

Le specialità farmaceutiche possono essere vendute in farmacia; per i farmaci di impatto sociale occorre la ricetta del medico curante autorizzato.

Drug forms

liquid	**liquido (-a)**
capsular	**capsulare**

Branches of medicine

clinical medicine	**medicina clinica**
preventive medicine	**medicina di prevenzione**
fringe medicine	**medicina marginale**
alternative medicine	**medicina alternativa**
complementary medicine	**medicina complementare**
holistic medicine	**medicina olistica**
unorthodox medicine	**medicina non ortodossa**
folk medicine	**medicina popolare**

PROPERTY

The types of property

apartment/flat	**l'appartamento** *m*
furnished apartment	**l'appartamento ammobiliato**
studio apartment	**il monolocale**
apartment block/block of flats	**il palazzo**
bungalow	**il bungalow**
castle	**il maniero**
chalet	**la baita**
consulate	**il consolato**
duplex/two-storey house	**la villetta bifamigliare a due piani**
embassy	**l'ambasciata** *f*
estate	**la tenuta**
farmhouse	**la fattoria**
field	**il campo**
grounds	**i terreni**
hall	**l'ingresso** *m*
house	**la casa**
country house	**la casa di campagna**
manor house	**la casa padronale**
ranch house	**il podere**
tenement house	**la casa popolare**
terraced (row) house	**la villetta a schiera**
town house	**la residenza cittadina**
lodge	**la casetta**
mansion	**il palazzo signorile**
office	**l'ufficio** *m*
palace	**la reggia**
park	**il parco**
penthouse	**l'attico** *m*
plot	**l'appezzamento** *m* **di terreno**
property	**le proprietà (beni)**
stately home	**la casa signorile**
villa	**la villa**
Our client requires 350 square metres of office space, fully equipped with telecommunications connections, and in a central location.	***Il nostro cliente richiede un ufficio di 350 metri quadri, completamente attrezzato con apparecchiatura ed allacciamenti per rete telematica, e in una posizione centrale.***

CONSTRUCTION, see page 97

The relationship with property

boarder	**il convittore (-trice)**
homeowner	**il locatario (-a) di casa**
householder	**l'affittuario** *m*
leaseholder/tenant	**l'inquilino (-a)**
lessee	**il locatore (-trice)**
lessor	**l'inquilino (-a)**
lodger	**il locatario (-a)**
occupier	**il padrone (-a) di casa**
owner	**la proprietà**
resident	**il/la residente**
paying guest	**il/la pensionante**
renter	**l'affittuario** *m/f*
Under the terms of this lease the landlord, Mr Marchi, grants possession and use of the property at this address to you as tenant or lessee for a term of 25 years.	***Secondo le condizioni di questo contratto di locazione il proprietario, Sig. Marchi, concede il possesso ed usufrutto della proprietà a questo indirizzo a Lei come inquilino o locatario per un periodo di 25 anni.***

The legal aspects of property

assign	**assegnare**
convey	**cedere**
conveyance	**la cessione**
freehold	**la proprietà assoluta di un terreno**
lease (v)	**dare in affitto, affittare**
leasehold/tenancy	**la locazione**
hereditament	**l'eredità** *f*
let (v)	**affittare**
sublet (n)	**il subaffitto, la sublocazione**
sublet (v)	**subaffittare**
rent (v)	**dare in affitto**
rental	**l'affitto** *m*
tenure	**il diritto di possesso**
trust, in	**in fede**
As a potential buyer of the freehold, it is important to check the seller's title to the property.	***Come possibile compratore del terreno, è fondamentale che si controllino i diritti di proprietà del venditore.***

TELECOMMUNICATIONS

Systems in telecommunications

cable (v)	**cablografare**
cablegram	**il cablogramma**
electronic mail	**la posta elettronica**
facsimile/fax	**il fax**
radio telegraphy	**la radio telegrafia**
teleconferencing	**la teleconferenza**
telegram	**il telegramma**
telephony	**la telefonia**
videoconferencing	**la videoconferenza**
wire (v)	**telegrafare**
wireless telegraphy	**telegrafia *f* senza fili**

Our new videoconferencing equipment allows two or more people at different locations to communicate written, spoken and visual information to each other.

La nostra nuova attrezzatura per videoconferenze permette a due o più persone situate in diversi luoghi di scambiare informazioni per iscritto, oralmente e visivamente.

Technology in telecommunications

asynchronous transfer mode (ATM)	**il modo di trasferimento asincrono**
bandwidth	**la larghezza di banda**
converter	**il convertitore**
data	**i dati**
analog data	**i dati analogici**
digital data	**i dati digitali**
transfer (v) data	**trasferire dati**
modem	**il modem**
fax modem	**il modem fax**
multiplexing	**la multiplazione**
time-division multiplexing	**la multiplazione a divisione di tempo**
network	**la rete**
Internet	**Internet**
local area net (LAN)	**rete locale**
wide-area networks	**reti ad ampia diffusione**
signal	**il segnale**
switching	**la commutazione**
packet switching	**la commutazione di pacchetto**

The A44 modem enables computer data to be transmitted over a telephone line at very high speeds.

Il modem A44 consente di trasmettere dati elettronici su una linea telefonica a velocità elevate.

Equipment and devices in telecommunications

amplifier	**l'amplificatore** *m*
antenna	**l'antenna** *f*
cable	**il cavo**
coaxial cables	**i cavi coassiali**
fibre/fiber optic cables	**i cavi a fibre ottiche**
circuit	**il circuito**
integrated circuit	**il circuito integrato**
printed circuit	**il circuito stampato**
communications satellite	**le comunicazioni satellitari**
electric	**elettrico (-a)**
electric circuit	**il circuito elettrico**
electric switch	**il commutatore elettrico**
headphone	**la cuffia telefonica**
headset	**la cuffia**
loudspeaker	**l'altoparlante** *m*
microphone	**il microfono**
microprocessor	**il microprocessore**
microwave	**la microonda**
photoelectric cell	**la cellula fotoelettrica**
radar	**il radar**
receiver	**il ricevitore**
semiconductor	**il semiconduttore**
switchboard	**il tavolo di commutazione**
telephone	**il telefono**
car telephone	**il telefono veicolare**
cellular phone	**il telefono cellulare**
radio telephone	**il radio telefono**
telephone exchange	**il centralino**
videophone	**il videotelefono**
transistor	**il transistor**
transmitter	**il trasmettitore**

Standard coaxial cable can carry up to 132,000 messages simultaneously.

Il cavo coassiale standard è in grado di trasmettere fino a 132.000 messaggi simultaneamente.

TEXTILES AND CLOTHING

Types of textiles

canvas	**la canapa**
cashmere	**il cashmere**
chintz	**il chintz**
corduroy	**il velluto a coste**
cotton	**il cotone**
damask	**il damascato**
denim	**il tessuto jeans**
fibre/fiber	**la fibra**
flannel	**la flanella**
gauze	**il velo**
hessian	**la tela grezza**
jute	**l'iuta** *f*
linen	**il lino**
mohair	**il mohair**
net	**la rete**
satin	**il raso**
silk	**la seta**
synthetics	**i tessuti sintetici**
nylon	**il nylon**
polyester	**il poliestere**
polymer	**il polimero**
rayon	**il rayon**
vinyl fibre/fiber	**la fibra vinilica**
velvet	**il velluto**
wool	**la lana**

Synthetics such as nylon and polyester, which are stronger than silk and lower in price, have led to a tremendous reduction in silk production and consumption.

L'uso di tessuti sintetici come ad esempio il nylon e il poliestere, i quali sono più resistenti e di minor costo, hanno comportato una riduzione drastica nella produzione e consumo della seta.

Processes in textile manufacture

to crochet	**lavorare all'uncinetto**
to darn	**rammendare**
to dye	**tingere**
to felt	**infeltrire**
to knit	**lavorare a maglia**
to press	**stirare**

to spin	**filare la lana**
to twill	**tessere in diagonale**
to weave	**tessere**
We use a wide range of natural dyes to colour/color our textiles.	***Si usa una vasta gamma di tinte per la colorazione dei nostri tessuti.***

Types of clothes

blouse	**la camicetta**
boots	**gli stivali**
bra	**il reggiseno**
cagoule	**la giacca a vento**
coat	**il soprabito, il cappotto**
glove	**il guanto**
handkerchief	**il fazzoletto**
hat	**il cappello**
jacket	**la giacca**
jeans	**i jeans**
jersey	**il pullover, la maglia**
knitwear	**la maglieria**
lingerie	**la biancheria intima**
pyjamas/pajamas	**i pigiama**
raincoat	**l'impermeabile *m***
sandals	**i sandali**
scarf	**la sciarpa**
shirt	**la camicia**
shoe	**la scarpa**
skirt	**la gonna**
sneakers	**le scarpe da tennis**
sock	**il calzino**
stockings	**le calze**
suit	**il vestito**
sweater	**il maglione di lana**
swimming trunks	**i calzoncini da bagno**
swimsuit/bathing suit	**il costume da bagno**
tie	**la cravatta**
tights	**i collant**
trainers	**le scarpe sportive**
trousers/pants	**i pantaloni, i calzoni**
t-shirt	**la camicietta**
underwear	**la biancheria intima**
vest	**la maglietta**

BANKING

The business of banking

retail banking	**l'attività *f* bancaria al dettaglio**
wholesale/corporate banking	**l'attività bancaria all'ingrosso/ di corporate**
universal/full-service banking	**l'attività bancaria universale**
investment banking	**l'attività di collocamento**
merchant banking	**l'attività di intermediazione finanziaria**
trustee banking	**l'attività bancaria fiduciaria**
We specialise in wholesale banking for corporate and institutional investors.	***Siamo specializzati nell'attività bancaria all'ingrosso, a favore di investitori istituzionali o legalmente costituiti in società.***

The services provided

account	**il conto corrente**
bank account	**il conto bancario**
current/checking account	**il conto corrente**
deposit account	**il conto vincolato**
savings account	**il conto di risparmio**
time deposit account	**il deposito a tempo**
correspondent banking	**l'attività *f* bancaria in corrispondenza**
credit	**il credito**
credit card	**la carta di credito**
credit limit	**il limite di credito**
credit line	**la linea di credito (fido bancario)**
debit card	**la carta di addebito-bancomat**
deposit (n)/(v)	**il deposito/depositare**
deposit account	**il conto di deposito**
deposit box	**la cassetta di deposito**
foreign exchange	**la valuta estera**
interest	**l'interesse *m***
interest rate	**il tasso d'interesse**
fixed interest rate	**il tasso d'interesse fisso**
variable interest rate	**il tasso d'interesse variabile**
investment	**l'investimento *m***
investment services	**i servizi d'investimento**

FINANCE DEPARTMENT, see page 73

loan	**il mutuo**
short-term loan	**il mutuo a breve termine**
long-term loan	**il mutuo a lungo termine**
lend	**prestare**
letter of credit	**la lettera di credito**
mortgage	**l'ipoteca** *f*
overdraft	**lo scoperto** *m* **di conto**
portfolio management	**la gestione di portafoglio**
project financing	**il finanziamento (dello sviluppo) di un progetto**
risk analysis	**l'analisi** *f* **dei rischi**
safe-deposit box	**la cassetta di sicurezza**
save	**risparmiare**
savings	**i risparmi** *m/pl*
savings account	**il conto di risparmio**
transfer	**il bonifico**
travellers' cheques/checks	**gli assegni** *m* **(turistici), i travellers' cheques** *m*

Our savings accounts offer very attractive rates of interest. — ***I nostri conti di risparmio offrono tassi di interesse estremamente convenienti.***

The profession of banking

bank manager	**il direttore (-trice) di banca**
cashier	**il cassiere (-a)**
customer advisor	**l'assistente** *m/f* **alla clientela**
dealer	**l'operatore** *m/f* **commerciale**
financial analyst	**l'analista** *m/f* **finanziario (-a)**
financier	**il finanziere**
investment advisor	**il/la consulente per gli investimenti**
investor	**l'investitore** *m/f* **(risparmiatore)**
market maker	**l'operatore** *m/f* **indipendente**
portfolio manager	**il gestore di portafoglio**
security guard	**la guardia giurata**
teller	**il cassiere (-a)**
trader	**il trader (operatore indipendente)**

A portfolio manager can make day-to-day decisions about your investments. — ***Il gestore di portafoglio può rivedere quotidianamente le condizioni relative ai Vs./vostri investimenti.***

INSURANCE

Types of insurance

aviation insurance	**l'assicurazione *f* aerea**
credit insurance	**l'assicurazione-credito**
fire insurance	**l'assicurazione contro l'incendio**
group insurance	**l'assicurazione collettiva**
group life insurance	**l'assicurazione collettiva sulla vita**
group health insurance	**l'assicurazione collettiva contro le malattie**
group annuities	**le rendite di gruppo**
health insurance	**l'assicurazione contro le malattie**
permanent health insurance	**l'assicurazione continuativa contro le malattie**
liability insurance	**l'assicurazione contro la responsabilità civile**
life insurance/assurance	**l'assicurazione sulla vita**
marine insurance	**l'assicurazione marittima**
motor/car insurance	**l'assicurazione auto**
comprehensive	**l'assicurazione contro tutti i rischi**
third party, fire and theft	**l'assicurazione contro la responsabilità civile, l'incendio e il furto**
re-insurance	**la riassicurazione**
theft insurance	**l'assicurazione contro il furto**
title insurance	**l'assicurazione per titolo imperfetto**
Under the terms of your motor insurance, you are not covered for damage caused to your own car.	***Secondo i termini della polizza auto stipulata, l'assicurato non è coperto per eventuali danni alla vettura.***

The elements of insurance

accidental occurrence	**l'evento *m* accidentale**
agreement	**l'accordo *m***
claim	**la richiesta di risarcimento**
reimburse	**il rimborso**
commission	**la commissione**
pay commission	**pagare la commissione**

contract	**il contratto**
hazard	**il pericolo**
loss	**la perdita**
mutuality	**la mutualità**
peril	**il rischio**
insurable peril	**il rischio assicurabile**
uninsurable peril	**il rischio non assicurabile**
policy	**la polizza**
cancel a policy	**disdire una polizza**
issue a policy	**emettere una polizza**
policy coverage	**la copertura della polizza**
premium	**il premio**
annual premium	**il premio annuo**
monthly premium	**il premio mensile**
pay a premium	**pagare il premio**
regular premium	**il premio abituale**
single premium	**il premio unico**
rating	**la tariffazione**
risk	**il rischio**
insurable risk	**il rischio assicurabile**
underwriting	**l'assunzione** *f* **di un rischio**
underwriting rates	**le quote assicurative**

If you want to make a claim, you must complete the form giving precise details of how the accident happened.

Per chiedere un risarcimento danni, è necessario compilare un formulario nel quale si è tenuti a specificare cgni dato relativo all'incidente.

Risks

accident	**l'infortunio** *m*
accidental damage	**il danno accidentale**
accidental loss	**la perdita accidentale**
breakdown	**il guasto**
business interruption	**l'interruzione** *f* **di esercizio**
death	**la morte**
explosion	**l'esplosione** *f*
fire	**l'incendio** *m*
flood	**l'inondazione** *m*
illness	**la malattia**

If you insure yourself against business interruption, then we

Stipulando una polizza di "interruzione di esercizio",

will pay out in the event that you are prevented for carrying out your normal business activities.	***l'assicurato ha diritto ad un indennizzo qualora non sia in grado di svolgere la propria normale attività professionale.***

The people involved in insurance

actuary	**l'attuario** *m*
adjuster	**il liquidatore d'avaria**
agent	**l'agente** *m/f* **mandatario (-a)**
broker	**il mediatore (-trice)**
insurer	**l'assicuratore (-trice)**
insured	**l'assicurato (-a)**
policy holder	**il titolare di polizza**
underwriter	**l'assicuratore (-trice)**
Our actuaries apply the theories of probability and statistics and the principles of finance to problems of insurance.	***I nostri attuari applicano alle questioni assicurative le teorie del calcolo probabilistico e statistico nonché i principi di base della finanza.***

Claims

cash	**il contante**
cash value	**il valore monetario**
claim damages	**la richiesta di risarcimento**
compensation	**l'indennizzo** *m*
damages	**il risarcimento**
depreciation	**il deprezzamento**
make a claim for damage	**presentare una richiesta di risarcimento danni**
make a claim for loss	**presentare una richiesta di risarcimento perdite**
new for old	**nuovo per vecchio**
wear and tear	**il logorio**
If you make a claim for damage or loss, then your compensation will be either on the basis of new for old or with a deduction for normal wear and tear.	***La richiesta di risarcimento per danno o perdita dà diritto ad un indennizzo calcolato sulla base del "nuovo per vecchio" oppure comprendente una detrazione a titolo di "logorio".***

LAW

General elements of law

action	**l'azione giudiziaria** *f*
bring an action against someone	**intentare una causa contro qualcuno**
award (n)/(v)	**il lodo arbitrale/assegnare**
capacity	**la capacità**
case	**la causa giudiziaria**
civil case	**la causa civile**
criminal case	**la causa penale**
claim (n)	**la querela**
make a claim against someone	**sporgere querela contro qualcuno**
compensation	**l'indennizzo** *m*
court	**la corte**
take someone to court	**citare qualcuno in giudizio**
damage	**il danno**
damages	**il risarcimento**
defendant	**il convenuto, l'imputato (-a)**
dispute	**la vertenza**
to settle a dispute	**comporre una vertenza**
duty	**il dovere**
duty of care	**dovere di diligenza**
impose a duty	**imporre un dovere**
fine (n)	**la sanzione**
gross (adj)	**grave**
gross incompetence	**la grave incompetenza**
gross misconduct	**la condotta grave**
gross negligence	**la colpa grave**
grounds	**le basi giuridiche**
guilty	**colpevole**
not guilty	**non colpevole**
imprisonment	**la reclusione**
invalid	**nullo (-a)**
judge (n)	**il giudice**
law	**la legge**
lawyer	**l'avvocato** *m*
legislation	**la legislazione**
liability	**la responsabilità civile**
offence	**il reato**
offend	**commettere un reato**
offender	**l'autore (-trice) del reato**

LEGAL DEPARTMENT, see page 78

party	**la parte**
guilty party	**la parte convenuta (in causa)**
responsible party	**il/la responsabile**
plaintiff	**il/la querelante**
prison	**la prigione**
proceedings	**gli atti giudiziari**
prosecute	**ricorrere in giudizio**
remedy	**la riparazione**
sentence	**la condanna**
terms	**i termini**
title	**il titolo**
valid	**valido (-a)**
validity	**la validità**

Contract Law

accept	**accettare**
acceptance	**l'accettazione *f***
agreement	**l'accordo *m***
conditions of an agreement	**le condizioni di un accordo**
terms of an agreement	**i termini di un accordo**
bid (n)	**la licitazione**
breach (n)	**la violazione**
breach of contract	**l'inadempienza *f* contrattuale**
clause	**la clausola**
compensation	**l'indennizzo *m***
consideration	**prestazione *f* corrispettiva, controprestazione *f***
contract	**contratto *m***
break a contract	**rompere un contratto**
enter into a contract	**stipulare un contratto**
make a contract	**concludere un contratto**
oral contract	**il contratto verbale**
rescind a contract	**rescindere un contratto**
terminate a contract	**rescindere un contratto**
written contract	**il contratto scritto**
intention to create legal relations	**l'intenzione *f* di stabilire rapporti giuridici**
offer (n)	**l'offerta *f***
make an offer	**fare un'offerta**
withdraw an offer	**ritirare un'offerta**
party	**la parte**
sue	**citare in giudizio**

LEGAL ASPECTS OF NEGOTIATIONS, see page 55

Employment law

discriminate	**discriminare**
discriminate against someone on the basis of sex, race or religion	**discriminare qualcuno sulla base del sesso, della razza o della religione**
dismiss	**licenziare**
dismissal	**il licenziamento**
fire (v)	**licenziare (per motivi disciplinari)**
lump sum	**la somma forfettaria**
misconduct	**la cattiva condotta**
pension	**la pensione**
pensionable age	**l'età *f* pensionabile**
pension off	**collocare a riposo**
re-engage	**riassumere**
re-engagement	**la riassunzione**
redundant/laid off	**in esubero**
make someone redundant/lay someone off	**mettere qualcuno in cassa integrazione**
redundancy/dismissal payment	**l'assegno *m* di cassa integrazione**
reinstate	**reintegrare**
reinstatement	**la reintegrazione**
retire	**andare in pensione**
retirement	**il pensionamento**
sack (n)	**il licenziamento**
strike	**lo sciopero**
trade union	**il sindacato**

If you are in breach of the terms of your contract of employment, you can be dismissed.

Violando i termini del contratto di lavoro, il dipendente può essere licenziato.

Civil law

arbitrate	**sottoporre ad arbitrato**
arbitration	**l'arbitrato *m***
conveyancing	**il trasferimento**
damages	**il risarcimento**
claim for damages	**la richiesta di risarcimento**
liable	**il responsabile**
litigate	**essere parte di una lite (causa)**
litigation	**la causa**
statute	**la legge**

PERSONNEL DEPARTMENT, see page 86

TOURISM AND LEISURE

Outdoor leisure activities

archery	**il tiro con l'arco**
bobsleighing/bobsledding	**il bob**
camping	**il campeggio**
caving	**la speleologia**
curling	**il curling**
cycling	**il ciclismo**
diving	**i tuffi**
deep-sea diving	**l'immersione *f* a grande profondità**
skin diving	**lo sport subacqueo, l'immersione *f***
exploring	**l'esplorazione *f***
flying	**il volo**
gliding	**il volo a vela (aliante)**
hang gliding	**il deltaplano**
paragliding	**il parapendio**
hiking	**l'escursionismo (a piedi) *m***
hunting	**la caccia**
jogging	**il jogging (corsa a piedi)**
luging	**luging**
mountaineering	**l'alpinismo *m***
orienteering	**l'orientamento *m***
riding	**l'equitazione *f***
rock-climbing	**la scalata su roccia**
shooting	**il tiro**
skating	**il pattinaggio**
ice hockey	**l'hockey *m* su ghiaccio**
ice skating	**il pattinaggio su ghiaccio**
skiing	**lo sci**
downhill skiing	**lo sci da discesa**
cross-country skiing	**lo sci da fondo**
langlauf	**lo sci da fondo pattinato**
ski-jumping	**il salto con gli sci**
water skiing	**lo sci d'acqua**
snorkling	**lo snorkelling**
surfing	**il surf**
wind-surfing	**il wind-surf**
swimming	**il nuoto**

tobogganing	**il toboga**
walking	**la camminata**
weight-training	**l'apesistica** *f*
weightlifting	**il sollevamento pesi**

Many people now take two holidays/vacations a year: a skiing holiday/vacation in winter and beach holiday/vacation in summer. — ***Oggigiorno, molte persone vanno in vacanza due volte all'anno: d'inverno per praticare lo sci, d'estate per godersi il sole e il mare.***

Travel and Tourism

biking	**il ciclo turismo**
bus tour	**l'escursione** *f* **in autobus**
business trip	**il viaggio d'affari**
cruise	**la crociera**
cycling	**il ciclismo**
driving	**la guida (di automobili)**
excursion	**l'escursione** *f*
expedition	**la spedizione**
grand tour	**il viaggio (nel Continente Europeo)**
hiking	**l'escursionismo** *m*
journey/tour	**il viaggio**
package tour	**il viaggio organizzato**
joy ride	**la gita di piacere in automobile**
motoring	**l'automobilismo** *m*
outing/trip	**la gita**
package tour	**un viaggio organizzato**
pleasure trip	**un viaggio di piacere**
ramble	**la passeggiata (camminata)**
ride	**la passeggiata a cavallo**
riding	**l'equitazione** *f*
safari	**il safari**
trek	**la camminata**
visit	**la visita**
voyage	**il viaggio, la traversata**
walking	**la camminata**

Meditours are offering an autumn/fall cruise around the Mediterranean. — ***Meditours propone una crociera autunnale nel Mediterraneo.***

English–Italian Business Dictionary

f	**feminine**
m	**masculine**
pl	**plural**
(adj)	**adjective**
(adv)	**adverb**
(n)	**noun**
(v)	**verb**
qc.	**qualcosa**
qu.	**qualcuno**
so.	**someone**
sth.	**something**

A

abandon an action rinunciare ad un'azione *f*
abroad all'estero
absent assente
absolute monopoly monopolio *m* perfetto
accelerated depreciation ammortamento *m* accellerato
accept *(agree, take sth.)* accettare
accept delivery of a shipment prendere in consegna un carico di merce
accept liability for sth. assumersi la responsabilità di qc.
acceptable accettabile, soddisfacente
acceptance accettazione *f*
account conto *m*
account for rendere conto
account in credit conto *m* in credito
account on stop conto *m* bloccato
account, on in acconto
accounts department reparto contabilità *m*
accounts payable conti *m* passivi
accounts receivable conti *m* attivi
accrue maturare, accumularsi
acknowledge receipt of a letter accusare ricevuta di una lettera
acquisition acquisizione, acquisto
across-the-board uniforme, indiscriminato (-a)
act of God causa *f* di forza maggiore
acting manager direttore (-trice) facente funzione
action for damages causa *f* per risarcimento
actuals prezzi effettivi *m* di vendita
ad valorem ad valorem, in base al valore di
add on 10% for service aggiungere il 10% per il servizio
additional charges spese *f* supplementari
additional premium premio *m* addizionale
address (n) indirizzo *m*, recapito *m*
address a letter indirizzare una lettera
address list lista *f* di indirizzi
adjourn a meeting aggiornare una riunione
adjudication tribunal tribunale *m* di arbitrato
adjustment accomodamento *m*, accordo *m*
administration amministrazione *f*, gestione *f*
administrative expenses spese *f* di amministrazione
admission charge spese d'ammissione, spese d'entrata
advance (n) *(loan)* anticipo *m*
advance (v) *(lend)* prestare
advance booking prenotamento *m* anticipato
advance on account anticipazione *f* su un conto
advance payment pagamento *m* anticipato
advertise a new product reclamizzare un nuovo prodotto
advertise a vacancy fare un'inserzione *f* per un impiego disponibile
advertisement annuncio *m* pubblicitario, pubblicità *f*
advertiser inserzionista *m*, chi fa pubblicità
advertising agency agenzia di pubblicità *f*
advertising budget budget *m* pubblicitario
advertising rates tariffe *f* delle inserzioni pubblicitarie
advertising space spazio *m* pubblicitario

advice note bolletta *f* d'avviso
affidavit attestazione *f* ufficiale
after-sales service assistenza *f* post-vendita alla clientela
after-tax profit utile *m* al netto delle imposte
agency agenzia *f*
agenda ordine *m* del giorno
agent *(representative)* agente *m/f*, rappresentante *m/f*
agree *(approve)* approvare
agree *(be same as)* concordare, corrispondere a
agree to do sth. acconsentire di fare qc., accettare di fare qc.
agreed price prezzo *m* concordato
agreement accordo *m*
aim (n) scopo *m* , proposito *m*
aim (v) avere lo scopo di
air freight trasporto *m* merci via aerea
air freight charges/rates spese trasporto merci via aerea
airfreight (v) trasportare merci via aerea
airmail (n) posta *f* aerea
airmail (v) spedire per posta aerea
airport aeroporto *m*
airport tax tasse *f* aereoportuali
airtight packaging imballaggio *m* ermetico
all expenses paid tutte le spese pagate
all-in price prezzo *m* tutto compreso
all-risks policy polizza *f* contro tutti i rischi
allow 10% for carriage calcolare 10% per il trasporto
allowance for depreciation accantonamento *m* al fondo di ammortamento
amend correggere
amendment emendamento *m*, rettifica *f*
amortization ammortamento *m*
amortize ammortare, ammortizzare
amount *(of money)* ammontare *m*, importo *m*
amount owing importo *m* dovuto
amount paid importo *m* pagato
amount to ammontare a
analyze the market potential analizzare il potenziale del mercato
analysis analisi *f*
annual accounts rendiconti *m* annuali
annual general meeting (AGM) Assemblea *f* Generale degli Azionisti
annual report relazione *f* annuale al bilancio
annually annualmente
answer (n) risposta *f*
answer (v) rispondere
answer the telephone rispondere al telefono
answering machine segreteria *f* telefonica
answering service servizio *m* segreteria telefonica
appeal *(against a decision)* (n) ricorso *m*, appello *m*; (v) ricorrere in appello, appellare
appeal to (v) *(attract)* attirare
appendix appendice *f*
application domanda *f*, istanza *f*
application form modulo *m* per domanda di assunzione
apply for a job fare domanda d'impiego
apply to *(affect)* riguardare
appoint nominare
appointment *(job)* impiego *m*, posto *m*
appointment *(meeting)* appuntamento *m*
appointments book agenda *f*
appointments vacant impieghi *m* disponibili
appreciate apprezzare; *(increase in value)* aumentare di valore
appreciation apprezzamento *m*; *(in value)* rivalutazione *f*
approval, on in prova, in esame
approve the terms of a contract approvare i termini di un contratto
approximate approssimativo (-a)
approximately approssimativamente
arbitrate in a dispute arbitrare una vertenza
arbitration board/tribunal Tribunale *m* Arbitrale
area code codice *m* di zona
area manager direttore (-trice) di zona

arrange *(meeting)* organizzare
arrears arretrati *m*
article *(clause)* clausola *f*
article *(item)* articolo *m*, prodotto *m*
as per advice come consigliato
as per invoice come da fattura
as per sample come da campione
ask (so. to do sth.)
chiedere (a qu. di fare qc.)
ask for a refund
chiedere un rimborso
ask for further details chiedere
ulteriori dettagli
assess damages accertare i danni
assessment of damages
accertamento *m* dei danni
asset bene *m*, cespite *m*
asset value valore *m* patrimoniale
assist assistere
assistant assistente *m/f*,
collaboratore (-trice)
assistant manager
vice direttore (-trice)
associate (adj) associato (-a)
associate (n) associato (-a),
socio (-a)
assurance assicurazione *f*
assurance policy
polizza *f* di assicurazione
assure so.'s life
assicurare la vita di qu.
attend *(meeting)* assistere a
attend to occuparsi di
attention attenzione *f*
attorney procuratore (-trice)
attractive salary
stipendio *m* interessante
auction (n) asta *f*
auction (v) vendere all'asta
audit (n) revisione *f* contabile
audit the accounts verificare i conti
auditor
revisore (-a) ufficiale dei conti
authority autorità *f*
authorization autorizzazione *f*
authorize payment
autorizzare un pagamento
availability disponibilità *f*
available disponibile
average (adj) medio (-a)
average price prezzo *m* medio
await instructions
attendere istruzioni
award a contract to so. aggiudicare
un contratto a qu.

B

back orders ordine *m* arretrato,
ordine inevaso
back tax imposta *f* arretrata
backdate postdatare
backlog lavoro *m* arretrato
backup copy copia *f* a sostegno
bad debt credito *m* inesigibile
balance (n) bilancio *m*, bilancia *f*
balance (v) **(a budget)**
pareggiare un budget
balance brought down/forward
saldo *m* da riportare
balance carried down/forward
saldo *m* riportato
balance due to us saldo *m* dovuto
balance of payments
bilancia *f* dei pagamenti
balance sheet bilancio *m* d'esercizio
ban (n) bando *m*, interdizione *m*
ban (v) interdire, vietare
bank (n) banca *f*, istituto *m* di credito
bank (v) depositare in banca, avere
un conto in banca
bank account conto *m* bancario
bank balance saldo *m* in banca
bank base rate
tasso *m* ufficiale di sconto
bank charges spese *f* bancarie
bank draft assegno *m* circolare
bank holiday giorno *m* di chiusura
degli sportelli bancari, festa *f*
nazionale
bank statement
estratto *m* conto bancario
bank transfer bonifico *m*
banker's order ordine *m* bancario
banknote banconota *f*
bankrupt (adj) fallito (-a);
(n) fallito(-a)
bankrupt (v) fare fallire
bankruptcy fallimento *m*
bar chart diagramma *m* a barre
bar code codice *m* a barre
bargain (n) *(cheaper than usual)*
affare *m*, occasione *f*; *(deal)*
affare *m*
bargain (v)
contrattare, tirare sul prezzo

bargaining position situazione *f* permettente di trattare
barter (n) baratto *m*, scambio *m*
barter (v) barattare
base (n) *(initial position)* base *f*
basic (adj) *(most important)* di base, fondamentale
basic discount sconto *m* di base
basic tax tassa *f* di base
batch (n) **(of products)** partita *f* (di merce)
batch (v) mettere insieme
batch number numero *m* di partita
bear (v) *(interest)* fruttare
bearer portatore *m*, portatrice *f*
bearer bond obbligazione *f* al portatore
begin cominciare, iniziare
behalf of, on a nome di, per conto di
benchmark punto *m* di riferimento
beneficiary beneficiario *m*
benefit from (v) trarre vantaggio da
berth (v) ormeggiare
bid (n) *(offer to buy)* offerta *f*
bilateral bilaterale
bill (n) *(in a restaurant)* conto *m*
bill (n) *(list of charges)* fattura *f*
bill (v) fatturare
bill of exchange cambiale *f*
bill of lading polizza *f* di carico
bill of sale fattura *f*, atto *m* di vendita
bills payable effetti *m* passivi, cambiali *m* da pagare
bills receivable effetti *m* attivi, cambiali *m* da incassare
black economy economia *f* nera
black list (n) lista *f* nera
black market mercato *m* nero
blacklist (v) lista *f* di proscrizione
blank cheque/check assegno *m* in bianco
block (v) bloccare
block booking noleggio *m* in blocco
board (n) *(group of people)* Consiglio *m* di Amministrazione
board meeting riunione *f* del consiglio di amministrazione
board of directors Consiglio *m* di Amministrazione
bond *(borrowing by government)* obbligazione *f*
bonus gratifica *f*, premio *m*
book (v) prenotare
book value valore *m* contabile
bookkeeper contabile *m/f*, ragioniere (-a)
bookkeeping contabilità *f*
boom industry industria *f* che si è sviluppata rapidamente
border frontiera *f*
borrow prendere a prestito, mutuare
borrower mutuatario *m*
boss *(informal)* capo *m*
bottleneck strozzatura *f* (nel processo aziendale)
bought ledger mastro *m* dei conti dei creditori
bounce *(cheque/check)* respingere
box number casella *f* postale
bracket together raggruppare
branch settore *m*
branch manager direttore *m* di filiale
brand marchio *m*, marca *f*
brand loyalty fedeltà *f* alla marca
brand name marca *f*, nome *m* del prodotto
breach of contract inadempimento *m* del contratto
break an agreement infrangere un accordo
break down (v) *(itemize)* dettagliare; *(machine)* rompersi
break even (v) giungere al punto di pareggio
break off negotiations sospendere le trattative
break the law violare la legge
breakdown (n) *(items)* ripartizione *f*; *(machine)* guasto *m*
breakeven point punto *m* di pareggio fra costi e ricavi
bribe (n) tangente *f*, bustarella *f*
bribe (v) corrompere
briefcase borsa *f*, cartella *f*
brochure fascicolo *m*
budget (n) *(personal, company)* bilancio *m* preventivo, budget *m*
budget (v) budgettare
budget account *(in bank)* contabilità *f* di bilancio
budgetary control controllo *m* budgetario
built-in incorporato (-a), inserito (-a)
bulk buying acquisto *m* in massa
bureau de change ufficio *m* cambio
business *(commerce)* affari *mpl*

business *(company)* impresa *f*
business *(discussion)* affare *m*
business, on per affari
business address
indirizzo *m* d'ufficio
business class classe *f* business
business hours ore *f* d'ufficio
business lunch pranzo *m* d'affari
business premises locali *m*
d'azienda, locali commerciali
business strategy
strategia *f* commerciale
businessman, businesswoman
uomo *m* d'affari, donna *f* d'affari
busy occupato (-a)
buy (v) comperare
buy forward comperare a termine
buyer *(person)* compratore (-trice)
buying department ufficio *m* acquisti

C

calculate calcolare
calculation calcolo *m*
calculator calcolatore *m*
calendar month mese *m* solare
calendar year anno *m* solare
call (n) *(phone)* chiamata *f*
call (n) *(visit)* visita *f*
call (v) *(phone)* chiamare
call off a deal disdire un affare
cancel cancellare, annullare
cancel a contract
annullare un contratto
cancellation clause
clausola *f* di rescissione
cancellation of an appointment
revoca *f* di una nomina
capacity *(ability)* abilità *f*, capacità *f*
capacity *(production)*
capacità *f* produttiva
capacity *(space)* capacità *f*
capital capitale *m*, capitali *mpl*
capital equipment
immobilizzi *m* tecnici
capital expenditure
spese *f* conto capitali
capital gains plusvalenza *f*
capitalization capitalizzazione *f*
capitalize capitalizzare
capitalize on trarre vantaggio da
captive market mercato *m*
controllato da un solo fornitore
capture impadronirsi
card *(business card)* biglietto *m*
card index schedario *m*
card phone
telefono *m* a schede, Telemat *m*
cardboard box scatola *f* di cartone
care of (c/o) presso
cargo carico *m*
carriage trasporto *m*
carriage forward porto *m* assegnato
carriage free franco di porto *m*
carriage paid porto *m* pagato
carrier *(company)* trasportatore *m*,
impresa *f* di trasporti
carry *(approve in a vote)*
far approvare
carry *(have in stock)* avere
carry *(transport)* portare, trasportare
carry forward riportare a nuovo
carry on a business svolgere
esercizio d'impresa
carton *(box)* cartone *m*, imballo *m*
di cartone
case (n) *(box)* cassa *f*
cash (adv) in contanti
cash (n) *(money)* denaro *m* contanti
cash a cheque/check
incassare un assegno
cash advance anticipo *m* in contanti
cash balance saldo *m* di cassa
cash book libro *m* cassa
cash card tessera *f* prelievo contanti
cash discount sconto *m* cassa,
sconto per pagamento in contanti
cash dispenser
cassa *f* automatica prelievi
cash flow flusso *m* di cassa
cash flow forecast previsioni *f* del
flusso di cassa
cash offer
offerta *f* reale, offerta per contanti
cash on delivery (c.o.d.)
pagamento *m* alla consegna
cash price prezzo *m* per contanti,
condizioni *f* per pagamento in
contanti
cash purchase
acquisto *m* per contanti
cash sale vendita *f* per contanti
cash terms condizioni *f* per
pagamento in contanti
casting vote voto *m* decisivo
casual work lavoro *m* saltuario

catalogue/catalog catalogo *m*
catalogue/catalog price prezzo *m* di catalogo
cater for provvedere di generi alimentari
caveat emptor l'acquirente presti la dovuta attenzione
ceiling price prezzo *m* massimo
cellular telephone telefono *m* cellulare
central bank banca *f* centrale
central purchasing acquisto *m* centralizzato
centralize centralizzare
certificate of approval certificato *m* di accettazione
certificate of deposit certificato *m* di deposito
certificate of origin certificato *m* d'origine
certified cheque/check assegno *m* a copertura garantita
certified copy copia *f* autentica
certify certificare, autenticare
chain store negozio *m* a catena
chairman *(of company)* presidente *m*
chairman and managing director presidente e amministratore delegato
Chamber of Commerce Camera *f* di Commercio
change (n) *(cash)* spiccioli *m; (difference)* cambiamento *m*
change (v) *(money)* cambiare
change hands essere venduto (-a)
channels of distribution canali *m* di distribuzione
charge (n) *(money)* carico *m*
charge (v) *(money)* far pagare
charge a purchase addebitare un acquisto
charge card carta *f* di credito
charter flight volo *m* charter
chase *(an order)* dare la caccia a
cheap economico (-a), a basso prezzo
cheap labour/labor manodopera *m* a basso prezzo
cheap rate tariffa *f* ridotta
check (n) *(examination)* controllo *m*
check (v) *(examine)* esaminare, controllare
check in *(at airport)* presentarsi al check in
check in *(at hotel)* firmare il registro
check-in *(at airport)* controllo *m* passeggeri
check-in counter check in *m*
check-in time ora *f* di accetazzione
check out (of hotel) lasciare libera la camera (dell'albergo)
checkout *(in supermarket)* cassa *f*
cheque/check assegno *m*
cheque/check book libretto *m* assegni
chief (adj) principale
chief executive officer (CEO) direttore (-trice) generale
choice (n) *(of items)* scelta *f*
choose scegliere
Christmas bonus gratifica *f* natalizia, tredicesima *f*
circular (n) lettera *f* circolare
circular letter of credit lettera *f* di credito circolare
claim (n) domanda d'indennizzo *m*, reclamo *m*
claim (v) *(insurance)* rivendicare, presentare una domanda d'indennizzo
claims department ufficio *m* indennità
classified advertisements annunci *m* economici
classified directory elenco *m* classificato
classify classificare
clause clausola *f*
clear (adj) *(understandable)* chiaro(-a)
clear (v) *(stock)* liquidare
clear a cheque/check compensare un assegno
clear profit utile *m* netto
clearing bank banca *f* di compensazione
clerical error errore *m* di trascrizione
clerk impiegato (-a)
client cliente *m/f*
clientele clientela *f*
clinch concludere definitivamente
close the meeting togliere la seduta
close an account chiudere un conto
close down chiudere/sospendere un'attività

closed chiuso (-a)
closed market mercato *m* chiuso
closing balance
bilancio *m* di chiusura
closing date termine *m* ultimo, data *f* di chiusura
closing price prezzo *m* di chiusura
closing stock giacenze *f* finali alla chiusura dell'esercizio
closing time ora *f* di chiusura
co-operate cooperare
co-operation cooperazione *m*, collaborazione *f*
co-opt so. cooptare qu.
code of practice
codice *m* di etica professionale
coin moneta *f*
cold call visita *f* a freddo
cold store magazzino *m* frigorifero
collaborate collaborare
collaboration collaborazione *f*
collapse (n) crollo *m*
collapse (v) crollare, cadere
collateral (n) garanzia *f* collaterale
collect (v) *(fetch)*
cogliere, raccogliere
collect a debt ricuperare un debito
collect call
telefonata *f* a carico del ricevente
collection *(of goods)* ritiro *m*
collective ownership
proprietà *f* collettiva
collector raccoglitore (-trice)
commerce commercio *m*
commercial (adj) commerciale
commercial (n) *(TV)*
pubblicità *f*, spot *m*
commercial law
diritto *m* commerciale
commission *(money)*
commissione *m*, percentuale *f*
commission rep rappresentante (-a) commissionario (-a)
commit funds to a project affidare fondi ad un progetto
commitments impegni *m*
commodity merce *f*, bene *m*
commodity exchange Borsa Merci *f*
commodity market mercato *m* delle materie prime
common pricing prezzi *mpl* correnti
communicate comunicare
communications comunicazioni *f*
commute *(travel)* fare il pendolare
commuter pendolare *m/f*
company compagnia *f*, società *f*
company director amministratore (-trice) di società
comparable paragonabile
compare confrontare, paragonare
compared with, be
essere paragonabile a
comparison confronto *m*
compensate compensare
compensation for damage
risarcimento *m* di danni
competing products prodotti *m* che si fanno concorrenza
competition
concorrenza *f*, competizione *f*
competitive price prezzo *m* allineato
competitive products
prodotti *m* competitivi
competitiveness competività *f*
competitor concorrente *m/f*
complain *(about)*
protestare, reclamare
complaint protesta *f*, reclamo *m*
complaints department
ufficio *m* reclami
complete (adj) completo (-a)
complete (v) finire, portare a termine
complimentary ticket
biglietto *m* d'omaggio
comply with
conformarsi a, osservare
compound interest interesse *m* composto
comprehensive insurance
assicurazione *f* globale
compromise (n) compromesso *m*
compromise (v)
venire a un compromesso
compulsory obbligatorio (-a)
compulsory purchase
espropriazione *f* per pubblica utilità
computer computer *m*
computer error
errore *m* di computer
computer file
archivio *m* (di un computer)
computer printout tabulato *m*
computer program
programma *m* di computer
computer system sistema *m* elettronico di elaborazione

computer terminal
terminale *m* di computer
computerize computerizzare
concern (n) *(worry)* preoccupazione *f*
concern (v) *(deal with)* interessarsi di
conclude *(agreement)* concludere
condition *(state, terms)* condizione *f*
condition that, on a condizione che
conditional soggetto (-a) a condizioni
conditions of employment
condizioni *f* di assunzione
conditions of sale
condizioni *f* di vendita
conduct negotiations
condurre una negoziazione
conference phone
telefono *m* per conferenze
conference room sala *f* riunioni
confidential riservato (-a)
confirm a booking
confermare una prenotazione
confirmation conferma *f*
conflict of interest
conflitto *m* di interressi
connecting flight
volo *m* di coincidenza
connection coincidenza *f*
consignment *(sending)* spedizione *f*
consignment *(things sent)* invio *m*
consignment note lettera *f* di vettura
consist of consistere in
consolidate (shipments)
consolidare (spedizioni)
consortium consorzio *m*
constant costante
consult consultarsi
consultancy firm ditta *f* di consulenza
consultant consulente *m/f*
consumer consumatore (-trice)
consumer goods beni *m* di consumo
consumer price index indice *m* dei
prezzi al consumo
consumer research ricerca *f* di
mercato sui bisogni dei
consumatori
contact (n) *(person)* contatto *m*
contact (v) mettersi in contatto con
contain contenere
container *(box, tin)* contenitore *m*
container *(for shipping)* container *m*
container terminal
terminal *m* per container
containerization containerizzazione *f*
containerize containerizzare
contents contenuto *m*
contingency plan
piano *m* di contingenza
continual continuo (-a)
continually continuamente
continue continuare
continuous continuo (-a)
contra account
conto *m* di contropartita
contra an entry
stornare una registrazione
contra entry
registrazione *f* di storno
contract (n) contratto *m*
contract (v) contrarre
contract note fissato *m* bollato
contract of employment contratto *m*
di lavoro
contractor imprenditore (-trice)
contractual liability
responsabilità *f* contrattuale
contractually contrattualmente
contrary contrario (-a)
control (n) *(check)* controllo *m*,
verifica *f*; *(power)* controllo *m*,
potere *m*
control a business detenere il
controllo azionario
control key tasto *m* di comando
convene convocare
convenient conveniente
conversion price/rate
tasso *m* di conversione
convert convertire
convertible loan stock
obbligazioni *f* convertibii
cooling off period periodo *m* che
permette un ripensamento
copy (n) *(of document)* copia *f*
copy (v) copiare, riprodurre
corner the market
accaparrarsi il mercato *m*
corporate image
immagine *f* aziendale
corporate plan
programma *m* aziendale
corporate profits utili *m* societari
corporation corporazione *f*
corporation tax
imposta *f* sulla società
correspond with so. essere in
corrispondenza con qu.

correspond with sth.
equivalere con qc.
correspondence corrispondenza *f*
cost (n) costo *m*
cost (v) costare
cost analysis analisi *f* dei conti
cost centre/center centro *m* di costi
cost of living
costo *m* della vita, carovita *m*
cost of sales costo *m* delle vendite
cost plus
costo *m* più una percentuale
cost price prezzo *m* sotto costo
cost, insurance and freight (c.i.f.)
costo *m* , assicurazione *f* e nolo *m*
cost-effective redditizio (-a)
cost-effectiveness
redditività *f* dei costi
cost-of-living index indice *m* del costo della vita
costs spese *f*
counter banco *m*
counter-claim (n) controrichiesta *f*
counter-claim (v)
presentare una controrichiesta
counter-offer controfferta *f*
counterfoil matrice *f*
countermand fermare
countersign contrassegno *m*
country of origin paese *m* d'origine
coupon ad
materia pubblicitaria con buono
courier *(guide)* guida *f* (turistica); *(messenger)* messaggero *m*, corriere *m*
court corte *f* di Giustizia
covenant (n) convenzione *f*
cover (n) *(insurance)*
copertura *f* assicurativa
cover (n) *(top)* copertura *f*
cover a risk
assicurarsi contro un rischio
cover costs coprire i costi
cover note polizza *f* provvisoria
covering letter
lettera *f* di accompagnamento
credit (n) credito *m*
credit (v) accreditare (un conto)
credit account conto *m* creditori
credit balance differenza *f* a credito
credit card sale
vendita *f* con carta di credito
credit control controllo *m* del credito
credit entry registrazione *f* contabile a credito
credit freeze blocco *m* del credito
credit limit limite *m* di credito
credit note nota *f* di accredito
credit, on a credito
creditor creditore (-trice)
cumulative cumulativo (-a)
cumulative interest
interesse *m* composto
currency moneta *f* legale
current account conto *m* corrente
current assets attività *f* liquide
current liabilities passività *f* correnti
current rate of exchange
tasso *m* di cambio corrente
curriculum vitae (CV)
curriculum *m* vitae
customer cliente *m/f*
customer satisfaction
soddisfazione *f* dei clienti
customer service department
ufficio *m* assistenza ai clienti
customs dogana *f*
customs clearance
svincolo *m* doganale
customs declaration form modulo *m* di dichiarazione doganale
customs entry point punto *m* per la dichiarazine doganale d'entrata
customs examination
controllo *m* doganale
customs official
ufficiale *m* di dogana
cut (n) taglio *m*
cut (v) tagliare
cut price (n) prezzo *m* ridotto
cut-price goods
merce *f* a prezzo ridotto
cycle ciclo *m*
cyclical ciclico (-a)
cyclical factors elementi *m* ciclici

D

damage (n) danno *m*
damage (v) danneggiare
damages danni *m*
data dati *m*
database base *f* di dati
date (n) data *f*
date (v) datare
date stamp datario *m*

day *(24 hours/working day)* giorno *m*
dead account conto *m* chiuso
deadline data *f* di scadenza, termine *m* ultimo
deadlock (n) punto *m* morto
deadlock (v) essere a un punto morto
deadweight cargo carico *m* lordo
deal (n) operazione *f*, affare *m*
deal (v) commerciare, negoziare
deal with an order dare corso ad un'operazione
dealer commerciante *m/f*
dear caro (-a)
debenture obbligazione *f* (di società private)
debit (n) addebito *m*
debit an account addebitare un conto
debit entry registrazione *f* a debito
debit note nota *f* di addebito
debt debito *m*
debt collection recupero *m* di crediti
debt collection agency agenzia *f* per il recupero dei crediti
debtor debitore (-trice)
decide on a course of action decidere una linea di condotta
deciding factor elemento *m* decisivo
decimal point virgola *f* decimale
declare goods to customs dichiarare le merci alla dogana
declared value valore *m* dichiarato
decrease (n) diminuzione *f*
decrease (v) diminuire
decrease in value diminuzione *f* del valore
decreasing (adj) decrescente
deduct dedurre
deductible detraibile
deduction detrazione *f*
deed atto *m*
default (v) essere contumace
default (n) **on payments** inadempienza *f* nel pagamento
defaulter inadempiente *m/f*
defect difetto *m*
defective *(faulty)* difettoso (-a)
defer payment differire un pagamento
deferment of payment rinvio *m* di pagamento
deferred creditor creditore (-trice) differito (-a)
deficit deficit *m*, disavanzo *m*
deficit financing finanziamento *m* del disavanzo *m*
defray *(costs)* pagare
delay (n) ritardo *m*
delay (v) ritardare
delete eliminare
deliver consegnare
delivered price prezzo *m* franco
delivery *(goods)* consegna *f*
delivery date data *f* di consegna
delivery note bolla *f* di spedizione
delivery time data *f* di consegna
demand (n) *(for payment)* domanda *f*, richiesta *f*; *(need)* domanda *f*
demand (v) domandare
demonstrate dimostrare
demonstration model campione *m* per dimostrazione
department *(in office)* reparto *m*, sezione *f*; *(in shop)* reparto *m*
department store grande magazzino *m*
depend on contare su
depending on a condizione che
deposit (n) *(in bank)* deposito *m*; *(paid in advance)* acconto *m*
deposit (v) versare soldi
deposit account conto *m* di deposito
deposit slip distinta *f* di versamento
depositor depositante *m/f*
depreciate *(lose value)* svalutare
depreciation *(loss of value)* svalutazione *f*
depreciation rate quota *f* d'ammortamento
deputize for so. rappresentare qu.
deputy delegato *m*, sostituto *m*
deputy managing director amministratore (-trice) delegato (-a)
design (n) design *m*, progettazione *f*
design (v) progettare
design department dipartimento *m*/ufficio *m* design
desk scrivania *f*
destination destinazione *f*
detail (n) dettaglio *m*
detailed account resoconto *m* dettagliato
devaluation svalutazione *f*
devalue svalutare
diagram diagramma *m*

dial a number
comporre un numero *m*
dialling code prefisso *m* telefonico
dialling tone suono m di linea libera
differ dissentire
differences in price
differenze *f* di prezzo
direct (adj) diretto (-a)
direct (v) dirigere
direct debit addebito *m* diretto
direct mail vendita *f* diretta tramite corrispondenza
direct tax imposta *f* diretta
direct-mail advertising pubblicita *f* a mezzo posta
directions for use
istruzioni *f* per l'uso
director amministratore (-trice)
directory annuario *m*
disclaimer smentita *f*
disclose a piece of information
divulgare un'informazione *f*
discontinue interrrompere
discount (n) sconto *m*
discount (v) vendere sotto costo
discount price prezzo *m* scontato
discounted cash flow (DCF) sconto *m* del valore attuale
discrepancy discrepanza *f*
discuss discutere
discussion discussione *f*
disk disco *m*
disk drive unità *f* a dischi magnetici
dismiss an employee
licenziare un dipendente
dismissal licenziamento *m*
dispatch (n) *(sending)* spedizione *f*
dispatch (v) *(send)* spedire
dispatch note bolla *f* di spedizione
display (n) esposizione *f*, mostra *f*
display (v) esporre
display material
materiale *m* da esposizione
display stand
banco *m* di esposizione
disposable
da non restituire, da gettare
disposal disposizione *f*
dispose of excess stock eliminare le scorte in eccesso
distress sale
vendita *f* di merce sotto costo
distribute *(goods)* distribuire
distribution distribuzione *f*
distribution costs
costi *m* di distribuzione
distribution manager direttore (-trice) delle distribuzioni
distributor distributore (-trice)
diversification diversificazione *f*
diversify diversificare
dividend dividendo *m*
dividend yield reddito *m* da dividendi
division *(part of a company)*
reparto *m*
dock (n) bacino *m*
dock (v) *(ship)*
entrare in porto, attraccare
documentation documentazione *f*
dollar dollaro *m*
dollar balance
bilancia *f* commerciale in dollari
domestic market mercato *m* interno
domestic production
produzione *m* nazionale
domestic sales vendite *f* interne
door-to-door a domicilio *m*
door-to-door selling
vendita *f* porta a porta
dossier dossier *m*, pratica *f*
dot-matrix printer
stampante *f* a matrice
double (v) raddoppiare
double taxation doppia tassazione *f*
double-booking riservazione *f* di una camera a due clienti
down payment
versamento *m* d'acconto
downside factor fattore *m* negativo
downturn regresso *m*
draft (n) *(money)* tratta *f*; *(rough plan)* bozza *f*
draft a contract preparare lo schema di un contratto
draft plan bozza *f* di un piano
draw (a cheque/check)
emettere (un assegno)
draw up a contract
stipulare un contratto *m*
drawee trattario (-a)
drawer traente *m*
drop (n) caduta *f*, ribasso *m*
drop (v) cadere, calare
drop in sales ribasso *m* delle vendite
due *(awaited)* atteso (-a); *(owing)* dovuto (-a)

dues ordine *m* inevaso
dummy fittizio (-a), falso (-a)
dummy pack confezione *f* finta
dump goods on a market svendere delle merci *m* sul mercato *m*
dumping vendita *f* sotto costo
duplicate (n) duplicato *m*
duplicate (v) duplicare
duty *(tax)* dazio *m*
duty-free esente da dazio *m*
duty-free shop 'duty free shop', negozio *m* esente da tasse

E

earmark funds for a project accantonare fondi *m* per un progetto
earn *(interest)* fruttare
earn *(money)* guadagnare
earnings *(profit)* utile *m*, profitto *m*
earnings *(salary)* guadagni *m*
easy terms condizioni *f* moderate
economic cycle ciclo *m* economico
economic development sviluppo *m* economico
economic growth crescita *f* economica
economic indicators indicatori *m* economici
economic trends congiuntura *f*
economical economico (-a)
economies of scale economia *f* di massa *f*
economize economizzare
economy *(saving)* economia *f*
economy class classe *f* turistica
ecu (European currency unit) ecu *m*
effect (n) effetto *m*
effect (v) effettuare
effective effettivo (-a)
effective yield rendimento *m* effettivo (-a)
effectiveness efficacia *f*
efficiency efficienza *f*
efficient efficiente
electronic mail posta *f* elettronica
electronic point of sale (EPOS) punto *m* di vendita elettronico
embargo (n) embargo *m*
embargo (v) mettere l'embargo su
embark imbarcare, imbarcarsi
embark on imbarcarsi in
employ impiegare, assumere
employee dipendente *m/f*
employer datore (-trice) di lavoro
employment impiego *m*
empty (adj) vuoto (-a)
enclose allegare
enclosure allegato *m*
end (n) fine *f*, termine *m*
end (v) finire, concludere
end of season sale svendite *f* di fine stagione
end product prodotto *m* finito
end user utenti *mpl* finali
endorse a cheque/check girare un assegno
endorsement *(action)* girata *f*; *(on insurance)* restrizione *f*
energy-saving (adj) che risparmia energia
engaged *(telephone)* occupato (-a)
engaged tone segnale *m* di linea occupata
enter *(go in)* entrare
enter *(write in)* registrare
enter into *(discussion)* predere parte in
enterprise impresa *f*
entitle conferire diritto
entitlement diritto *m*
entrepreneur imprenditore (-trice)
entry *(going in)* entrata *f*
entry *(writing)* scrittura *f* contabile
entry visa visto *m* d'ingresso
equip equipaggiare
equipment apparecchiatura *f*
equities azioni ordinarie
equity capital capitale *m* effettivo
error errore *m*
errors and omissions excepted (e. & o.e.) salvo errori e omssioni (S.E & O)
escape clause clausola *f* di salvaguardia
escrow account conto *m* a garanzia
establish stabilire, istituire
establishment *(business)* azienda *f* commerciale
estimate (n) *(calculation)* valutazione *f*
estimate (n) *(quote)* preventivo *m*
estimate (v) stimare, valutare
estimated sales vendite *f* presunte

Eurocheque/Eurocheck euroassegno *m*
European Union (EU) Unione Europea (UE)
evaluate costs valutare i costi
evaluation valutazione *f*
exact (v) esigere
examination *(inspection)* esame *f*
examination *(test)* esame *f*
examine esaminare
exceed sorpassare, superare
excellent eccellente
excess capacity capacità *f* produttiva in eccesso
excessive eccessivo (-a)
exchange (n) *(currency)* cambio *m*
exchange (v) *(currency)* cambiare
exchange (v) *(swap)* scambiare con
exchange rate tasso *m* di cambio
excise duty imposta *f* indiretta
excluding escluso (-a)
exclusion clause clausola *f* di esclusione *f*
exclusive agreement accordo *m* in esclusiva
exclusive of tax tassa *f* esclusa
exclusivity esclusività f
executive (adj) esecutivo (-a)
executive (n) dirigente *m*
exempt (adj) esente
exempt (v) esentare
exempt from tax esente da tassa/imposta
exemption from tax esenzione *f* da tassa
exercise an option esercitare un'opzione
exercise of an option esercizio *m* di un'opzione
exhibit (v) esibire
exhibition esposizione *f*, mostra *f*
exhibitor espositore (-trice), standista *m/f*
expand ampliare
expenditure spesa *f*, spese *fpl*
expense spesa *f*, conto *m*
expense account conto *m* spese
expensive costoso (-a)
experienced esperto (-a)
expire terminare, scadere
expiry fine *f*, scadenza *f*
expiry date data *f* di scadenza
export (n) esportazione f
export (v) esportare
export department reparto *m* esportazioni
export licence/permit licenza *f* d'esportazione
export manager direttore (-trice) del reparto esportazioni
exporter esportatore *m/f*
exports esportazioni *f*
exposure rischio *m* finanziario
express (adj) *(fast)* espresso (-a)
express delivery spedizione *f* per espresso
extend *(make longer)* prolungare
extended credit credito *m* prorogato
extension *(making longer)* prolungamento *m*
extension *(telephone)* interno *m*
external audit revisione *f* esterna
external auditor revisore *m* esterno
external trade commercio *m* estero
extra charges spese *f* extra
extras spese *f* supplementari

F

face value valore *m* nominale
facilities servizi *m*, mezzi *m*
facility *(credit)* agevolazione *f*
factor (n) *(influence)* fattore *m*
factor (n) *(person, company)* agente *m/f* di factoring; *(company)* società *f* di factoring
factoring charges costi *m* di factoring
factors of production fattori *m* di produzione
factory fabbrica *f*
factory price prezzo *m* di fabbrica
fail *(go bust, not to succeed)* fallire
failing that se non è possibile
failure insuccesso *m*
fair giusto (-a), equo (-a)
fair price prezzi *mpl* equi
fair wear and tear normale usura *f* e degrado *m*
faked documents documenti *m* falsi
fall behind *(worse position)* rimanere indietro
fall behind *(late)* essere in ritardo
fall due essere dovuto (-a)
fall through fallire, non arrivare a compimento
false pretence millantato credito *m*

fare tariffa *f*
farm out work appaltare del lavoro
fast-selling items articoli *m* che vendono rapidamente
favourable/favorable balance of trade bilancia *f* commerciale attiva
fax (n) fax *m*
fax (v) inviare per fax
feasibility report studio *m* della fattibilità
fee *(admission)* quota *f* d'iscrizione
fee *(for services)* emolumento *m*, compenso *m*
field sales manager direttore (-trice) vendite esterne
figure cifra *f*
figures cifre *f*, numeri *m*
file (n) *(computer)* file *m*, archivio *m*; *(documents)* fascicolo *m*
file documents depositare documenti *m*
filing cabinet schedario *m*
fill a gap colmare una lacuna
final demand domanda *f* finale
final dividend dividendo *m* finale
finalize completare
finance (n) finanza *f*, attività *f* finanziaria
finance (v) finanziare
finance director direttore (-trice) delle finanze
finances finanze *f*
financial finanziario (-a), economico (-a)
financial institution istituto *m* finanziario
financial position posizione *f* finanziaria
financial resources risorse *f* finanziarie
financial risk rischio *m* finanziario
financial year esercizio *m* finanziario
financing finanziamento *m*
fine (n) multa *f*
fine (v) multare
fire damage danno *m* causato da un incendio
fire insurance assicurazione *f* contro gli incendi
firm (n) ditta *f*, azienda *f*, impresa *f*
firm price prezzo *m* stabile
first in first out (FIFO) primo ad entrare primo ad uscire
first option prima opzione *f*
first-class di prima classe
fiscal measures provvedimenti *m* fiscali
fix *(mend)* riparare
fix a meeting for 3 p.m. fissare una riunione per le 15
fixed costs costi *m* fissi
fixed income reddito *m* fisso
fixed scale of charges tabella *f* fissa dei prezzi
fixed-price agreement contratto *m* a prezzo fisso
flat rate importo *m* fisso
flexibility flessibilità *f*
flexible flessibile
flight information informazioni *m* di volo
flight of capital capitale *m* in fuga
flip chart blocco *m* di fogli per lavagna
float (n) *(money)* anticipo *m*
float (v) *(a currency)* far fluttuare
float a company lanciare una società
floating exchange rate tasso *m* fluttuante di cambio
floor *(level)* piano *m*
floor plan planimetria *f*
floor space superficie *f* di pavimento
flop (n) insuccesso *m*
flop (v) fare fiasco
flotation lancio *m* di una società
flourishing fiorente
flow chart schema *m* del ciclo
fluctuate fluttuare, oscillare
fluctuation fluttuazione *f*
follow up aggiornamento *m*, sollecito *m*
follow-up letter lettera *f* di sollecito
for sale in vendita
force majeure causa *f* di forza maggiore
forced sale vendita *f* coatta
forecast (n) previsione *f*
forecast (v) prevedere
foreign currency divise *f*, moneta *f* straniera
foreign exchange *(currency)* divise *f*, valuta *f* estera
foreign money order ordine *m* di pagamento di valuta estera
forfeit a deposit perdere un deposito
forfeiture perdita *f* (di un diritto)

fork-lift truck
carrello *m* elevatore (a forche)
form (n) modulo *m*
form of words formulazione *f*
formal formale
forward buying acquisto *m* a termine
forward market mercato *m* a termine
forward rate corso *m* per operazioni a termine
forwarding address
indirizzo *m* d'inoltro
forwarding instructions istruzioni *f* per la spedizione
franchise (n) concessione *f*
franchise (v)
concedere il diritto di esclusiva
franchisee concessionario (-a)
franchiser concedente *m/f*
franchising concessione *f* di vendita
franking machine
macchina *f* affrancatrice
fraud frode *f*
free (adj) *(no payment)* gratis; (adv) gratis, gratuitamente
free (adj) *(no restrictions; not busy)* libero (-a)
free delivery consegna *f* gratuita
free of charge gratuito (-a), franco (-a) di spese
free of tax esente da tasse *f*
free on board (f.o.b.)
franco (-a) a bordo
free sample campione *m* gratuito
free trade zone
zona *f* di libero scambio
freeze (v) *(prices)* congelare
freight *(carriage)*
trasporto *m* (via mare)
freight costs spese *f* di trasporto
freight forward porto assegnato
freight plane aereo *m* da carico
frequent frequente
frozen account conto *m* congelato
frozen assets cespiti *m* congelati
fulfil an order evadere un ordine
full pieno (-a), intero (-a)
full price prezzo *m* intero
full refund rimborso *m* totale
full-time orario *m* pieno
fund (n) fondo *m*, fondi *mpl*
fund (v) finanziare
further to in seguito a
future delivery futura consegna *f*

G

gain (n) *(getting bigger)* aumento *m*; *(increase in value)* guadagno *m*
gap in the market
apertura *f* sul mercato
gearing rapporto *m* di indebitamento
general generale
general manager
direttore (-trice) generale
general strike sciopero *m* generale
gentleman's agreement accordo *m* sulla parola *f*
genuine purchaser
acquirente *m* genuino
get rid of sth. liberarsi di qc.
gift regalo *m*
gift voucher buono premio *m*
give *(as gift)* regalare
glut (n) saturazione *m*
go into business mettersi negli affari
going rate tariffa *f* en vigore
gold card carta *f* di credito d'oro
good buy buon affare *m*
good quality buona qualità f
good value *(for money)*
di buon valore
goods merce *f*
goodwill avviamento *m* commerciale
government bonds titoli *m* di stato
government contractor
fornitore (-trice) statale/allo stato
graded hotel albergo *m* selezionato
graduated income tax imposta *f* progressiva sul reddito
gram/gramme grammo *m*
grand total totale *m* generale
gratis gratis
gross (n) *(144)* grossa *f*
gross (v)
avere un ricavo lordo, incassare
gross domestic product (GDP)
prodotto *m* interno lordo (PIL)
gross national product (GNP)
prodotto *m* nazionale lordo (PNL)
gross profit utile *m* lordo
gross salary stipendio *m* lordo
gross weight peso *m* lordo
growth crescita *f*
growth rate percentuale *f* di crescita
guarantee (n) garanzia *f*
guarantee (v) garantire
guideline direttiva f

H

half (n) metà *f*
half-price sale saldo *m* a metà prezzo
half-year semestre *m*
hand luggage bagaglio *m* a mano
hand over
passaggio *m* delle consegne
handle (v) *(deal with)* occuparsi di; *(sell)* commerciare
handling charge
spese *f* di manutenzione
handwritten scritto (-a) a mano
harbour/harbor porto *m*
hard bargain
affare *m* poco vantaggioso
hard currency valuta *f* solida
hard disk hard disk *m*
harmonization armonizzazione *f*
haulage costs/rates
prezzo *m* del trasporto *m*
head of department capo *m* reparto
head office sede *f*
headquarters (HQ) sede *f* centrale
heavy costs/expenditure
forti costi *m*/spese *f*
heavy equipment
apparecchiatura *f* pesante
heavy goods vehicle (HGV)
veicolo *m* per merci pesanti
hectare ettaro *m*
hidden asset attività *f* occulte
hidden reserves riserve *f* occulte
high interest interesse *m* alto
high rent affitto *m* alto
high-quality di qualità superiore
highly-paid altamente retribuito (-a)
highly-priced ad alto prezzo
hire a car noleggiare una macchina
hire purchase (HP)
acquisto *m* rateale
hire staff assumere del personale
historical figures cifre *f* effettive
hold (n) *(ship)* stiva *f*
hold (v) *(contain)* contenere
hold a meeting tenere una seduta *f*
hold over posporre
hold up (v) *(delay)* trattenere
hold-up (n) (delay) ritardo *m*
holding company 'holding' *m*,
società *f* controllante
home address
indirizzo *m* personale
home sales vendite *f* nazionali,
vendite sul mercato interno
honour/honor a bill
onorare una cambiale
hotel hotel *m*, albergo *m*
hotel bill conto *m* dell'albergo
hour ora *f*
hourly rate retribuzione *f* a ore
hourly wage salario *m* orario
hourly-paid workers dipendenti *m*
pagati a ore
house *(company)* ditta *f*, impresa *f*
house insurance
assicurazione *f* sulla casa
hurry up affrettarsi

I

illegal illegale
illegally illegalmente
immediate immediato (-a)
immediately immediatamente
imperfect imperfetto (-a)
implement (n) strumento *m*
implement an agreement
perfezionare un accordo
implementation attuazione *f*
import (n) importazione *f*
import (v) importare
import duty dazio *m* doganale
import licence/permit
licenza *f* di importazione
import quota
contingente *m* di importazione
import-export (adj)
importazioni-esportazioni
importer importatore (-trice)
imports importazioni *f*
impulse buyer acquirente *m/f* che
compra per impulso
in-house interno (-a)
incentive incentivo *m*
incidental expenses
spese *f* impreviste
include includere
inclusive incluso (-a)
inclusive charge spesa *f* compresa
inclusive of tax comprese tasse *f*
income reddito *m*
income tax imposta *f* sul reddito
incoming call telefonata *f* in arrivo
incorporate *(a company)* costituire
incorrect scorretto

incorrectly scorrettamente
increase (n) aumento *m*
increase (v) aumentare
increase (v) **in price**
aumentare di prezzo
incur costs sostenere spese
incur debts contrarre debiti *m*
indebted indebitato (-a)
indemnification
indennità *f*, indennizzo *m*
indemnify so. for a loss risarcire qu. per una perdita
indemnity garanzia *f*, assicurazione *f*
index (n) *(of prices)* indice *m*
index (v) elencare
index-linked indicizzato
indexation indicizzazione *f*
indicator indicatore *m*
indirect labour/labor costs costi *m* indiretti del lavoro
indirect taxation
tassazione *f* indiretta
induction course/training
corso *m* introduttivo
industrial accident
infortunio *m* sul lavoro
industrial espionage
spionaggio *m* industriale
industrial relations
relazioni *f* industriali
industrial tribunal
tribunale *m* del lavoro
industrialist industriale *m/f*
industry *(companies)* industria *f*
inefficiency inefficienza *f*
inefficient inefficiente
inflation inflazione *f*
inflationary inflazionistico (-a)
influence (n) influenza *f*
influence (v) influenzare
information informazione *f*
infrastructure infrastruttura *f*
infringe a patent
usurpare un brevetto
infringement of patent usurpazione *f* di brevetto *m*
initial (v) siglare
initial capital capitale *m* d'apporto
initiate discussions
iniziare un dibattito *m*
initiative iniziativa *f*
input information informazioni *f* immesse nel computer
inquire indagare
inquiry richiesta *f*
insolvent insolvente
inspect esaminare
inspection ispezione *f*
instalment rata *f*
instant credit credito *m* immediato
institution istituzione *f*
institutional investors
investitore *m* istituzionale
instrument *(document)*
documento *m*, strumento *m*
insurance assicurazione *f*
insurance broker mediatore (-trice) assicurativo (-a)
insurance company
compagnia *f* di assicurazioni
insurance policy
polizza *f* di assicurazione
insure assicurare
intangible assets
attività *f* immateriali
interest (n) *(paid on investment)*
interesse *m*
interest (v) interessare
interest charges
addebiti *m* per interessi
interest rate tasso *m* d'interesse
interface (n) interfaccia *f*
interim payment
pagamento *m* provvisiorio
intermediary intermediario *m*
internal audit revisione *f* interna
international call
telefonata *f* internazionale
international law
diritto *m* internazionale
international trade
commercio *m* internazionale
interpret interpretare
interpreter interprete *m/f*
intervention price
prezzo *m* d'intervento
interview (n) *(for a job)* intervista *f*
interview (v) *(for a job)* avere un colloquio con
introduce introdurre
introductory offer
offerta *f* di propaganda
inventory (n) *(list of contents)*
inventario *m*
inventory (n) *(stock)* inventario *m*, scorte *f*, stock *m*

inventory control
controllo *m* di magazzino
invest investire
investment investimento *m*
investment income
reddito *m* da investimenti
invisible earnings proventi *m* da partite invisibili
invisible trade
commercio *m* invisibile
invite invitare
invoice (n) fattura *f*
invoice (v) fatturare
invoice number numero *m* di fattura
invoice price prezzo *m* di fattura
irrecoverable debt
debito *m* inesigibile
irredeemable bond
obbligazione *f* irredimibile
irregularities irregolarità *f*
irrevocable letter of credit lettera *f* di credito irrevocabile
issue a letter of credit aprire una lettera *f* di credito
issue instructions
diramare delle istruzioni
item *(on agenda)* argomento *m*, questione *f*; *(thing for sale)* articolo *m*
itemized account
conto *m* dettagliato
itemized invoice fattura *f* dettagliata

J

job *(employment)* impiego *m*, lavoro *m*; *(piece of work)* lavoro *m*
job description
descrizione *f* dei compiti
job security
sicurezza *f* del posto di lavoro
job title
denominazione *f* della mansione
join (v) unire
joint account conto *m* congiunto
joint managing director
condirettore (-trice)
joint signatory firmatario (-a) congiunto (-a)
joint venture 'joint venture' *m*, associazione *f* in partecipazione
journal *(accounts book)*
libro *m* giornale
junior clerk apprendista *m/f*
junk bonds
obbligazioni *f* 'cartastraccia'
junk mail opuscoli *mpl* pubblicitari
jurisdiction giurisdizione f

K

keen competition
concorrenza *f* accanita
keen prices prezzi *m* concorrenziali
keep a promise
mantenere una promessa
keep up with the demand stare al passo con la richiesta
key *(on keyboard)* tasto *m*
key post posto *m* chiave
kilo/kilogram
chilo *m*, chilogrammo *m*
knock down (v) *(price)*
ridurre, abbassare
knock off *(reduce price)* abbassare, ridurre il prezzo di
knock off *(stop work)*
cessare di lavorare

L

label (n) etichetta *f*
label (v) etichettare
labour/labor costs
costo *m* della manodopera
labour/labor disputes
vertenza *f* di lavoro
lack of funds mancanza *f* di fondi
land (n) terra *f*, terreno *m*
land goods at a port scaricare della merce in un porto
landed costs costi *m* fondiari
landing charges spese *f* di scarico
landlord locatore (-trice)
lapse (v) scadere
late (adv) tardi, in ritardo
latest recentissimo (-a)
lawful trade commercio *m* legittimo
lawsuit causa *f*
lawyer avvocato *m*
lay off workers licenziare personale
lease (n) affitto *m*
lease (v) *(of landlord)* affittare, dare in affitto; *(of tenant)* affittare, tenere in affitto
lease equipment affitare impianti *m*

lease-back leasing *m* immobiliare
leasing 'leasing' *m*
ledger libro *m* mastro
legal *(referring to law)* giuridico (-a)
legal advice consulenza *f* legale
legal costs/charges spese *f* legali
legal proceedings vie *f* legali
legal status stato *m* giuridico
lend prestare
lender prestatore (-trice), chi presta
lending limit limite *m* del prestito
lessee affittuario (-a)
lessor locatore (-trice)
letter of complaint lettera *f* di reclamo
letter of credit (L/C) lettera *f* di credito
letter of reference lettera *f* di referenze
level piano (-a), livello (-a)
level off/out stabilizzarsi
leverage leva *f* finanziaria
levy (n) imposta *f*
levy (v) imporre
liabilities passività *f*
liable for responsabile per
liable to passibile di
licence/license (n) licenza *f*
license (v) autorizzare
lien privilegio *m*
life assurance assicurazione *f* sulla vita
lift an embargo togliere l'embargo *m*
limit (n) limite *m*
limit (v) limitare
limited liability responsabilità *f* limitata
limited liability company (Ltd) società *f* di capitali a responsabilità limitata
liquid assets liquidità *f*
liquidate a company mettere in liquidazione una società
liquidate stock mettere in liquidazione delle scorte di magazzino
liquidation liquidazione *f*
liquidator liquidatore (-trice)
liquidity liquidità *f*
lira *(currency)* lira *f* (italiana)
list (n) *(catalogue/catalog)* listino *m*, catalogo *m*
list price prezzo *m* di listino
load (v) *(computer program)* caricare
load a lorry/a ship caricare un camion/una nave
loan (n) prestito *m*, mutuo *m*
loan (v) prestare, dare in prestito
loan capital capitale *m* mutuato
local labour/labor manodopera *m* locale
lock (n) serratura *f*
lock (v) chiudere a chiave
lock up a shop chiudere a chiave un negozio
lock up capital investire capitali
logo logogramma *m*
long credit redito *m* a lungo termine
long-dated bill effetto *m* a lunga scadenza
long-haul flight volo *m* a lungo raggio
long-standing agreement accordo *m* di lunga data
long-term a lungo termine
long-term debts debiti *m* a lungo termine
long-term loan mutuo *m* a lunga scadenza
long-term planning pianificazione *f* a lunga scadenza
loose sciolto (-a)
lose an order perdere un'ordinazione
lose money perdere dei soldi
loss *(not a profit)* perdita *f*
loss *(of sth.)* perdita *f*
loss-leader articolo *m* di richiamo per la clientela
low sales vendite *f* basse
lower (v) **prices** abbassare i prezzi
luggage bagaglio *m*
lump sum importo *m* forfettario

M

magazine rivista *f*
magazine insert fascicolo *m* supplementare
mail (n) *(letters/postal system)* posta *f*
mail (v) spedire per posta
mail shot campagna *f* promozionale a mezzo posta
mail-order ordinazioni *f* per corrispondenza

mail-order catalogue/catalog catalogo *m* di vendita per corrispondenza
mailing list elenco *m* di indirizzi
mailing shot campagna *f* promozionale a mezzo posta
main office sede centrale, direzione centrale
maintain *(keep going)* tenere in efficienza
maintenance *(keeping in working order)* manutenzione *f*
maintenance of supplies mantenimento *m* delle provvigioni
major shareholder azionista *m* principale
majority maggioranza *f*
majority shareholder azionista *m/f* di maggioranza
make good *(a defect, loss)* indennizzare, risarcire
make money fare soldi *mpl*
make out *(invoice)* compilare
make up for compensare
man (v) fornire il personale
man-hour ora *f* lavorativa
manage property amministrare un patrimonio
manage to riuscire a
management *(action)* gestione *f*; (*managers)* direzione *f*
management team quadri *m* direttivi
manager *(of branch, shop)* direttore (-trice)
managerial staff personale *m* dirigente
managing director (MD) amministratore (-trice) delegato (-a), direttore (-trice) generale
manning levels livello *m* di organico
manpower manodopera *f*
manpower shortage carenza *f* di manodopera
manual (adj) manuale
manual (n) manuale *m*
manual worker manovale *m/f*
manufacture (v) produrre, fabbricare
manufactured goods manufatti *m*
manufacturer produttore *m*, fabbricante *m*
manufacturing costs costi *m* di produzione
margin *(profit)* margine *m*
marginal pricing determinazione *f* marginale del prezzo
maritime law diritto *m* della navigazione *f*
maritime trade commercio *m* marittimo
mark (n) impronta *f*
mark (n) **(D-mark)** marco *m* tedesco
mark (v) notare
mark down abbassare il prezzo
mark up aumentare il prezzo
mark-up *(profit margin)* margine *m*, utile *m* lordo
market (n) *(possible sales)* mercato *m*
market (v) vendere, commercializzare
market analysis analisi *f* di mercato
market forces forze *f* di mercato
market leader prodotto-guida *m* del mercato, azienda *f* primaria sul mercato
market opportunities possibilità *f* di mercato
market penetration penetrazione *f* di mercato
market research ricerca *f* di mercato
market share quota *f* di mercato
market trends tendenza *f* di mercato
marketing marketing *m*
marketing department servizio *m* di marketing
marketing manager direttore (-trice) di marketing
marketing strategy strategia *f* di marketing
mass market product prodotto *m* per il mercato di massa
mass media mass-media *m*, mezzi *m* di comunicazione di massa
mass production produzione *f* in serie
maternity leave congedo *m* per maternità
matter (n) *(to be discussed)* argomento *m*, questione *f*
matter (v) importare
maturity date data *f* di scadenza
maximum (adj) massimo (-a)
maximum (n) massimo *m*
mean (n) media *f*
mean annual increase aumento *m* medio annuale

means *(money)* mezzi *mpl*
measurement of profitability misura *f* della redditività
medium-sized di medie dimensioni
medium-term a medio termine
meet *(be satisfactory)* soddisfare
meet *(so.)* incontrare
meet a deadline rispettare una scadenza *f*
meet a demand andare incontro ad una richiesta
meet a target raggiungere un obiettivo
meeting riunione *f*
memo memorandum *m*
merchandise (n) merce *f*
merchandize a product esercitare il commercio di un prodotto
merchandizing attività *f* promozionale
merchant bank 'merchant bank' *m*, banca *f* mercantile
merge incorporare
merger fusione *f*
message messaggio *m*
middle management quadri *mpl* intermedi
middle-sized company società *f* di mezza misura
middleman intermediario *m*
minimum (adj) minimo (-a)
minimum (n) minimo *m*
minimum payment pagamento *m* minimo
minimum wage salario *m* minimo
minority minoranza *f*
minority shareholder azionista *m* di minoranza
minus factor fattore *m* negativo
minute (v) verbalizzare, mettere a verbale
minutes (n) *(meeting)* verbale *m*
miscalculate fare male i propri calcoli
miscalculation calcolo *m* sbagliato
miscellaneous miscellaneo, vario
miss *(not to hit)* mancare; *(not to meet)* mancare; *(train, plane)* perdere
mistake errore *m*
misunderstanding malinteso *m*
mixed economy economia *f* di tipo misto
mobilize capital mobilizzare capitali
mock-up modello *m* in scala
mode of payment modalità *f* di pagamento
model (n) modello *m*
model agreement accordo-tipo *m*
modem modem *m*
moderate (adj) moderato (-a)
monetary monetario (-a)
money denaro *m*
money order vaglia *m* postale
money supply disponibilità *f* di capitali
money up front soldi *m* in anticipo
monitor (n) *(screen)* monitor *m*
monitor (v) controllare
monopoly monopolio *m*
month-end accounts contabilità *f* di fine mese
monthly (adj) mensile
monthly payments pagamenti *m* mensili
monthly statement resoconto *m* mensile
moratorium moratoria *f*
mortgage (n) ipoteca *f*
mortgage (v) ipotecare
most-favoured/favored nation nazione *f* più favorita
motivated motivato (-a)
motivation motivazione *f*
multilateral agreement accordo *m* multilaterale
multinational (n) multinazionale *f*
multiple (adj) multiplo (-a)
multiple entry visa visto *m* consolare multiplo
multiplication moltiplicazione *f*
multiply moltiplicare

N

nationalized industry industria *f* statalizzata
nationwide di dimensioni nazionali
natural resources risorse *f* naturali
negotiable negoziabile
negotiable instrument strumento *m* negoziabile
negotiate negoziare
negotiation negoziato *m*, negoziazione *f*
negotiator negoziatore *m*
net (adj) netto (-a)

net assets/worth
valore *m* patrimoniale netto
net income/salary reddito *m* netto
net margin margine *m* netto
net price prezzo *m* netto
net profit utile *m* netto
net weight peso *m* netto
net yield rendimento *m* netto
network (v) *(computers)*
collegare in rete
niche nicchia *f*
nil return ricavo *m* nullo
nominal capital capitale *m* nominale
nominal value valore *m* nominale
nominee (n) candidato (-a)
non profit-making
senza scopo di lucro
non-negotiable instrument
strumento *m* non negoziabile
non-payment *(of a debt)* omesso
pagamento *m* di un debito
non-refundable deposit deposito *m*
non rimborsabile
non-returnable packing
imballo *m* a perdere
note (n) nota *f*, biglietto *m* di banca
notice *(time allowed)* preavviso *m*
notification notificazione *f*
notify notificare
null nullo (-a)
number (n) *(figure)* numero *m*
number (v) numerare

O

objective (n) obiettivo *m*
obligation *(duty)*
dovere *m*, impegno *m*
obsolescence invecchiamento *m*
obsolete antiquato (-a)
obtain ottenere
obtainable conseguibile, ottenibile
odd numbers numeri *m* dispari
off *(away from work)* assente;
(cancelled) annullato (-a)
off-peak non di punta
off-season fuori stagione *f*
offer (n) offerta *f*
offer (v) *(to buy)* offrire, proporre
office ufficio *m*
office hours orario *m* d'ufficio
office staff personale *m* d'ufficio
official (adj) ufficiale
official (n)
funzionario (-a), dirigente *m/f*
offshore offshore, all'estero
oil *(petroleum)* petrolio *m*
oil price prezzo *m* del petrolio *m*
old vecchio (-a)
old-fashioned antiquato (-a)
on account in acconto
on approval salvo vista e verifica
on behalf of per conto di
on business per affari
on order stato (-a)/ordinato (-a)
on sale in vendita
on time puntuale
one-off unico (-a)
open (adj) *(not closed)* aperto (-a)
open (v) *(start new business)* aprire
open a bank account
aprire un conto bancario
open a line of credit aprire una linea
di credito
open a meeting aprire una seduta
open account conto *m* aperto
open credit credito *m* aperto
open market mercato *m* libero
open-plan office
ufficio *m* senza divisioni
opening balance
bilancio *m* d'apertura
opening hours orario *m* d'apertura
opening stock rimanenze *f* iniziali
opening time orario *m* d'apertura
operate operare, funzionare
operating costs/expenses costi *m*
d'esercizio, spese *f* d'esercizio
operating manual
manuale *m* operativo
operating profit utile *m* d'esercizio
operation operazione *f*
operational costs costi *m* di gestione
operator operatore (-trice)
option to purchasee
opzione *f* per l'acquisto
optional extras
spese *f* supplementari
order (n) *(for goods)* ordine *m*;
(instruction) ordine *m*
order (n) *(money)* mandato *m* di
pagamento, vaglia *f*
order (v) *(goods)* ordinare
order fulfilment
evasione *f* di un ordine
order number numero *m* d'ordine

order processing elaborazione *f* degli ordini
order, on essere stato (-a) ordinato (-a)
ordinary shares azioni *f* ordinarie
organization chart organigramma *m*
organize organizzare
origin origine *f*
original (adj) originario (-a)
out of date non attuale
out of stock esaurito (-a)
out of work disoccupato (-a)
outgoing mail posta *f* in partenza
outgoings spese *f*
outlay esborso *m*
output (n) *(goods)* produzione *f*
outside office hours fuori orario d'ufficio
outsize (OS) di taglia forte
outstanding *(exceptional)* straordinario (-a); *(unpaid)* non pagato (-a)
outstanding debts debiti *m* insoluti
outstanding orders ordinazioni *f* da evadere
overbook prenotare più di quanti siano disponibili
overbooking prenotazione *f* di più di quanti siano disponibili
overcapacity capacità *f* in eccedenza
overcharge (n) prezzo *m* eccessivo
overcharge (v) far pagare troppo
overdraft scoperto *m*
overdrawn account conto *m* scoperto
overdue scaduto (-a)
overhead costs/expenses spese *f* generali
overheads spese *f* generali
overproduction produzione *f* in eccesso
overseas markets mercati *m* esteri
overseas trade commercio *m* estero
overspend one's budget spendere oltre il proprio budget
overstocks sovraccarico *m* di scorte
overtime lavoro *m* straordinario
overtime pay compenso *m* per lavoro straordinario
owe essere debitore
owing to a causa di
own label goods prodotti con etichetta propria
owner proprietario (-a)
ownership proprietà *f*

P

pack (n) pacco *m*
pack (v) imballare, impacchettare
package *(of services)* contratto *m* globale
package deal pacchetto *m* rivendicativo
packaging material materiale *m* d'imballaggio
packer impacchettatore (-trice)
packing list/slip distinta *f* d'imballaggio
paid *(invoice)* pagato (-a)
pallet paletta *f*
palletize palettizzare, trasportare a mezzo di palette
paper loss perdita *f* sulla carta
paper profit utili *mpl* ipotetici
paperwork lavoro *m* d'ufficio
par value valore *m* nominale
parcel (n) pacco *m*
parcel post servizio *m* pacchi postali
parent company società *f* controllante
part exchange permuta *f* come pagamento parziale
part-time work/employment lavoro *m* a orario ridotto
partial payment pagamento *m* parziale
particulars dettagli *m*
partner socio (-a), compagno (-a)
party *(legal)* parte *f*
patent brevetto *m*
patent applied for/pending brevetto *m* richiesto, in attesa di brevetto
pay (n) *(salary)* paga *f*, retribuzione *f*, salario *m*
pay a bill pagare un conto
pay an invoice pagare una fattura
pay back rimborsare
pay by credit card pagare con carta di credito
pay cash pagare in contanti
pay cheque/check (n) assegno *m* dello stipendio
pay in advance pagare anticipatamente
pay out sborsare
pay rise aumento *m* salariale

payable in advance pagabile anticipatamente
payable on delivery pagabile alla consegna
payable on demand pagabile su richiesta
payee beneficiario (-a)
payer chi paga
paying-in slip distinta *f* di versamento
payment pagamento *m*
payment by cheque/check pagamento *m* tramite assegno
payment in cash pagamento *m* in contanti
payment on account pagamento *m* in acconto
peak period periodo *m* di massima attività
peg prices bloccare i prezzi *m*
penalize penalizzare
penalty clause clausola *f* di penalità
pending pendente
penetrate a market realizzare la penetrazione di un mercato
pension pensione *f*
per annum all'anno
per hour/day/week/year all'ora/al giorno/alla settimana/all'anno
percentage percentuale *f*
percentage discount sconto *m* percentuale
period periodo *m*
perishable goods merci *f* deperibili
permission autorizzazione *f*
permit (n) permesso *m*
permit (v) autorizzare
personal allowances detrazioni *f* personali
personal assistant (PA) segretaria *f* personale
personal computer (PC) personal computer *m*, elaboratore *m* ad uso personale
personnel personale *m*
personnel manager capo *m* del personale
petty cash piccola cassa *f*
petty expenses piccole spese *f*
phase in introdurre gradualmente
phase out eliminare gradualmente
phone (n) telefono *m*
phone (v) telefonare
phone call chiamata *f* telefonica
phone card carta *f* di credito telefonica
phone number numero *m* del telefono, numero telefonico
photocopier fotocopiatrice *f*
photocopy (n) fotocopia *f*
photocopy (v) fotocopiare
pie chart grafico *m* a settori
piece rate retribuzione *f* a cottimo
piecework lavoro *m* a cottimo
pilferage/pilfering furto *m* di scarsa entità
pilot scheme progetto *m* pilota
place an order fare un ordine
place of work posto *m* di lavoro
plaintiff querelante *m/f*
plan (n) *(drawing)* pianta *f*
plan (n) *(project)* piano *m*, progetto *m*
plan (v) progettare, organizzare
plane aereo *m*
plant (n) *(machinery)* impianti *mpl*
plug (n) *(electric)* presa *f* elettrica
plug (v) *(publicize)* pubblicizzare
plus factor fattore *m* positivo
point of sale (POS) punto *m* di vendita
policy politica *f*, polizza *f*
poor quality qualità *f* scadente
poor service servizio *m* scadente
popular prices prezzi *m* popolari
port *(computer)* connettore *m*; *(harbour/harbor)* porto *m*
port of call porto *m* di scalo
port of embarkation porto *m* d'imbarco
portable portatile
portfolio portafoglio *m*
POS (point of sale) material materiale *m* per punto di vendita
position *(job)* impiego *m*, lavoro *m*
positive positivo (-a)
possess possedere
post (n) *(job)* posto *m* di lavoro, impiego *m*
post (n) *(letters)* posta *f*
post (v) spedire per posta
post free franco (-a) posta
postage spesa *f* postale
postage and packing (p & p) spese *fpl* postali e imballo
postage paid porto *m* pagato

postal charges/rates spese *f* postali
postcode
codice *m* d'avviamento postale
poste restante fermoposta *m*
postpaid affrancatura *f* pagata
postpone differire, rinviare
postponement dilazione *f*, rinvio *m*
potential market
mercato *m* potenziale
pound *(money)* sterlina *f*; *(weight: 0.45kg)* libbra *f* peso
power of attorney procura *f*
preference shares azioni *f* privilegiate
premises locali *mpl*
premium *(insurance)*
premio *m* di assicurazione
premium offer offerta *f* premio
prepack/prepackage preconfezionare
prepaid pagato (-a) in anticipo
prepayment pagamento *m* anticipato
present (adj) *(being there)* presente; *(now)* attuale
present (n) *(gift)* regalo *m*
present (v) *(show a document)*
presentare
present a bill for acceptance
presentare un effetto *m* per l'accettazione
presentation *(exhibition)*
presentazione *f*; *(showing a document)* presentazione *f*
press conference
conferenza *f* stampa
press release comunicato *m* stampa
pretax profit
utile *m* al lordo delle imposte
prevention prevenzione *f*
price (n) prezzo *m*
price (v) stabilire il prezzo
price ceiling tetto *m* dei prezzi
price controls
regolamentazione *f* dei prezzi
price ex warehouse
prezzi *m* franco magazzino
price ex works
prezzi *m* franco stabilimento
price label/tag
cartellino *m* del prezzo
price list listino *m* prezzi
price war guerra *f* dei prezzi
price/earnings ratio (P/E ratio)
rapporto *m* corso/utili
pricing policy politica *f* della determinazione dei prezzi
primary industry industria *f* primaria
prime cost costi *m* diretti
principal (adj) principale
principal (n) *(money)* capitale *m*
principal (n) *(person)* capo *m*, direttore (-trice)
principle principio *m*
print out stampare
printer *(machine)* stampante *f*
printout stampato *m*
private enterprise
iniziativa *f* privata
private property proprietà *f* privata
private sector settore *m* privato
privatization privatizzazione *f*
privatize privatizzare
pro forma *(invoice)*
(fattura) proforma
pro rata prorata, proporzionale
problem area area *f* problematica
problem solver
persona *f* che risolve problemi
process (v) *(deal with)* trattare
processing of information
elaborazione *f* delle informazioni
product prodotto *m*
product design
progettazione *f* del prodotto
product line linea *f* di prodotti
product mix gamma *f* di prodotti
production *(making)* produzione *f*
production department
ufficio *m* produzioni
production manager direttore (-trice) di produzione
production targets
obiettivi *m* di produzione
productive discussions
discussione *f* produttiva
productivity produttività *f*
productivity agreement accordo *m* sulla produttività
professional (n) *(expert)*
professionista *m/f*, esperto (-a)
professional qualifications
qualificazioni *f* professionali
profit profitto *m*, utile *m*
profit after tax
utile *m* al netto delle imposte
profit and loss account conto *m* profitti e perdite

profit before tax utile *m* al lordo delle imposte
profit centre/center centro *m* di profitto
profit margin margine *m* di utile
profitability redditività *f*
profitable rimunerativo (-a), proficuo (-a), redditizio (-a)
program a computer programmare un computer
programme/program programma *m*
progress chaser addetto (-a) al controllo dell'avanzamento
progress report relazione *f* sull'avanzamento
project *(plan)* progetto *m*
project manager direttore (-trice) del progetto
projected sales vendite *f* previste
promissory note pagherò *m*
promote *(advertise; give better job)* promuovere
promote a new product pubblicizzare un nuovo prodotto
promotion *(publicity; to better job)* promozione *f*
promotional budget stanziamento *m* promozionale
prompt payment pagamento *m* in contanti
prompt service servizio *m* sollecito
proportion proporzione *f*
proportional proporzionale
propose to *(do sth.)* intendere
proprietor proprietario *m*
proprietress proprietaria *f*
prosecution *(legal action)* procedimento *m* giudiziario
prospective buyer possibile acquirente *m/f*
prospects prospettive *f*
prospectus prospetto *m*
protest strike sciopero *m* di protesta
provided that/providing a patto che
provision *(condition)* condizione *f*, clausola *f*
provisional budget budget *m* provvisorio
proviso clausola *f* condizionale
proxy *(person)* mandatario *m*
proxy vote voto *m* per delega
public finance finanza *f* pubblica
public holiday festa *f* nazionale
Public Limited Company (Plc) società *f* di capitali a sottoscrizione pubblica
public relations (PR) pubbliche relazioni *f*
public relations department ufficio *m* delle pubbliche relazioni
public sector settore *m* pubblico
public transport trasporti *m* pubblici
publicity pubblicità *f*
publicity budget budget *m* pubblicitario
publicity department ufficio *m* della pubblicità
publicity manager direttore (-trice) della pubblicità
publicize pubblicizzare
purchase (n) acquisto *m*
purchase (v) acquistare, comperare
purchase tax imposta *f* generale sugli acquisti
purchaser compratore (-trice)
purchasing acquisto *m*
purchasing power potere *m* d'acquisto
put in writing mettere per iscritto

Q

qualified *(skilled)* abile, qualificato (-a)
qualify as qualificarsi
quality control controllo *m* di qualità
quantity quantità *f*
quantity discount sconto *m* sul quantativo
quarter *(25%)* quarto *m*; *(three months)* trimestre *m*
quarterly (adj) trimestrale
quay molo *m*
quorum numero *m* minimo legale
quota quota *f*
quotation/quote *(estimate of cost)* quotazione *f*
quote (v) *(estimate costs)* indicare un prezzo, quotare

R

rail/railway ferrovia *f*
railway station stazione *f* ferroviaria
raise (v) *(increase)* aumentare; *(obtain money)* raccogliere fondi

raise an invoice emettere una fattura
random check sondaggio *m*
random error errori *m* casuali
rate (n) *(amount)* tasso *m*; *(price)* quota *f*, tariffa *f*, tasso *m*
rate of exchange tasso *m* di cambio
rate of inflation tasso *m* d'inflazione
ratio rapporto *m*
rationalize razionalizzare
raw materials materie *f* prime
reach a decision arrivare ad una decisione *f*
reach an agreement giungere ad un accordo *m*
ready pronto (-a)
ready cash pronta cassa *f*
real estate proprietà *f* immobiliare
real income/wages reddito *m* effettivo
realizable assets attivo *m* esigibile, cespiti *m* realizzabili
realize *(sell for money)* realizzare
realize assets realizzare cespiti *m*
reapply riapplicare
reappoint ricollocare
reassess fare una nuova stima
rebate rimborso *m*
receipt *(paper)* ricevuta *f*; *(receiving)* ricevimento *m*
receipts entrate *f*
receivables effetti *m* attivi
receive ricevere
receiver *(liquidator)* liquidatore (-trice)
reception portineria *f*
reception desk banco *m* d'albergo
receptionist receptionist (-a)
recession recessione *f*
reciprocal trade commercio *m* bilaterale
recognize a union riconoscere un sindacato
recommend *(say sth. is good)* raccomandare; *(suggest action)* consigliare
reconcile riconciliare
reconciliation riconciliazione *f*
record (n) *(better than before)* primato *m*; *(of events)* rapporto *m*
record (v) registrare
record sales vendite *f* record
records documentazione *f*, archivio *m*
recover *(get better)* riprendersi; *(get sth. back)* ricuperare
recovery *(getting better)* ripresa *f*; *(getting sth. back)* ricupero *m*
red tape lungaggine *f* burocratica
redeem estinguere
redemption (of a loan) riscatto *m* (di un prestito)
redemption date data *f* di rimborso
reduce ridurre
reduce a price ridurre un prezzo
reduced rate tasso *m* ridotto
redundant in esubero
refer *(pass to so.)* sottoporre; *(to item)* riferirsi, fare riferimento a
reference *(report on person)* referenze *fpl*, attestato *m*
reference number numero *m* di riferimento
refund (n) rimborso *m*
refund (v) rimborsare
refundable deposit caparra *f* rimborsabile
refusal rifiuto *m*
refuse (v) rifiutare
regarding riguardante
regardless of senza riguardo per
register (n) *(official list)* registro *m*
register (v) *(in official list)* iscriversi; *(letter)* fare una lettera raccomandata
register a company iscrivere una società
registered office sede *f* legale
registered trademark marchio *m* di fabbrica *m* depositato
Registrar of Companies Conservatore *m* del Registro delle Società
registration registrazione *f*
registration fee tassa *f* di registrazione
registry registrazione *f*
regular *(always at same time)* consueto (-a), fisso (-a)
regular *(ordinary)* regolare, normale
regular customer cliente *m* abituale
regulate *(by law)* regolarizzare
regulations regolamenti *m*, disposizioni *f*
reinvest reinvestire
reinvestment reinvestimento *m*
reject (n) scarto *m*

reject (v) rifiutare, respingere
relating to relativo (-a) a
relations parenti *m*
release (v) *(make public)* rilasciare
release dues
liquidare gli ordini arretrati
reliability attendibilità *f*
reliable attendibile
remain *(be left)* restare
remainder *(things left)*
saldi *mpl*, giacenze *fpl*
remit by cheque/check inviare
rimessa a mezzo assegno
remittance rimessa *f*
remunerate retribuire
remuneration retribuzione *f*
render an account
presentare un conto
renew a bill of exchange rinnovare
una cambiale
renewal of a lease rinnovo *m* di un
contratto d'affitto
rent (n) affitto *m*
rent (v) *(pay money for)*
prendere in affitto
rental affitto *m*
reorder (n) nuova ordinazione *f*
reorder (v) riordinare
reorder level livello *m* di riordinazione
reorganization riorganizzazione *f*
reorganize riorganizzare
repay ripagare
repayable rimborsabile
repeat an order ripetere un ordine
repeat order ordinazione *f* rinnovata
replacement *(item)* sostituzione *f*
replacement value
valore *m* di sostituzione
reply (n) risposta *f*
reply (v) rispondere
report (n) rapporto *m*
report (v) riferire
report to so. dover rispondere a qu.
represent rappresentare
representative *(person)*
rappresentante *m* di commercio
request (n) richiesta *f*
request (v) richiedere, domandare
request, on su richiesta
requirements richieste *f*
resale rivendita *f*
research and development (R & D)
ricerca *f* e sviluppo *m* (RS)
researcher ricercatore (-trice)
reservation prenotazione *f*
reserve (n) *(money)* fondo *m*;
(supplies) riserva *f*
residence permit
permesso *m* di soggiorno
resign dimettersi
resources risorse *f*
response reazione *f*
responsibility responsabilità *f*
responsible (for) responsabile (di)
responsible to so.
che deve rispondere a qu.
restock rifornire
restrict limitare
restrictive practices
pratiche *f* restrittive
restructure ristrutturare
restructuring (of a loan)
rifinanziamento *m* (di un prestito)
result from derivare
result in avere come risultato
results *(profit or loss)* risultati *mpl*
resume negotiations
riprendere le negoziazioni
retail (v) *(goods)*
vendere al dettaglio
retail (v) *(sell for a price)* vendersi a
retail goods
merce *f* per la vendita al dettaglio
retail price prezzo *m* al dettaglio
retailer dettagliante *m/f*
retire *(from one's job)*
andare in pensione
retirement age età *f* della pensione
retrain riaddestrare
retrenchment riduzione *f* delle spese
retroactive retroattivo (-a)
return (n) *(declaration)*
dichiarazione *f*; *(profit)* profitto *m*,
guadagno *m*
return (n) *(going back)* ritorno *m*;
(sending back) rinvio *m*
return a letter to sender rimandare
una lettera al mittente
return address
indirizzo *m* del mittente
return on investment (ROI) reddito *m*
sugli investimenti
returns *(unsold goods)*
merce *f* non venduta
revenue reddito *m*
revoke revocare

revolving credit credito *m* rinnovabile automaticamente
right (adj) *(not left)* destro (-a); *(not wrong)* corretto (-a)
right (n) *(legal title)* diritto *m*
right of way diritto *m* di precedenza
rightful owner proprietario (-a) legittimo (-a)
rights issue emissione *f* di diritti
rise (n) *(increase)* aumento *m*; *(salary)* aumento *m*
rise (v) aumentare
risk (n) rischio *m*
risk (v) *(money)* rischiare
risk capital capitale *m* di rischio
risky rischioso (-a)
rival company società *f* rivale
road strada *f*
road transport trasporto *m* su strada
rock-bottom prices prezzo *m* ridottissimo
room *(hotel)* camera *f*; *(space)* spazio *m*
room service servizio *m* in camera
rough calculation calcolo *m* approssimativo
rough estimate valutazione *f* approssimativa
round down arrotondare diminuendo
routine work lavoro *m* di routine
royalty diritto *m* di concessione
rule (n) norma *f*
rule (v) *(give decision)* decretare
ruling (n) decreto *m*
run (v) *(be in force)* essere valido (-a), entrare in vigore
run (v) *(manage)* dirigere
run into debt contrarre debiti
run out of esaurirsi
running costs/expenses spese *f* d'esercizio, costi *m* di gestione di un'azienda
running total totale *m* corrente
rush hour ora *f* di punta
rush order ordine *m* urgente

S

sack so. licenziare qu.
safe (n) cassaforte *f*
safe investment investimento *m* sicuro
safeguard salvaguardia *f*
safety precautions misure *f* di sicurezza
safety regulations norme *f* di sicurezza
salaried stipendiato (-a)
salary stipendio *m*
salary review revisione *f* dello stipendio
sale (n) *(at a low price)* saldo *m*; *(selling)* vendita *f*
sales vendite *f*, fatturato *m*
sales budget previsione *f* di vendita
sales campaign campagna *f* di vendite
sales conference raduno *m* dei venditori
sales department ufficio *m* vendite
sales figures volume *m* d'affari
sales forecast previsione *f* di vendita
sales manager direttore (-trice) commerciale
sales target obiettivo *m* di vendita
sales tax imposta *f* sul volume di affari
salesman *(in shop)* commesso (-a); *(representative)* rappresentante *m/f*
salvage (n) *(action)* recupero *m*
salvage (v) salvare, ricuperare
sample (n) *(part)* campione *m*, saggio *m*
satisfy *(customer)* soddisfare
satisfy a demand soddisfare una richiesta
saturate the market rendere saturo il mercato
save (v) *(money)* risparmiare; *(data)* salvaguardare; *(not waste)* risparmiare, economizzare
savings account conto *m* di risparmio
scale down/up ridurre/aumentare proporzionalmente
scale of charges tariffa *f*
scheduled flight volo *m* di linea
seal (v) *(attach a seal)* sigillare
sealed tenders offerta *f* in busta chiusa
season *(time of year)* stagione *f*
season ticket tessera *f*
seasonal demand richiesta *f* stagionale

seasonal variations
variazioni *f* stagionali
secondary industry
industria *f* secondaria
secondhand
usato (-a), di seconda mano
seconds
prodotti *m* di seconda qualità
secretarial college scuola *f* per
segretarie d'azienda
secretary segretaria *f*, segretario *m*
sector settore *m*
secure funds procurarsi fondi *m*
secured creditor creditore (-trice)
privilegiato (-a)
secured loan mutuo *m* garantito
securities titoli *m*
security guard guardia *f* giurata
security of employment sicurezza *f*
dell'impiego
seize sequestrare
seizure sequestro *m*
self-employed che lavora in proprio
self-financing (adj)
che può autofinanziarsi
sell vendere
sell forward vendere a termine
sell-by date data *f* di scadenza
selling (n) vendita *f*
semi-skilled workers lavoratori *m*
parzialmente qualificati
send an invoice spedire una fattura
sender colui che spedisce
senior manager/executive
dirigente *m/f* in capo,
direttore (-trice)
separate (adj) separato (-a)
serial number numero *m* di serie
serve a customer servire un cliente
service (n) *(dealing with customers)*
servizio *m; (of machine)*
revisione *f*, manutenzione *f*
service (v) *(a machine)* revisionare
service centre/center
centro *m* di assistenza
service charge
percentuale *f* per il servizio
service department
ufficio *m* assistenza
service manual
manuale *m* di manutenzione
set (adj) fisso (-a)
set price prezzo *m* stabilito
set up a company
costituire una società *f*
setback battuta *f* d'arresto
settle (an invoice)
liquidare, pagare (una fattura)
settle an account saldare un conto
settlement *(payment)* pagamento *m*
share (n) *(in a company)* azione *f*
share (v) *(divide among)*
spartire, dividere
share (v) *(use with so.)* dividere
share certificate
certificato *m* azionario
shareholder azionista *m/f*
shareholding
partecipazione *f* azionaria
sheet of paper foglio *m* di carta
shelf scaffale *m*
shelf life of a product periodo *m*
medio di permanenza di un
prodotto
shelve accantonare, differire
shelving *(postponing)*
accantonamento *m*
shelving *(shelves)* scaffalatura *f*
shift (n) *(team of workers)* turno *m*
(di lavoro)
shift work lavoro *m* con turni
ship (n) nave *f*
ship (v) trasportare, spedire
shipment trasporto *m* marittimo
shipper spedizioniere *m* marittimo
shipping charges/costs costi *m* per la
spedizione marittima
shipping instructions istruzioni *f* per
la spedizione
shop negozio *m*
shop around chiedere informazioni
nei negozi
shop window vetrina *f*
shopper acquirente *m/f*, cliente *m/f*
shopping centre/mall
centro *m* commerciale
short credit
credito *m* a breve termine
short of a meno di
short-term (adj)
a breve, a breve termine
short-term contract contratto *m* a
breve termine
short-term loan
mutuo *m* a breve scadenza
shortage scarsità *f*

shortlist (n)
lista *f* ristretta (di candidati)
shortlist (v) inserire qu. in una rosa di candidati
show a profit indicare un profitto
sideline attività *f* secondaria
sight draft tratta *f* a vista
sign (n) insegna *f*
sign (v) firmare
signatory firmatario (-a)
signature firma *f*
simple interest interesse *m* semplice
sister company società *f* sorella
site luogo *m*
site engineer ingegnere *m* edile
situation *(state of affairs)* situazione *f*
situations vacant offerte *f* d'impiego
skeleton staff
personale *m* ridotto al minimo
skill abilità *f* tecnica
skilled labour/labor
manodopera *f* qualificata
slack lento (-a), stagnante
slash prices tagliare i prezzi
sleeping partner
socio *m* accomandante
slip (n) *(mistake)* errore *m*; *(piece of paper)* foglietto *m*
slow payer pagatore *m* tardivo
slump in sales discesa *f* delle vendite
small businesses piccole imprese *f*
small-scale in scala *f* ridotta
social costs costi *m* sociali
social security previdenza *f* sociale
socio-economic groups
gruppi *m* socioeconomici
soft currency valuta *f* debole
software software *m*
sole solo (-a), unico (-a)
sole agent
rappresentante esclusivo
sole owner unico proprietario *m*
solicit orders sollecitare un ordine
solution soluzione *f*
solve a problem
risolvere un problema
solvency solvibilità *f*
solvent (adj) solvente
source of income fonte *f* di reddito
spare part pezzo *m* di ricambio
special drawing rights (SDRs)
diritti *m* speciali di prelievo (DSP)
special offer offerta *f* speciale
specification specifica *f*
specify specificare
spend *(money)* spendere
spend time passare il tempo a
spinoff sottoprodotto *m*
sponsor (n) sponsor *m*, garante *m*
sponsor (v) garantire, sponsorizzare, patrocinare
sponsorship
sponsorizzazione *f*, avvallo *m*
spot cash pagamento *m* in contanti
spot price
prezzo *m* per merce pronta
spot purchase transazione *f* a pronti
spread a risk ripartire un rischio
stability stabilità *f*
stabilize stabilizzare
stable currency moneta *f* stabile
stable prices prezzi *m* stabili
staff meeting
assemblea *f* del personale
staged payments
pagamenti *m* scaglionati
stagger scaglionare
stamp (n) *(post)* francobollo *m*
stamp (v) *(letter)* affrancare, mettere francobolli
stand (n) *(at exhibition)* stand *m*
standard (adj) standard
standard (n) norma *f*
standard rate (of tax)
aliquota *f* d'imposta base
standardize standardizzare
standby ticket biglietto *m* aereo privo di prenotazione
standing standing *m*
staple industry industria *f* di base
start-up costs spese *f* di avviamento
starting date data *f* d'inizio
starting salary stipendio *m* iniziale
state (n) *(condition)*
condizione *f*, stato *m*
state-of-the-art all'avanguardia
statement of account
estratto *m* conto
statistical analysis analisi *f* statistica
statistics statistica *f*
status condizione *f* sociale
status inquiry
informazioni *f* commerciali
statute of limitations prescizione *f*
statutory holiday
giorno *m* festivo legale

sterling lira sterlina *f*
stipulate stipulare
stock (n) *(goods)* stock *m*, scorte *f*
stock (v) *(goods)* rifornire, tenere
stock control controllo *m* delle scorte
stock exchange
Borsa *f*, Borsa Valori *f*
stock list inventario *m*
stock market mercato *m* azionario
stock size dimensioni *f* delle scorte
stock up immagazzinare
stockbroker agente *m/f* di cambio
stockist rivenditore (-trice)
stocktaking inventario *m*
stocktaking sale
saldi *m* per inventario
stop (v) *(doing sth.)* cessare, finire
stop a cheque/check
bloccare un assegno
stop payments
sospendere i pagamenti
storage (n) *(computer)* memoria *f*
storage (n) *(cost)* spese *fpl* di immagazzinamento; *(in warehouse)* magazzinaggio *m*, deposito *m*
storage capacity
capienza *f* di magazzino
storage facilities
impianti *m* di magazzinaggio
store (n) *(large shop)* negozio *m*, grande magazzino *m*
store (n) *(place where goods are kept)* deposito *m*, magazzino *m*
store (v) *(keep in warehouse)*
immagazzinare
straight line depreciation
ammortamento *m* a quote costanti
strategic planning
pianificazione *f* strategica
strategy strategia *f*
strike (n) sciopero *m*
strike (v) scioperare
striker scioperante *m/f*
strong currency divisa *f* forte
sub judice in contenzioso
subcontract (n) subappalto *m*
subcontract (v) dare in subappalto
subcontractor subappaltatore (-trice)
subject to soggetto a
sublease (n) subaffitto *m*
sublease/sublet subaffittare
subsidiary (adj) sussidiario (-a)
subsidiary (n) filiale *f*
subsidiary company affiliata *f*
subsidize sussidiare
subsidy sussidio *m*, sovvenzione *f*
subtotal totale *m* parziale
succeed *(do well)*
riuscire, avere successo
success successo *m*
successful di successo
sue citare, intentare causa
sum *(of money)* somma *f*
sundries articoli *m* vari
supervise sorvegliare
supervision
supervisione *f*, vigilanza *f*
supervisor supervisore *m*
supervisory
ispettivo (-a), di supervisione
supplementary supplementare
supplier fornitore (-trice)
supply (n) *(action)* fornitura *f*
supply (v) fornire, approvvigionare
supply price prezzo *m* d'offerta
surcharge sovrapprezzo *m*
surplus surplus *m*, sovrappiù *m*
surrender (n) *(of insurance policy)*
riscatto *m*
surrender value valore *m* di riscatto
survey (n) *(examination)* indagine *f*, perizia *f*, studio *m*
survey (v) *(inspect)*
esaminare, ispezionare
surveyor perito *m*
suspend sospendere
suspension of payments
sospensione *m* dei pagamenti
swap (n) scambio *m*
swap (v) scambiare
switch over to passare a
switchboard centralino *m*
synergy sinergia *f*
system sistema *m*
systems analyst
analista *m/f* dei sistemi

T

tacit approval tacito consenso *m*
take a call prendere una telefonata
take action agire
take legal advice ricorrere a consulenza legale

take off *(deduct)* dedurre, fare uno sconto di; *(plane)* decollare
take on more staff assumere altro personale
take out a policy sottoscrivere una polizza
take over *(from so. else)* prendere il controllo di
take place avere luogo
take so. to court portare qu. in tribunale
take stock far l'inventario *m*
take the initiative prendere l'iniziativa *f*
takeover rilevamento *m*
takeover bid offerta *f* pubblica d'acquisto
takings incassi *m*
tangible assets beni *m* reali
target market mercato *m* prescelto
tariff *(price)* tariffa *f*
tariff barriers barriere *f* tariffarie
tax (n) tassa *f*, imposta *f*
tax (v) tassare, gravare d'imposta
tax assessment accertamento *m* fiscale
tax consultant consulente *m/f* fiscale
tax deducted at source imposta *f* trattenuta alla fonte
tax exemption esenzione *f* fiscale
tax inspector ispettore (-trice) delle tasse
tax paid imposta *f* pagata
tax rate aliquota *f* d'imposta
tax return/declaration denuncia *f* dei redditi
tax year anno *m* fiscale
tax-deductible detraibile dal reddito imponibile
tax-free esente da tasse
taxable income reddito *m* imponibile
taxpayer contribuente *m/f*
telephone (n) telefono *m*
telephone (v) telefonare
telephone directory elenco *m* telefonico
telephone number numero *m* telefonico, numero del telefono
telephonist telefonista *m/f*
temporary staff personale *m* avventizio
tenancy *(agreement)* contratto *m* di locazione
tenant inquilino (-a)
tender (n) *(offer to work)* licitazione *f*, offerta *f* d'appalto
term *(time of validity)* periodo *m*, durata *f*
term loan prestito *m* a termine
terminal (adj) *(at the end)* terminale
terminate an agreement rescindere un accordo
termination clause clausola *f* di rescissione
terms condizioni *f*
terms of employment condizioni *f* di impiego
terms of payment condizioni *f* di pagamento
terms of sale condizioni *f* di vendita
territory *(of salesman)* territorio *m*
tertiary industry industria *f* terziaria
test (n) prova *f*
test (v) provare
theft furto *m*
third party terza persona *f*
threshold price prezzo *m* d'entrata
throughput lavorazione *f*
tie-up *(link)* collegamento *m*
tighten up on restringere
time scale scala *f* temporale
time, on puntuale, in orario
timetable (n) *(appointments)* programma *m*
timetable (v) programmare
tip (v) *(give money)* dare la mancia a
token charge costo *m* simbolico
toll pedaggio *m*
toll free esente da pedaggio
ton tonnellata *f*
tonnage tonnellaggio *m*
top management direzione *f* al vertice
top quality qualità *f* superiore
total (adj) totale, globale
total (n) totale *m*
total (v) ammontare a
total amount importo *m* totale
total cost costo *m* totale
total invoice value valore *m* totale della fattura
track record curricolo *m*
trade (n) *(business)* commercio *m*
trade (v) commerciare, trafficare

trade directory annuario *m* commerciale
trade discount sconto *m* ai rivenditori
trade fair fiera *f* campionaria
trade journal giornale *m* di categoria
trade price prezzo *m* al rivenditore
trade terms sconti *m* al rivenditore
trade union sindacato *m*
trade-in price prezzo *m* di permuta
trademark/trade name marchio *m*
trader commerciante *m/f*
trading loss perdita *f* d'esercizio
trading partner partner *m* commerciale
trading profit utile *m* d'esercizio
train (v) *(learn)* fare pratica; *(teach)* istruire
trainee tirocinante *m/f*
transact business fare affari
transaction transazione *f*
transfer (n) trasferimento *m*
transfer of funds trasferimento *m* di capitali
transferred charge call telefonata *f* a carico del ricevente
transit transito *m*
transit visa visto *m* consolare di transito
translation traduzione *f*
translator traduttore (-trice)
transport (n) trasporto *m*
transport (v) trasportare
trial balance bilancio *m* di verifica
trial sample campione *m* di prova
triplicate, in in triplice copia
true copy copia *f* autentica
turn down rifiutare
turn over (v) *(make sales)* avere un giro d'affari di
turnkey operation operazione *f* chiavi in mano
turnover *(sales)* volume *m* d'affari

U

unaudited accounts contabilità *f* non sottoposta a revisione contabile
unauthorized expenditure spesa *f* non autorizzata
unavailable non disponibile
unconditional incondizionato (-a)
undated non datato (-a)
under *(according to)* secondo; *(less than)* meno di, inferiore
under contract sotto contratto
under new management sotto nuova gestione
undercharge far pagare meno
undercut a rival vendere a minor prezzo di un concorrente
undersell vendere sotto costo
undersigned sottoscritto
understanding intesa *f*
undertaking *(company)* azienda *f*, impresa *f*; *(promise)* compito *m*, impegno *m*
underwrite *(guarantee)* garantire
unemployed disoccupato (-a)
unemployment disoccupazione *f*
unfair competition concorrenza *f* sleale
unfavourable/unfavorable exchange rate tasso *m* di cambio sfavorevole
unfulfilled order ordine *m* inevaso
unilateral unilaterale
union sindacato *m*
unique selling point/proposition (USP) proposta *f* unica di vendita
unit cost costo *m* unitario
unit price prezzo *m* unitario
unload *(goods)* scaricare
unobtainable non ottenibile
unpaid invoices fatture *f* insolute
unsecured creditor creditore (-trice) non garantito (-a)
unsuccessful che non ha successo
up front anticipato (-a)
up to date *(complete)* aggiornato (-a); *(modern)* moderno (-a), attuale
up-market rivolto (-a) a una fascia alta del mercato
update (v) aggiornare, mettere al corrente
urgent urgente
use (n) uso *m*
use (v) usare
user-friendly facile da usare, accessibile
utilization utilizzazione *f*

V

vacancy *(for job)* posto *m* vacante
valid valido (-a)
valuation valutazione *f*
value (n) valore *m*
value (v) valutare
value added tax (VAT) imposta *f* sul valore aggiunto (IVA)
variable costs costi *m* variabili
VAT invoice fattura *f* con IVA
vendor venditore (-trice/-a)
venture capital capitale *m* di rischio
verbal agreement accordo *m* verbale
verification verifica *f*
verify verificare
vested interest interessi *mpl* costituiti
veto a decision porre il veto a una decisione
visa visto *m* consolare
visible trade partite *f* visibili
void (adj) *(not valid)* nullo (-a)
void (v) invalidare, annullare
volume of trade/business volume *m* degli scambi commerciali
voluntary liquidation liquidazione *f* volontaria
vote of thanks ringraziamento *m*
voucher buono *m*

W

wage salario *m*
wage negotiations negoziato *m* salariale
waive rinunciare
waiver clause clausola *f* di recessione
warehouse (n) magazzino *m*
warehouse (v) immagazzinare
warehousing magazzinaggio *m*
warrant (n) *(document)* autorizzazione *f*
warrant (v) *(guarantee)* garantire
warranty (n) garanzia *f*
wastage spreco *m*
waste (n) spreco *m*
waste (v) *(use too much)* sprecare
waybill lettera *f* di vettura
wear and tear deterioramento *m* naturale
weekly settimanale
weigh pesare
weight peso *m*
weighted index indice *m* ponderato
whole-life insurance assicurazione *f* sulla vita
wholesale (adv) all'ingrosso
wholesale discount sconto *m* all'ingrosso
wholesaler commerciante *m/f* all'ingrosso
win a contract vincere un contratto
wind up *(a company)* mettere in liquidazione
withdraw *(an offer)* ritirare; *(money)* prelevare
witness (n) testimone *m/f*
witness (v) *(a document)* firmare come testimone
word-processing elaborazione *f* della parola
work (n) lavoro *m*
work (v) lavorare
work permit permesso *m* di lavoro
worker lavoratore (-trice)
working conditions condizioni *f* di lavoro
world mondo *m*
worldwide (adj) mondiale
worth, be valere
wrap up impaccare
writ mandato *m*
write down *(assets)* ridurre il valore
write off *(debt)* annullare
write out a cheque/check compilare un assegno
write-off *(loss)* svalutazione *f*
written agreement accordo *m* scritto

Y

yearly payment pagamento *m* annuale
yellow pages Pagine *f* Gialle
yield (n) *(on investment)* rendita *f*
yield (v) *(interest)* rendere

Z

zip code codice *m* d'avviamento postale

Italian–English Business Dictionary

f	**feminine**
m	**masculine**
pl	**plural**
(adj)	**adjective**
(adv)	**adverb**
(n)	**noun**
(v)	**verb**
qc.	**qualcosa**
qu.	**qualcuno**
so.	**someone**
sth.	**something**

A

abbassare reduce, knock down *(price)*
abile qualified *(skilled)*
abilità *f* ability, capacity
abilità tecnica skill
accantonamento *m* shelving, postponing
accantonare shelve, postpone
accantonare fondi per un progetto earmark funds for a project
accaparrarsi il mercato corner the market
accertamento *m* **dei danni** assessment of damages
accertamento fiscale tax assessment
accertare i danni assess damages
accessibile user-friendly
accettare accept
accettare di fare qc. agree to do sth.
accettazione *f* acceptance
accomodamento *m* adjustment
acconsentire di fare qc. agree to do sth.
acconto *m* deposit, payment in advance
acconto, in on account, in advance
accordo *m* agreement; adjustment
accordo che stabilisce il divieto di sciopero no-strike agreement
accordo di lunga data long-standing agreement
accordo in esclusiva exclusive agreement
accordo scritto written agreement
accordo sulla parola gentleman's agreement
accordo-tipo *m* model agreement
accreditare credit
accumularsi accrue
accusare ricevuta di una lettera acknowledge receipt of a letter
accusato *m* defendant
acquirente *m/f* shopper
acquirente che compra per impulso impulse buyer
acquirente genuino genuine purchaser
acquirente presti la dovuta attenzione, l' caveat emptor
acquisizione *f* acquisition
acquistare purchase
acquisto *m* purchase, purchasing; acquisition
acquisto a termine forward buying
acquisto centralizzato central purchasing
acquisto in massa bulk buying
acquisto per contanti cash purchase
acquisto rateale hire purchase
addebitare un acquisto charge a purchase
addebitare un conto debit an account
addebitare una telefonata al ricevente reverse the charges
addebiti *mpl* **per interessi** interest charges
addebito *m* debit
addebito diretto direct debit
addetto *m* **al controllo dell'avanzamento** progress chaser
addetto commerciale commercial attaché
aereo *m* **da carico** freight plane
affare *m* operation, deal; bargain
affare poco vantaggioso hard bargain
affari *mpl* business *(commerce)*
affari, fare do business
affari, per on business
affidare fondi ad un progetto commit funds to a project
affiliata *f* subsidiary company
affittare lease
affitto *m* lease; rent
affittuario *m* lessee
affrancare stamp *(letter)*

affrancatura *f* **pagata** postpaid
affrettarsi hurry up
agenda *f* appointments book
agenda tascabile pocket diary
agente *m/f* agent *(representative)*
agente di cambio stockbroker
agente di factoring factor
agenzia *f* **di pubblicità** advertising agency
agenzia per il recupero dei crediti debt collection agency
agevolazione *f* facility *(credit)*
aggiornamento *m* follow up
aggiornare update
aggiornare una riunione adjourn a meeting
aggiornato (-a) up to date
aggiudicare un contratto a qu. award a contract to so.
aggiungere il 10% per il servizio add on 10% for service
agire take action
albergo *m* hotel
aliquota *f* rate
aliquota d'imposta tax rate
allegare enclose
allegato *m* enclosure
altamente retribuito (-a) highly-paid
amministrare un patrimonio manage property
amministratore (-trice) company director
amministratore (-trice) delegato (-a) managing director (MD)
amministrazione (-trice) administration
ammontare *m* amount
ammontare a amount to, total
ammortamento *m* amortization
ammortare/ammortizzare amortize
ampliare expand
analisi *f* **dei conti** cost analysis
analisi delle mansioni job analysis
analisi di mercato market analysis
analista *m/f* **dei sistemi** systems analyst
andare in pensione retire *(from one's job)*
andare incontro ad una richiesta meet a demand
anno *m* **fiscale** tax year
anno solare calendar year
anno, all' per year, per annum
annualmente annually
annuario *m/f* directory
annuario commerciale trade directory
annullare write off *(debt)*; cancel; void
annullato (-a) cancelled, off
annunci *mpl* **economici** classified advertisements
annuncio *m* **pubblicitario** advertisement
anticipato (-a) up front, in advance
anticipazione *f* **su un conto** advance on account
anticipo *m* advance, loan
anticipo in contanti cash advance
antiquato (-a) old-fashioned, obsolete
aperto (-a) open
apertura *f* **sul mercato** gap in the market
appaltare del lavoro farm out work
apparecchiatura *f* equipment
apparecchiatura pesante heavy equipment
appellare appeal *(against a decision)*
appello *m* appeal *(against a decision)*
apprendista *m/f* junior clerk
apprendista in direzione aziendale management trainee
apprezzamento *m* appreciation *(how good sth. is)*
apprezzare appreciate *(how good sth. is)*
approssimativamente approximately
approvare approve, agree
approvare i termini di un contratto approve the terms of a contract
approvare, far carry, approve in a vote
approvvigionare supply
appuntamento *m* appointment
aprire open
aprire una lettera di credito issue a letter of credit
aprire una seduta open a meeting
arbitrare una vertenza arbitrate in a dispute
archivio *m* computer file; documentation, records
area *f* **problematica** problem area
argomento *m* matter *(to be discussed)*, item *(on agenda)*

armonizzazione *f* harmonization
arretrati *m* arrears
arrivare ad una decisione reach a decision
arrotondare aumentando round up
arrotondare diminuendo round down
articoli *mpl* **che vendono rapidamente** fast-selling items
articoli vari sundries
articolo *m* article *(item)*
articolo di richiamo per la clientela loss-leader
ascensore *m* lift/elevator
assegno *m* cheque/check
assegno a copertura garantita certified cheque/check
assegno circolare bank draft
assegno dello stipendio pay cheque/check
assegno in bianco blank cheque/ check
assemblea *f* **del personale** staff meeting
Assemblea Generale degli Azionisti annual general meeting
assente absent, away from work
assicurare insure
assicurare la vita di qu. assure so.'s life
assicurarsi contro un rischio cover a risk
assicuratore (-trice) insurer
assicurazione *f* insurance, indemnity
assicurazione globale comprehensive insurance
assicurazione sulla vita life assurance
assistenza *f* **post-vendita alla clientela** after-sales service
assistere assist
assistere a attend *(meeting)*
associato (-a) associate (adj/n)
associazione *f* **in partecipazione** joint venture
assumere employ
assumere del personale hire staff
assumersi la responsabilità di qc. accept liability for sth.
asta *f* auction
attendere istruzioni await instructions
attendibile reliable
attendibilità *f* reliability
atterrare land *(of plane)*
atteso (-a) due *(awaited)*
attestato *m* reference *(report on person)*
attestazione *f* **ufficiale** affidavit
attirare appeal to *(attract)*
attività *f* activity, business
attività *fpl* asset(s)
attività finanziaria finance
attività immateriali intangible assets
attività liquide current assets
attività occulte hidden asset
attività promozionale merchandizing
attività secondaria sideline
attività trascurata neglected business
attivo *m* **esigibile** realizable assets
atto *m* deed
atto di vendita bill of sale
attraccare dock *(ship)*
attuale present *(now)*; up to date
attuale, non out of date
attuazione *f* implementation
aumentare rise; increase, raise
aumentare di valore appreciate, increase in value
aumentare il prezzo mark up
aumentare proporzionalmente scale up
aumento *m* increase, rise
aumento medio annuale mean annual increase
aumento salariale pay rise
autenticare certify
autofinanziarsi, che può self-financing (adj)
autorità *f* authority
autorizzare permit, license
autorizzare un pagamento authorize payment
autorizzazione *f* authorization, permission
avanguardia, all' state-of-the-art
avaria *f* average *(insurance)*
avere carry *(have in stock)*
avere come risultato result in
avere lo scopo di aim (v)
avere luogo take place
avere un colloquio con interview so. *(for a job)*
avere un giro d'affari di turn over (v)
avere un ricavo lordo gross (v)

avviamento commerciale goodwill
avvocato *m* lawyer
azienda *f* firm, business, company
azienda autonoma independent company
azienda commerciale business establishment
azione *f* share/stock *(in a company)*
azioni ordinarie ordinary shares
azioni privilegiate preference shares
azionista *m/f* shareholder, stockholder
azionista di maggioranza majority shareholder/stockholder
azionista di minoranza minority shareholder/stockholder

B

bacino *m* dock
bagagli *mpl* **non reclamati** unclaimed baggage
bagaglio *m* luggage
banca *f* **di compensazione** clearing bank
banco *m* counter
banco d'albergo reception (desk)
banco di esposizione display stand
banconota *f* banknote
bando *m* ban
barattare barter (v)
baratto *m* barter
base *f* **di dati** database
base, di basic, fundamental
battuta *f* **d'arresto** setback
bene *m* asset, commodity
beneficiario *m* beneficiary; payee
beni di consumo consumer goods
beni reali tangible assets
biglietto *m* card; ticket
biglietto aereo privo di prenotazione standby ticket
biglietto aperto open ticket
biglietto d'omaggio complimentary ticket
biglietto di banca banknote
bilancia *f* balance
bilancia commerciale attiva favourable/favorable balance of trade
bilancia dei pagamenti balance of payments
bilancio *m* balance
bilancio d'apertura opening balance
bilancio d'esercizio balance sheet
bilancio di chiusura closing balance
bilancio di verifica trial balance
bilancio preventivo budget
bloccare i prezzi peg prices
bloccare un assegno stop a cheque/check
blocco *m* **del credito** credit freeze
blocco di fogli per lavagna flip chart
bolla *f* **di spedizione** delivery note, dispatch note
bolletta *f* **d'avviso** advice note
bonifico *m* bank transfer
borsa *f* briefcase
Borsa *f* stock exchange
Borsa Merci commodity exchange
bozza *f* draft, rough plan
bozza di un piano draft plan
breve (termine), a short-term (adj)
brevetto *m* patent
brevetto richiesto/in attesa di brevetto patent applied for, patent pending
budget *m* **provvisorio** provisional budget
budget pubblicitario advertising budget, publicity budget
budgettare budget
buon affare good buy
buona qualità good quality
buono *m* voucher
buono premio gift voucher
buon valore, di good value *(for money)*
bustarella *f* bribe

C

cadere drop, fall, collapse
caduta *f* drop
calare drop
calcolare calculate
calcolare 10% per il trasporto allow 10% for carriage
calcolatrice *f* **tascabile** pocket calculator
calcolo *m* **approssimativo** rough calculation
calcolo sbagliato miscalculation
cambiale *f* bill of exchange
cambiali da incassare receivables, bills receivable
cambiali da pagare bills payable

cambiamento *m* change *(difference)*
cambiare change; exchange *(currency)*
cambio *m* exchange *(currency)*
camera *f* room
Camera di Commercio Chamber of Commerce
campagna *f* **di vendite** sales campaign
campagna promozionale a mezzo posta mail/mailing shot
campionamento *m* sampling
campione *m* sample *(part)*
campione casuale random sample
campione di prova trial sample
campione gratuito free sample
campione, come da as per sample
cancellare cancel
candidato (-a) nominee
capacità *f* capacity *(space/ability)*
capacità in eccedenza overcapacity
capacità produttiva production capacity
capacità produttiva in eccesso excess capacity
caparra *f* **rimborsabile** refundable deposit
capienza *f* **di magazzino** storage capacity
capire realize *(understand)*
capitale *m*, **capitali** *mpl* capital
capitale d'apporto initial capital
capitale di rischio risk capital, venture capital
capitale effettivo equity capital
capitale in fuga flight of capital
capitale mutuato loan capital
capitalizzare capitalize
capitalizzazione *f* capitalization
capo *m* boss *(informal)*
capo del personale personnel manager
capo reparto head of department
capo servizio departmental manager
carenza *f* **di manodopera** manpower shortage
carica *f* office, position
caricare (un programma) load (a computer program)
caricare un camion/una nave load a truck/ship
carico *m* cargo; charge *(money)*
carico lordo deadweight cargo
carovita *m* cost of living
carrello *m* **elevatore** fork-lift truck
carta *f* paper
carta di credito credit card; charge card
carta di credito telefonica phone card
carta riciclata recycled paper
cartella *f* briefcase
cartellino *m* **del prezzo** price label, price tag
cartone *m* carton *(box)*
casella *f* **postale** box number
cassa *f* cash desk, checkout *(in supermarket)*; case, box
cassa automatica prelievi cash dispenser, automatic teller
cassa integrazione, in redundant
cassaforte *f* safe
cassiere *m*/**cassiera** *f* cashier
catalogo *m* catalogue/catalog, list
catalogo di vendita per corrispondenza mail-order catalogue/catalog
causa *f* lawsuit
causa di forza maggiore force majeure, act of God
causa per risarcimento action for damages
causa di, a owing to
centralino *m* **telefonico** telephone switchboard
centro *m* **commerciale** shopping centre/mall
centro di assistenza service centre/center
certificato *m* **azionario** share/stock certificate
certificato di accettazione certificate of approval
cespite *m* asset
cespiti congelati frozen assets
cespiti realizzabili realizable assets
cessare di lavorare stop work, knock off
chiamare call, phone
chiamata *f* **telefonica** phone call
chiaro (-a) clear, easy to understand
chiedere (a qu. di fare qc.) ask (so. to do sth.)
chiedere informazioni nei negozi shop around
chiedere ulteriori dettagli/particolari ask for further details/particulars

chiedere un rimborso ask for a refund
chilo *m*/**chilogrammo** *m* kilogram
chiudere close down
chiudere a chiave lock, lock up
chiudere un conto close an account
chiuso (-a) closed
ciclico (-a) cyclical
ciclo *f* **economico** economic cycle
cifra *f* figure
cifre effettive historical figures
citare sue
classe turistica economy class
clausola *f* article, clause; provision, condition
clausola condizionale proviso
clausola di esclusione exclusion clause
clausola di rescissione cancellation clause, termination clause
clausola di salvaguardia escape clause
cliente *m/f* customer, client, shopper
cliente abituale regular customer
clientela *f* clientele
codice *m* code
codice a barre bar code
codice d'avviamento postale postcode, zip code
codice di etica professionale code of practice
codice di zona area code
cogliere collect (v) *(fetch)*
coincidenza *f* connection
collaborare collaborate
collaborazione *f* collaboration
collegamento *m* tie-up *(link)*
collegare in rete network (v) *(computers)*
colmare una lacuna fill a gap
come consigliato as per advice
come da campione as per sample
come da fattura as per invoice
cominciare begin
commercializzare market (v)
commerciante *m/f* dealer, trader
commerciante all'ingrosso wholesaler
commerciare deal; trade, handle, sell
commercio *m* commerce, trade
commercio bilaterale reciprocal trade
commercio estero external trade, overseas trade
commesso (-a) di negozio shop assistant, salesman/saleswoman
commissione *m* commission *(money)*
compagno (-a) partner
compagnia *f* company
compagnia di assicurazioni insurance company
compensare compensate, make up for
compensare un assegno clear a cheque/check
compenso *m* fee *(for services)*
compenso per lavoro straordinario overtime pay
comperare buy, purchase
comperare a termine buy forward
competività *f* competitiveness
competizione *f* competition
compilare make out *(invoice)*
compilare un assegno write out a cheque/check
compito *m* undertaking *(promise)*
completare finalize
completo (-a) complete (adj)
comporre un numero dial a number
compratore *m* buyer, purchaser
comprese tasse *f* inclusive of tax
compromesso *m* compromise
computerizzare computerize
comunicare communicate
comunicato *m* **stampa** press release
concedente *m/f* franchiser
concedere il diritto di esclusiva franchise (v)
concessionario *m* franchisee
concessione *f* franchise
concessione di vendita franchising
concludere conclude, wrap up *(agreement)*; end
concordare agree *(be same as)*
concorrente *m/f* competitor
concorrenza *f* competition
concorrenza accanita keen competition
concorrenza dura stiff competition
concorrenza sleale unfair competition
concorrenza, in competing (adj)
condirettore (-trice) joint managing director

condizione *f* condition, terms, provision
condizione sociale status
condizione che, a on condition that, depending on
condizioni *fpl* terms
condizioni di assunzione conditions of employment
condizioni di impiego terms of employment
condizioni di vendita conditions/ terms of sale
condizioni moderate easy terms
condizioni per pagamento in contanti cash terms
condurre una negoziazione conduct negotiations
conferenza *f* **stampa** press conference
conferire diritto entitle
conferma *f* confirmation
confermare una prenotazione confirm a booking
confezione *f* **finta** dummy pack
conformarsi a comply with
confrontare compare
confronto *m* comparison
congedo *m* **per maternità** maternity leave
congelare freeze *(prices)*
congiuntura *f* economic trends
connettore *m* port *(computer)*
consegna *f* delivery *(goods)*
consegna gratuita free delivery
consegnare deliver
conseguibile obtainable
Conservatore *m* **del Registro delle Società** Registrar of Companies
consigliare recommend *(suggest action)*
consigliato, come as per advice
Consiglio *m* **di Amministrazione** board of directors
consistere in consist of
consolidare (spedizioni) consolidate (shipments)
consorzio *m* consortium
consueto (-a) regular, usual
consulente *m/f* consultant
consulente fiscale tax consultant
consulenza *f* **legale** legal advice
consultarsi consult
consumatore (-trice) consumer
contabile *m/f* bookkeeper
contabilità *f* bookkeeping
contabilità di bilancio budget account *(in bank)*
contabilità di fine mese month-end accounts
contabilità non sottoposta a revisione contabile unaudited accounts
contanti, in cash (adv)
contare su depend on
contatto *m* contact *(person)*
contatto con, mettersi in contact (v)
contenere contain
contenitore *m* container *(box, tin)*
contenuto *m* contents
contenzioso, in sub judice
conti *mpl* **attivi** accounts receivable
conti passivi accounts payable
contingente *m* **di importazione** import quota
continuare continue
continuo (-a) continual; continuous
conto *m* account, bill, expense
conto a garanzia escrow account
conto aperto open account
conto bloccato account on stop
conto chiuso dead account
conto congelato frozen account
conto congiunto joint account
conto corrente current account
conto dettagliato itemized account
conto di contropartita contra account
conto di risparmio savings account
conto profitti e perdite profit and loss account
conto scoperto overdrawn account
conto spese expense account
conto di, per on behalf of
contraffazione *f* forgery *(action)*
contrario (-a) contrary
contrarre contract (v)
contrarre debiti run into debt, incur debts
contrassegno *m* countersign
contrattare bargain
contratto *m* contract
contratto collettivo salariale collective wage agreement
contratto di lavoro contract of employment
contratto di locazione tenancy (agreement)

contratto globale
package *(of services)*
contrattualmente contractually
contribuente *m* taxpayer
controfferta *f* counter-offer
controllare monitor; check, examine
controllo *m* control *(power)*; check, examination
controllo delle scorte stock control
controllo di magazzino inventory control
controllo doganale customs examination
controllo passeggeri check-in *(at airport)*
controrichiesta *f* counter-claim
contumace, essere default (v)
convenire covenant (v)
convenzione *f* covenant
convertire convert
convocare convene
cooptare qu. co-opt so.
copertura *f* cover *(top)*
copertura assicurativa insurance cover
copia *f* **a sostegno** backup copy
copia autentica certified copy, true copy
copiare copy (v)
copiatrice *f* copier
coprire i costi cover costs
correggere amend
corretto (-a) right (adj) *(not wrong)*
corriere *m* courier *(messenger)*
corrispondenza con qu., essere in correspond with so.
corrispondere a agree *(be same as)*
corrompere bribe
corso *m* **in amministrazione** management course
corso introduttivo induction courses, induction training
corso per operazioni a termine forward rate
corte *f* **di Giustizia** lawcourt
costare cost
costi *mpl* **d'esercizio** operating costs
costi di gestione operational/running costs
costi di produzione manufacturing costs
costi diretti prime cost
costi fissi fixed costs
costi fondiari landed costs
costi indiretti del lavoro indirect labour/labor costs
costi per la spedizione marittima shipping charges, shipping costs
costituire una società incorporate, set up a company
costo *m* cost
costo, assicurazione e nolo cost, insurance and freight (c.i.f.)
costo della manodopera labour/labor costs
costo delle vendite cost of sales
costo più una percentuale cost plus
costo simbolico token charge
costo unitario unit cost
costoso (-a) expensive
credito a breve termine short credit
credito a lungo termine long credit
credito d'imposta tax credit
credito immediato instant credit
credito inesigibile bad debt
credito prorogato extended credit
credito rinnovabile automaticamente revolving credit
credito, a on credit
creditore *m/f* creditor
creditore differito (-a) deferred creditor
creditore non garantito unsecured creditor
creditore privilegiato (-a) secured creditor
crescita *f* growth
crescita economica economic growth
crollare collapse
crollo *m* collapse
cronico (-a) chronic
curricolo *m* track record

D

danneggiare damage
danni *mpl* damages
danno *m* damage
danno causato da un incendio fire damage
dare corso ad un'operazione deal with an order
dare in subappalto subcontract (v)
dare la caccia a chase *(an order)*
dare la mancia a tip *(give money to)*

data *f* d'inizio starting date
data di chiusura closing date
data di consegna delivery date/time
data di rimborso redemption date
data di scadenza sell-by date; expiry date; deadline
datare date
datario *m* date stamp
datato (-a), non undated
dati *mpl* data
datore *m* **di lavoro** employer
dazio *m* duty *(tax)*
dazio doganale import duty
debiti *mpl* **a lungo termine** long-term debts
debiti insoluti outstanding debts
debito *m* debt
debito inesigibile irrecoverable debt
debitore (-trice) debtor
debitore (-trice) riconosciuto (-a) da tribunale judgment debtor
debitore (-trice), essere owe
decidere una linea di condotta decide on a course of action
decollare take off *(plane)*
decrescente decreasing (adj)
decretare rule, give decision
decreto *m* ruling
dedurre deduct, take off
deficit *m* **della bilancia commerciale** trade deficit/gap
delegato (-a) deputy
denaro *m* money
denaro contante cash *(money)*
denominazione *f* **della mansione** job title
denuncia *f* **dei redditi** tax return/declaration
deperibile perishable *(goods, items, cargo)*
depositante *m* depositor
depositare documenti file documents
depositare in banca bank *(a cheque/check)*
deposito *m* deposit *(in bank)*; warehousing; store, warehouse
deposito a termine time deposit
deposito non rimborsabile non-refundable deposit
derivare result from
descrizione *f* **dei compiti** job description
design, dipartimento/ufficio design department
destro (-a) right (adj) *(not left)*
detenere il controllo azionario control a business
deterioramento *m* **naturale** wear and tear
determinazione *f* **marginale del prezzo** marginal pricing
detraibile deductible
detraibile dal reddito imponibile tax-deductible
detrazione *f* allowance, deduction
detrazioni personali personal allowances
dettagli *m* particulars
dettagliante *m* retailer
dettagliare break down *(itemize)*
dettaglio *m* detail
diagramma *f* **a barre** bar chart
dichiarare le merci alla dogana declare goods to customs
dichiarazione *f* declaration, return
dichiarazione dei redditi declaration of income
dichiarazione doganale customs declaration
difendere una causa defend a lawsuit
difesa *f* defence *(legal)*
difetto *m* defect
difettoso (-a) defective *(faulty)*
differenza *f* **a credito** credit balance
differenze di prezzo differences in price
differire postpone
differire un pagamento defer payment
digitare key in, keyboard
dilazione *f* postponement
dimensioni *f* **delle scorte** stock sizes
dimettersi resign
diminuire decrease
diminuzione *f* **del valore** decrease (n) in value
dimostrare demonstrate
dipendente *m/f* employee
dipendenti *mpl* staff
dipendenti pagati a ore hourly-paid workers
diramare delle istruzioni issue instructions
direttiva *f* guideline
diretto (-a) direct (adj)

direttore (-trice) manager *(of branch, shop)*; principal *(person)*
direttore commerciale sales manager
direttore del reparto esportazioni export manager
direttore di filiale branch manager
direttore di zona area manager
direttore facente funzione acting manager
direttore generale general manager
direttore vendite esterne field sales manager
direzione *f* management *(managers)*
direzione al vertice top management
direzione centrale main office, headquarters
dirigente *m/f* executive, manager; official
dirigente delle vendite sales executive
dirigente in capo senior manager/ executive
dirigere direct, run, manage
diritto *m* right, legal title, entitlement
diritto commerciale commercial law
diritto di concessione royalty
diritto di precedenza right of way
diritto internazionale international law
disavanzo *m* deficit
discesa *f* **delle vendite** slump in sales
disco *m* disk
discrepanza *f* discrepancy
discussione *f* **produttiva** productive discussion
discutere discuss
disdire un affare call off a deal
disegno *m* **industriale** industrial design
disoccupato (-a) out of work, unemployed
disoccupazione *f* unemployment
disponibile available
disponibile, non unavailable
disponibilità *f* availability
disponibilità di capitali money supply
disposizione *f* disposal
disposizioni *fpl* arrangements, regulations
dissentire differ
distinta *f* list
distinta d'imballaggio packing list, packing slip
distinta di versamento deposit/paying-in slip
distribuire distribute *(goods)*
distributore (-trice) distributor
distribuzione *f* distribution
ditta *f* firm, business
ditta di consulenza consultancy firm
dividendo *m* **finale** final dividend
dividere share
divisa *f* foreign currency, foreign exchange
divisa forte strong currency
divulgare un'informazione disclose a piece of information
documentazione *f* documentation, records
documenti *mpl* **falsi** faked documents
dogana *f* customs
domanda *f* request, demand
domanda d'indennizzo claim
domanda finale final demand
domanda d'impiego, fare apply for a job
domandare demand; request
domicilio, a house-to-house, door-to-door
donna *f* **d'affari** businesswoman
doppia tassazione *f* double taxation
dovere *m* obligation *(duty)*
dovuto (-a) due *(owing)*
dovuto (-a), essere fall due
dozzina *f* dozen

E

economia *f* economy *(saving)*
economia di massa economies of scale
economia di tipo misto mixed economy
economia nera black economy
economico (-a) economical, cheap; financial
economizzare economize, save
ecu *m* **(Unità di Conto Europea)** ecu/ECU (European currency unit)
edificio *m* **principale** main building
effetti *mpl* **attivi** receivables, bills receivable
effetti passivi bills payable

effettivo (-a) effective
effetto *m* effect; bill of exchange
effetto a lunga scadenza long-dated bill
effettuare effect
efficacia *f* effectiveness
efficiente efficient
efficienza *f* efficiency
elaboratore *m* **ad uso personale** personal computer
elaborazione *f* **degli ordini** order processing
elaborazione della parola word-processing
elaborazione delle informazioni processing of information
elementi *mpl* **ciclici** cyclical factors
elemento *m* element, factor
elemento decisivo deciding factor
elencare index (v)
elenco *m* **classificato** classified directory
elenco di indirizzi mailing list
elenco telefonico telephone directory
eliminare delete
eliminare gradualmente phase out
eliminare le scorte in eccesso dispose of excess stock
embargo su, mettere l' embargo (v)
emendamento *m* amendment
emettere un assegno draw a cheque/check
emettere una fattura raise an invoice
emissione *f* **di diritti** rights issue
emolumento *m* fee *(for services)*
energia, che risparmia energy-saving
entrare in porto dock (v) *(of ship)*
entrare in vigore run (v) *(be in force)*
entrata *f* entry *(going in)*
entrate *fpl* receipts
equipaggiare equip
equivalere con qc. correspond with sth.
equo (-a) fair
errore *m* error, mistake, slip
errore di trascrizione clerical error
errori *mpl* **casuali** random errors
esame *f* examination *(test)*; check, examination, inspection
esame, in on approval
esaminare check, examine; inspect
esaurirsi run out of
esaurito (-a) out of stock
esborso *m* outlay
escluso (-a) excluding
esecutivo (-a) executive (adj)
esentare exempt
esente exempt (adj)
esente da dazio duty-free
esente da tasse/da imposta tax-free, free of tax
esenzione *f* **da tassa** exemption from tax
esenzione fiscale tax exemption
esercitare il commercio di un prodotto merchandize a product
esercitare un'opzione exercise an option
esercizio *m* **di un'opzione** exercise of an option
esercizio finanziario financial year
esibire exhibit
esigere exact (v)
esperto (-a) experienced (adj); professional, expert (n)
esporre display
esportare export
esportatore (-trice) exporter
esportazione *f* export
esportazioni *fpl* exports
espositore (-trice) exhibitor
esposizione *f* display, exhibition
espresso (-a) express, fast
espropriazione *f* **per pubblica utilità** compulsory purchase
estero, all' abroad, offshore
estinguere redeem
estratto *m* **conto** statement of account, bank statement
età *f* **della pensione** retirement age
etichetta *f* label
etichettare label
ettaro *m* hectare
euroassegno *m* Eurocheque/ Eurocheck
evadere un ordine fulfil an order
evasione *f* **fiscale** tax avoidance, tax evasion
evasione di un ordine order fulfilment

F

fabbrica *f* factory
fabbricante *m/f* manufacturer
fabbricare manufacture

facile da usare user-friendly
factoring, agente/società di factor
fallimento *m* bankruptcy
fallire fail; go bankrupt; fall through
fallito (-a) bankrupt (adj/n)
fallito (-a) non riabilitato (-a) undischarged bankrupt
falso (-a) dummy
fare un ordine place an order
fascicolo *m* file *(of documents)*; brochure
fascicolo supplementare magazine insert
fattore *m* factor, influence
fattore negativo downside, minus factor
fattore positivo plus factor
fattori *mpl* **di produzione** factors of production
fattura *f* bill, invoice
fattura con IVA VAT invoice
fattura dettagliata itemized invoice
fattura di vendita bill of sale
fattura, come da as per invoice
fatturare bill, invoice
fatturato *m* sales
fatture *fpl* **insolute** unpaid invoices
fax, inviare per fax (v)
fedeltà *f* **alla marca** brand loyalty
fermare countermand
fermoposta *m* poste restante
ferrovia *f* rail, railway
festa *f* **nazionale** public/bank holiday
fiera *f* **campionaria** trade fair
file *m* file *(computer)*
filiale *f* subsidiary
finanza *f* **pubblica** public finance
finanze *fpl* finances
finanziamento *m* financing
finanziamento del disavanzo deficit financing
finanziare finance, fund
finanziario (-a) financial (adj)
fine *f* end; expiry
finire stop *(doing sth.)*; end, complete
fiorente flourishing
firma *f* signature
firmare sign
firmare come testimone witness (v) *(a document)*
firmare il registro check in *(at hotel)*
firmatario (-a) signatory
firmatario (-a) congiunto (-a) joint signatory
fissare una riunione per le 15 fix a meeting for 3 p.m.
fissato *m* **bollato** contract note
fisso (-a) set; regular *(always at same time)*
fittizio (-a) dummy
flessibile flexible
flessibilità *f* flexibility
flusso *m* **di cassa** cash flow
fluttuare fluctuate
fluttuare, far float *(a currency)*
foglietto *m* slip *(piece of paper)*
foglio *m* **di carta** sheet of paper
fondamentale basic, most important
fondo *m*, **fondi** *mpl* reserve, fund
fonte *f* **di reddito** source of income
forgiare forge
formulazione *f* form of words
fornire supply
fornire il personale man (v)
fornitore (-trice) supplier
fornitore (-trice) statale/allo stato government contractor
fornitura *f* supply
forti costi *mpl*, **forti spese** *fpl* heavy costs/expenditure
forze *f* **di mercato** market forces
fotocopiatrice *f* photocopier
franco a bordo free on board
franco di porto carriage free
franco di spese free of charge
franco posta post free
francobolli, mettere stamp (v) *(letter)*
francobollo *m* stamp *(post)*
frode *f* fraud
frontiera *f* border
fruttare bear, earn *(interest)*
funzionare function, operate
funzionario *m* official
fuori orario d'ufficio outside office hours
furto *m* theft
furto di scarsa entità pilferage, pilfering
fusione *f* merger
futura consegna *f* future delivery

G

gamma *f* **di prodotti** product mix
garante *m* sponsor

garantire guarantee; sponsor
garanzia *f* guarantee, warranty; indemnity
garanzia collaterale collateral
gelare freeze *(prices)*
gestione *f* management, administration
gettare, da disposable
giacenze *fpl* remainder *(things left)*
giacenze finali closing stock
giornale *m* **di categoria** trade journal
giorno *m* day
giorno festivo legale statutory holiday
giorno, al per day
girante *m/f* endorser
girare un assegno endorse a cheque/check
girata *f* endorsement *(action)*
giungere ad un accordo reach an agreement
giungere al punto di pareggio break even (v)
giuridico (-a) legal *(referring to law)*
giurisdizione *f* jurisdiction
giusto (-a) fair
globale total (adj)
grafico *m* **a settori** pie chart
grammo *m* gram/gramme
grande magazzino *m* department store
gratifica *f* bonus
gratifica natalizia Christmas bonus
gratuitamente free *(no payment)*
gratuito (-a) free of charge
gravare d'imposta tax (v)
grossa *f* gross (144)
guadagnare earn *(money)*
guadagni *mpl* earnings *(salary)*
guadagno *m* return, profit
guardia *f* **giurata** security guard
guasto *m* breakdown *(of machine)*
guerra *f* **dei prezzi** price war
guida *f* courier, tourist guide
guida stradale street directory
guidare lead

H

hard disk *m* hard disk
holding *m* holding company

I

imballaggio *m* **ermetico** airtight packaging
imballare pack (v)
imballo *m* **a perdere** non-returnable packing
imballo di cartone carton
imbarcare/imbarcarsi embark, board
imbarcarsi in embark on
imitazione *f* fake
immagazzinare store, warehouse, keep in warehouse
immagine *f* **aziendale** corporate image
immobilizzi *m* **tecnici** capital equipment
impaccare pack; wrap up *(goods)*
impacchettare pack
impacchettatore (-trice) packer
impadronirsi capture
impegni *mpl* commitments
impegno *m* obligation *(duty)*; undertaking, promise
impianti *mpl* facilities; equipment, plant, machinery
impianti di magazzinaggio storage facilities
impiegare employ
impiegato (-a) clerk
impiegato (-a) alla biglietteria booking clerk
impieghi *mpl* **disponibili** appointments vacant
impiego *m* employment; position, post, job
imporre levy
importare matter (v); import (v)
importatore (-trice) importer
importazione *f* import
importazioni *fpl* imports
importo *m* amount *(of money)*
importo dovuto amount owing
importo fisso flat rate
importo forfettario lump sum
importo pagato amount paid
importo totale total amount
imposta *f* tax, levy
imposta arretrata back tax
imposta di bollo stamp duty
imposta diretta direct tax
imposta generale sugli acquisti purchase tax

imposta indiretta excise duty
imposta pagata tax paid
imposta progressiva sul reddito graduated income tax
imposta sul reddito income tax
imposta sul valore aggiunto value added tax
imposta sul volume di affari sales tax
imposta sulla società corporation tax
imposta trattenuta alla fonte tax deducted at source
imposta, gravare d' tax (v)
imprenditore (-trice) contractor; entrepreneur
imprenditoriale entrepreneurial
impresa *f* business, company, firm
impresa di trasporti carrier, haulage company
impronta *f* mark
inadempiente *m/f* defaulter
inadempienza *f* default
inadempienza nel pagamento default on payments
inadempimento *m* **del contratto** breach of contract
incassare gross (v)
incassare un assegno cash a cheque/check
incassi *mpl* takings
includere include
incluso (-a) inclusive
incondizionato (-a) unconditional
incontrare meet *(so.)*
incorporare merge
incorporato (-a) built-in
indagare inquire
indagine *f* inquiry, survey, examination
indebitarsi get into debt
indebitato (-a) indebted
indennità *f* indemnification
indennità di contingenza cost-of-living allowance
indennizzare make good *(a defect)*
indennizzo *m* indemnification
indennizzo, presentare una domanda d' claim (v) *(insurance)*
indicare un prezzo quote, estimate costs
indicare un profitto show a profit
indice *m* index *(of prices)*
indice dei prezzi al consumo consumer price index
indice ponderato weighted index
indicizzato (-a) index-linked
indicizzazione *f* indexation
indirizzare una lettera/un pacco address a letter/a parcel
indirizzo *m* address
indirizzo d'inoltro forwarding address
indirizzo d'ufficio business address
indirizzo del mittente return address
indirizzo di comodo accommodation address
indirizzo personale home address
indiscriminato (-a) across-the-board
industria *f* industry *(companies)*
industria chiave key industry
industria di base staple industry
industria statalizzata nationalized industry
industriale *m* industrialist
inefficienza *f* inefficiency
inferiore under *(less than)*
inflazionistico (-a) inflationary
influenza *f* influence
influenzare influence
informazioni *fpl* **commerciali** status inquiry
informazioni immesse nel computer input information
infortunio *m* **sul lavoro** industrial accident
infrangere un accordo break an agreement
ingegnere *m* **edile** site engineer
ingrosso, all' wholesale
iniziare begin
iniziare un dibattito initiate discussions
iniziativa *f* initiative
iniziativa privata private enterprise
inquilino (-a) tenant
insegna *f* sign
inserire qu. in una rosa di candidati shortlist (v)
inserito (-a) built-in
inserzionista (-a) advertiser
insieme together
insieme, mettere batch (v)
insuccesso *m* failure, flop
intendere propose to *(do sth.)*
intentare causa sue
interdire ban (v)
interdizione *m* ban

interessare interest (v)
interessarsi di concern *(deal with)*
interesse *m* **alto** high interest
interesse composto compound interest; cumulative interest
interesse semplice simple interest
interessi *mpl* **costituiti** vested interest
interfaccia *f* interface
intermediario (-a) intermediary, middleman
interno (-a) in-house (adj)
interno *m* extension *(telephone)*
intero (-a) full
interprete *m/f* interpreter
interrrompere discontinue
intervista *f* interview *(for a job)*
intesa *f* understanding
introdurre introduce
introdurre gradualmente phase in
invalidare invalidate, void
invecchiamento *m* obsolescence
inventario *m* inventory, stock list; stocktaking
inventario, far l' take stock
inverso (-a) reverse (adj)
investimento sicuro safe investment
investire invest
investire capitali lock up capital
investitore *m* **istituzionale** institutional investors
inviare per fax fax (v)
inviare rimessa a mezzo assegno remit by cheque/check
invio *m* consignment *(things sent)*
ipermercato *m* hypermarket
ipoteca *f* mortgage
ipotecare mortgage
irregolarità *f* irregularities
iscritto, mettere per put in writing
iscrivere una società register a company
iscriversi register *(in official list)*
ispettivo (-a) supervisory
ispettore *m* **delle tasse** tax inspector
ispezionare inspect, survey
ispezione *f* inspection
istanza *f* request, application
istituire establish
istituto *m* **finanziario** financial institution
istituto di credito bank
istruire train, teach
istruzioni *fpl* instructions, directions
istruzioni per l'uso directions for use
istruzioni per la spedizione shipping/forwarding instructions
IVA (imposta sul valore aggiunto) VAT (value added tax)

L

lanciare una società float a company
lancio *m* **di una società** flotation
lasciare libera la camera dell'albergo check out *(of hotel)*
lavorare work
lavora in proprio, che self-employed
lavoratore (-trice) worker
lavoratori parzialmente qualificati semi-skilled workers
lavorazione *f* throughput
lavoro *m* job, work; position
lavoro a contratto a termine temporary employment
lavoro a cottimo piecework
lavoro a orario ridotto part-time work/employment
lavoro arretrato backlog
lavoro ben pagato well-paid job
lavoro con turni shift work
lavoro d'ufficio paperwork
lavoro di routine routine work
lavoro saltuario casual work
lavoro straordinario overtime
leasing *m* **immobiliare** lease-back
lento (-a) slack
lettera *f* **circolare** circular
lettera di accompagnamento covering letter
lettera di credito circolare circular letter of credit
lettera di reclamo letter of complaint
lettera di sollecito follow-up letter
lettera di vettura consignment note, waybill
lettera espresso express letter
lettera raccomandata, fare una register a letter
leva *f* **finanziaria** leverage
libbra *f* pound *(weight: 0.45kg)*
liberarsi di qc. get rid of sth.
libero (-a) free
libretto *m* **assegni** cheque/check book
libro cassa cash book

libro giornale journal *(accounts book)*
libro mastro ledger
licenza *f* licence/license
licenza d'esportazione export licence/permit
licenza di importazione import licence/permit
licenziamento *m* dismissal
licenziare qu. dismiss/sack so.
licenziato, essere get the sack
licitazione *f* tender
limitare limit, restrict
limite *m* limit
limite del prestito lending limit
limite di credito credit limit
linea *f* **di prodotti** product line
linea esterna outside line
linea telefonica telephone line
liquidare sell off, clear *(stock);* settle *(an invoice)*
liquidare gli ordini arretrati release dues
liquidatore (-trice) liquidator, receiver
liquidazione una società, mettere in liquidate/wind up a company
liquidità *f* liquidity; liquid assets
lira *f* Italian lira
lira sterlina pound sterling
lista *f* **di indirizzi** address list
lista di proscrizione blacklist (v)
lista nera black list
lista ristretta shortlist
listino *m* list
listino prezzi price list
litro *m* litre/liter
livello *m* floor, level
livello di organico manning levels
livello di riordinazione reorder level
locali *mpl* premises
locali d'azienda/commerciali business premises
locatore (-trice) landlord; lessor
logogramma *m* logo
lungaggine *f* **burocratica** red tape
lungo (-a) long
luogo *m* site

M

macchina *f* **affrancatrice** franking machine
magazzinaggio *m* warehousing, storage in warehouse
magazzino *m* storeroom; warehouse; store
magazzino frigorifero cold store
magazzino, grande store, large shop
maggioranza *f* majority
malinteso *m* misunderstanding
mancanza *f* **di fondi** lack of funds
mancare miss *(not to hit, not to meet)*
mancia *f* tip *(money)*
mandatario *m* proxy *(person)*
mandato *m* writ
mandato di pagamento money order
manodopera *f* manpower
manodopera a basso prezzo cheap labour/labor
manodopera qualificata skilled labour/labor
manovale *m* manual worker
mantenere una promessa keep a promise
mantenimento *m* **delle provvigioni** maintenance of supplies
manuale manual (adj)
manuale *m* **di manutenzione** service manual
manuale operativo operating manual
manufatti *m* manufactured goods
manutenzione *f* maintenance, service *(of machine)*
marca *f* **del prodotto** brand name; trademark, trade name
marchio *m* brand name; trademark, trade name
marchio di fabbrica depositato registered trademark
marco *m* **tedesco** Deutschmark, German mark
margine *m* **di utile** (profit) margin
mastro *m* **dei conti dei creditori** bought ledger
materia *f* **pubblicitaria con buono** coupon ad
materiale *m* **d'imballaggio** packaging material
materiale da esposizione display material
materiale per punto di vendita point of sale material
materiali *mpl* **di imballaggio** packing (material)
materie *f* **prime** raw materials

matrice *f* counterfoil
maturare accrue
media *f* mean
mediatore *m* **assicurativo** insurance broker
medie dimensioni, di medium-sized
medio (-a) average (adj)
memoria *f* storage *(computer)*
meno di under *(less than)*
meno di, a short of
mensile monthly (adj)
mercantile merchant, trading (adj)
mercati *m* **esteri** overseas markets
mercato *m* market
mercato a termine forward market
mercato azionario stock market
mercato chiuso closed market
mercato controllato da un solo fornitore captive market
mercato delle materie prime commodity market
mercato interno domestic market
mercato libero open market
mercato nero black market
mercato prescelto target market
merce *f* goods, merchandise; commodity
merce a prezzo ridotto cut-price goods
merce non venduta returns
merce per la vendita al dettaglio retail goods
mese *m* **solare** calendar month
messaggero (-a) messenger *(courier)*
messaggio *m* message
metà *f* half
mezzi *mpl* facilities; means *(money)*
mezzi di comunicazione di massa mass media
mezzo (-a) half (adj)
millantato credito *m* false pretences
minoranza *f* minority
misura *f* **della redditività** measurement of profitability
misure di sicurezza safety precautions
modalità di pagamento mode of payment
modello *m* model *(style of product)*; scale model *(small copy)*
modulo *m* form
modulo di dichiarazione doganale customs declaration form
modulo per domanda di assunzione application form
molo *m* quay
mondiale worldwide (adj)
mondo *m* world
moneta *f* coin
moneta legale currency
moneta stabile stable currency
moneta straniera foreign currency/exchange
monetario (-a) monetary
monopolio *m* **perfetto** absolute monopoly
multa *f* fine
multare fine (v)
multinazionale *f* multinational
multiplo (-a) multiple (adj)
mutuare borrow
mutuatario *m* borrower
mutuo *m* loan
mutuo a breve scadenza short-term loan
mutuo a lunga scadenza long-term loan
mutuo garantito secured loan

N

nazionali, di dimensioni nationwide
nazione *f* **più favorita** most-favoured/favored nation
negoziare negotiate, deal
negoziato *m* negotiation(s)
negoziato salariale wage negotiations
negoziatore (-trice) negotiator
negoziazione *f* negotiation
negozio *m* shop, store
negozio a catena chain store
negozio appartenente ad una catena multiple store
negozio esente da tasse duty-free shop
netto (-a) net (adj)
nicchia *f* niche
noleggiare una macchina hire/rent a car
noleggio *m* **in blocco** block booking
nome *m* **del prodotto** brand name
nome di, a on behalf of
nominare appoint

norma *f* rule, standard
normale normal, regular, ordinary
normale usura e degrado fair wear and tear
norme *fpl* **di sicurezza** safety regulations
nota *f* note, banknote
nota di accredito credit note
nota di addebito debit note
notaio *m* notary public
notare mark
nullo (-a) null, void, not valid
numerare number
numeri *mpl* figures
numeri dispari odd numbers
numero *m* number, figure
numero d'ordine order number
numero dell'assegno cheque/check number
numero di fattura invoice number
numero di partita batch number
numero di riferimento reference number
numero minimo legale quorum
nuova ordinazione *f* reorder, repeat order

O

obbligatorio (-a) compulsory
obbligazione *f* bond; debenture
obbligazione al portatore bearer bond
obbligazione irredimibile irredeemable bond
obbligazioni *fpl* **'cartastraccia'** junk bonds
obbligazioni convertibii convertible loan stock
obiettivi *mpl* **di produzione** production targets
obiettivo (-a) objective (adj)
obiettivo *m* objective, target
obiettivo di vendita sales target
occasione *f* bargain, good buy
occuparsi di attend to, handle, deal with
occupato (-a) busy; engaged *(tel.)*
offerta *f* offer, bid
offerta d'appalto tender
offerta di propaganda introductory offer
offerta in busta chiusa sealed tenders
offerta per contanti cash offer
offerta premio premium offer
offerta pubblica d'acquisto takeover bid
offerta reale cash offer
offerte *fpl* **d'impiego** situations vacant
offrire offer *(to buy)*
oggettivo (-a) objective (adj)
omesso pagamento (di un debito) non-payment (of a debt)
onorare una cambiale honour/honor a bill
operazione *f* operation, deal
operazione chiavi in mano turnkey operation
opusculi *mpl* **pubblicitari** junk mail
opzione *f* **per l'acquisto** option to purchase
ora di accettazione check-in time
ora di chiusura closing time
ora di punta rush hour
ora lavorativa man-hour
ora, all' per hour
orario *m* timetable *(trains, etc.)*
orario d'apertura opening hours/time
orario d'ufficio office hours
orario pieno full-time
orario, in on time
ordinare order *(goods)*
ordinato (-a) on order
ordinazione *f* **rinnovata** reorder, repeat order
ordinazioni *fpl* **da evadere** outstanding orders
ordinazioni per corrispondenza mail-order
ordine *m* order
ordine arretrato back order
ordine bancario banker's order
ordine del giorno agenda
ordine di pagamento di valuta estera foreign money order
ordine inevaso back order, unfulfilled order
ordine ripetuto repeat order
ordine urgente rush order
ore *fpl* **d'ufficio** business hours
organigramma *m* organization chart
organizzare organize, plan; arrange *(meeting)*

originario (-a) original (adj)
origine *f* origin
ormeggiare berth
oscillare fluctuate
osservare comply with
ottenere obtain
ottenibile obtainable
ottenibile, non unobtainable

P

pacchetto *m* **rivendicativo** package deal
pacco *m* parcel, pack
paese *m* **d'origine** country of origin
paga *f* pay, salary
pagabile payable
pagabile alla consegna payable on delivery
pagabile anticipatamente payable in advance
pagabile su richiesta payable on demand
pagamenti *mpl* **mensili** monthly payments
pagamenti scaglionati staged payments
pagamento *m* payment, settlement
pagamento alla consegna cash on delivery (c.o.d.)
pagamento anticipato advance payment, prepayment
pagamento in acconto payment on account
pagamento in contanti payment in cash; spot cash
pagamento provvisiorio interim payment
pagamento tramite assegno payment by cheque/check
pagare pay; defray costs
pagare anticipatamente pay in advance
pagare in contanti pay cash
pagare un conto pay a bill
pagare una fattura pay/settle an invoice
pagare, far charge (v)
pagare meno, far undercharge
pagare troppo, far overcharge
pagato (-a) paid *(invoice)*
pagato (-a) in anticipo prepaid
pagato (-a), non outstanding, unpaid
pagatore (-trice) tardivo (-a) slow payer
pagherò *m* promissory note, IOU
pagina *f* page
Pagine Gialle yellow pages
paletta *f* pallet
paliquota *f* **d'imposta base** standard rate (of tax)
paragonabile comparable
paragonare compare
pareggiare un budget balance a budget
parenti *m* relations
parte *f* party *(legal)*
partecipazione *f* **azionaria** shareholding
partenze *fpl* departures
partita *f* **di merci** batch (of products)
partite *fpl* **visibili** visible trade
partner *m* **commerciale** trading partner
passaggio *m* **delle consegne** hand-over (n)
passare a switch over to
passare il tempo a spend (time)
passare in testa ad una coda jump the queue/line
passibile di liable to
passività *f* liabilities
passività correnti current liabilities
patrociniare sponsor (v)
patto *m* agreement; covenant
patto che, a provided that, providing
pedaggio *m* toll
pendente pending
pendolare *m/f* commuter
pensione *f* pension
pensione, andare in retire
per affari on business
per conto di on behalf of
percentuale *f* percentage; commission *(money)*
percentuale di crescita growth rate
percentuale per il servizio service charge
perdere miss *(train, plane)*
perdere dei soldi lose money
perdere un deposito forfeit a deposit
perdere un'ordinazione lose an order
perdita *f* loss *(not a profit)*; forfeiture
perdita d'esercizio trading loss
perdita sulla carta paper loss
perfetta sintonia *f* fine tuning

perfezionare un accordo implement an agreement
periferici *m* peripherals
periodo *m* period, term
periodo di massima attività peak period
periodo medio di permanenza di un prodotto shelf life of a product
perito *m* surveyor
perizia *f* survey, examination
permesso *m* **di lavoro** work permit
permesso di soggiorno residence permit
permuta *f* trade-in *(in exchange)*
permuta come pagamento parziale part exchange
personale *m* personnel
personale avventizio temporary staff
personale d'ufficio office staff
personale dirigente managerial staff
personale ridotto al minimo skeleton staff
pesare weigh
peso *m* weight
peso lordo gross weight
peso netto net weight
petrolio *m* oil *(petroleum)*
pezzo *m* **di ricambio** spare part
pianificazione *f* **a lunga scadenza** long-term planning
piano *m* floor, level; plan, project
piano di contingenza contingency plan
pianta *f* plan *(drawing)*
piccola cassa *f* petty cash
piccole imprese *f* small businesses
piccole spese *f* petty expenses
pieno (-a) full
PIL (prodotto interno lordo) GDP (gross domestic product)
planimetria *f* floor plan
plusvalenza *f* capital gains
PNL (prodotto nazionale lordo) GNP (gross national product)
politica *f* policy
politica della determinazione dei prezzi pricing policy
polizza *f* policy
polizza contro tutti i rischi all-risks policy
polizza di assicurazione insurance/assurance policy
polizza di carico bill of lading
polizza provvisoria cover note
portafoglio *m* portfolio
portare carry, transport
portare a termine complete (v)
portare qu. in tribunale take so. to court
portatile portable
portatore (-trice) *f* bearer
portineria *f* reception (desk)
porto *m* port, harbour/harbor; carriage
porto assegnato carriage/freight forward
porto d'imbarco port of embarkation
porto di scalo port of call
porto pagato carriage/postage paid
posporre hold over
possedere possess
possibile acquirente prospective buyer
possibile, se non è failing that
possibilità *f* **di mercato** market opportunities
posta *f* post, mail
posta aerea airmail
posta elettronica electronic mail, e-mail
posta in partenza outgoing mail
postdatare backdate
posticipare put back *(later)*
posto *m* appointment, job
posto chiave key post
posto di lavoro post *(job);* place of work
posto vacante vacancy *(for job)*
potere *m* power, control
potere d'acquisto purchasing power
pranzo *m* **d'affari** business lunch
pratica *f* dossier, file
pratica, fare train, study (v)
pratiche *fpl* **restrittive** restrictive practices
preavviso *m* notice *(time allowed)*
preconfezionare prepack(age) (v)
predere parte in enter into *(discussion)*
prefisso *m* **telefonico** dialling code
prelevare withdraw *(money)*
premio *m* bonus
premio addizionale additional premium
premio di assicurazione insurance premium

premio di merito merit award, merit bonus
prendere a prestito borrow
prendere il controllo di take over
prendere in affitto rent, hire
prendere in consegna un carico di merce accept delivery of a shipment
prenotatione *f* **anticipata** advance booking
prenotare book (v)
prenotare più di quanti siano disponibili overbook
prenotazione *f* reservation
preoccupazione *f* concern, worry
preparare lo schema di un contratto draft a contract
prescizione *f* statute of limitations
presentare present, show *(a document)*
presentare un conto render an account
presentare un effetto per l'accettazione present a bill for acceptance
presentare una controrichiesta counter-claim (v)
presentarsi per un colloquio di lavoro report for an interview
presente present (adj) *(being there)*
presidente *m* chairman *(of company)*
presidente e amministratore delegato chairman and managing director
presso care of (c/o)
prestare lend, advance
prestatore (-trice) lender
prestito *m* loan
prestito a termine term loan
prevedere forecast
preventivo *m* estimate *(quote)*
previdenza *f* **sociale** social security
previsione *f* forecast
previsione della necessità di manodopera manpower forecasting
previsione di vendita sales forecast
previsioni *fpl* **del flusso di cassa** cash flow forecast
prezzi *mpl* **concorrenziali** keen prices
prezzi correnti common pricing
prezzi equi fair price
prezzi franco magazzino price ex warehouse
prezzi franco stabilimento price ex works
prezzo *m* price
prezzo al dettaglio retail price
prezzo al rivenditore trade price
prezzo allineato competitive price
prezzo concordato agreed price
prezzo d'entrata threshold price
prezzo d'offerta supply price
prezzo del coperto cover charge
prezzo del trasporto transport/haulage costs
prezzo di chiusura closing price
prezzo di fabbrica factory price
prezzo di fattura invoice price
prezzo di listino list price
prezzo di permuta trade-in price
prezzo di sostegno support price
prezzo eccessivo overcharge (n)
prezzo franco delivered price
prezzo intero full price
prezzo massimo ceiling price
prezzo medio average price
prezzo per contanti cash price
prezzo per merce pronta spot price
prezzo ridottissimo rock-bottom prices
prezzo ridotto cut price
prezzo scontato discount price
prezzo sotto costo cost price
prezzo stabile firm price
prezzo stabilito set price
prezzo tutto compreso all-in price
prezzo unitario unit price
prezzo, a basso economical, cheap
prezzo, ad alto highly-priced
primaria sul mercato, azienda *f* market leader *(company)*
primato *m* record *(best)*
primo ad entrare primo ad uscire first in first out
principale chief, principal (adj)
principio *m* principle
privatizzare privatize
privilegio *m* lien
procura *f* power of attorney
procurarsi fondi secure funds
procuratore (-trice) attorney
prodotti *mpl* **che si fanno concorrenza** competing products
prodotti con etichetta propria own label goods
prodotti di seconda qualità seconds

prodotto *m* product, article *(item)*
prodotto finito end product
prodotto interno lordo gross domestic product
prodotto nazionale lordo gross national product
prodotto per il mercato di massa mass market product
prodotto-guida *m* **del mercato** market leader *(product)*
produrre manufacture
produrre macchine in serie mass-produce cars
produttore (-trice) manufacturer
produzione *f* production, output
produzione in eccesso overproduction
produzione in serie mass production
produzione nazionale domestic production
professionista *m* professional, expert
proficuo (-a) profitable
profitto *m* earnings, profit
proforma, (fattura) pro forma (invoice)
progettare plan, design (v)
progettazione *f* design
progettazione del prodotto product design
progetto *m* project, plan
progetto pilota pilot scheme
programma *f* (computer) program
programma aziendale corporate plan
programmare timetable (v)
programmazione *f* **economica** economic planning
prolungamento *m* extension *(making longer)*
prolungare extend *(make longer)*
promozione *f* promotion *(to better job; publicity)*
promuovere promote *(give better job; advertize)*
pronta cassa *f* ready cash
pronto (-a) ready
proporre offer *(to buy)*
proposito *m* aim
proposta *f* **unica di vendita** unique selling point/proposition
proprietà *f* ownership
proprietà immobiliare real estate
proprietà privata private property
proprietario (-a) owner, proprietor
proprietario legittimo rightful owner
prospettive *f* prospects
prospetto *m* prospectus
protesta *f* complaint
protestare complain *(about)*
protestare contro qc. protest against sth.
prova *f* test
prova, in on approval
provare test
proventi *m* **da partite invisibili** invisible earnings
provvedere di generi alimentari cater for
provvedimenti *m* **fiscali** fiscal measures
pubbliche relazioni *f* public relations
pubblicità *f* publicity; advertisement, commercial *(TV)*
pubblicità a mezzo posta direct-mail advertising
pubblicità di un prodotto product advertising
pubblicizzare publicize, promote
pubblicizzare un nuovo prodotto promote a new product
punta *f* peak
punta, non di off-peak
punto *m* point
punto di pareggio fra costi e ricavi breakeven point
punto di riferimento benchmark
punto di vendita point of sale
punto morto deadlock
punto per la dichiarazine doganale d'entrata customs entry point
puntuale punctual, on time

Q

quadri *m* **direttivi** management team
quadri intermedi middle management
qualificarsi qualify as
qualificato (-a) qualified, skilled
qualificazioni *f* **professionali** professional qualifications
qualità *f* **scadente** poor quality
qualità superiore top quality
quantitativo *m* quantity
quarto *m* quarter *(25%)*
querelante *m/f* plaintiff

questione *f* matter *(to be discussed)*, item *(on agenda)*
quota *f* quota; rate, price
quota d'ammortamento depreciation rate
quota d'iscrizione fee *(admission)*
quota di mercato market share
quotare quote, estimate costs
quotazione *f* quotation, quote, estimate *(of cost)*

R

raccogliere collect *(fetch)*
raccogliere fondi raise (v)
raccoglitore (-trice) collector
raccomandare recommend
raccomandata *f* registered letter
raddoppiare double (v)
raduno *m* **dei venditori** sales conference
raggiungere un obiettivo meet a target
raggruppare group, bracket together
ragioniere (-a) bookkeeper
rapporto *m* record, report; ratio
rapporto corso/utili price/earnings ratio
rapporto di indebitamento gearing
rappresentante *m/f* representative, agent, salesman
rappresentante commissionario (-a) commission rep
rappresentante esclusivo (-a) sole agent
rappresentare represent
rappresentare qu. deputize for so.
rata *f* instalment
realizzare realize *(sell for money)*
realizzare beni realize property
reazione *f* response
recapito *m* address
recentissimo (-a) latest
reclamare complain (about)
reclamizzare un nuovo prodotto advertise a new product
reclamo *m* complaint, claim
redditività *f* profitability, making a profit
redditività dei costi cost-effectiveness
redditizio (-a) cost-effective, profitable
reddito *m* income, revenue
reddito da dividendi dividend yield
reddito da investimenti investment income
reddito dell'investimento return on investment
reddito effettivo real income/wages
reddito fisso fixed income
reddito imponibile taxable income
reddito netto net income/salary
reddito sugli investimenti return on investment
regalare give *(as gift)*
regalo *m* gift, present
registrare enter, record, write in
registrazione *f* registration
registrazione a credito credit entry
registrazione a debito debit entry
registrazione di storno contra entry
registro *m* register, official list
regolamentazione *f* **dei prezzi** price controls
regolamenti *m* regulations
regolare regular, normal, ordinary
regolarizzare regulate *(by law)*
regresso *m* downturn
relativo (-a) a relating to
relazione *f* **annuale al bilancio** annual report
relazione sull'avanzamento progress report
rendere yield (v) *(interest)*
rendere conto account for
rendere saturo il mercato saturate the market
rendersi conto di realize *(understand)*
rendiconti *m* **annuali** annual accounts
rendimento *m* return, yield
rendita *f* yield (on investment)
reparto *m* department *(shop/office)*
reparto contabilità accounts department
reparto esportazioni export department
rescindere un accordo terminate an agreement
residenza *f* residence
resoconto *m* account
resoconto dettagliato detailed account
resoconto mensile monthly statement

respingere refuse, reject, turn down; bounce *(cheque/check)*
responsabile (di) responsible (for)
responsabile per liable for
responsabilità *f* **contrattuale** contractual liability
responsabilità limitata limited liability
responsabilità limitata, a Ltd (limited company)
restare remain, be left
restituire give back, return
restituire, da non disposable
restringere tighten up on
restrizione *f* endorsement *(on insurance)*
retribuire remunerate
retribuzione *f* remuneration; pay, salary
retribuzione a cottimo piece rate
retribuzione a ore hourly rate
rettifica *f* correction, amendment
revisionare service *(a machine)*
revisione *f* service *(of machine)*
revisione contabile audit
revisione dello stipendio salary review
revisione esterna external audit
revisione interna internal audit
revisore (-a) ufficiale dei conti auditor
revisore (-a) esterno (-a) external auditor
revoca *f* **di una nomina** cancellation of an appointment
revocare revoke
riaddestrare retrain
riapplicare reapply
ribasso *m* drop
ricavi *mpl* **netti** net sales
ricavo *m* return, recipts
ricavo nullo nil return
ricerca *f* research
ricerca di mercato sui bisogni dei consumatori consumer research
ricerca e sviluppo research and development
ricercatore (-trice) researcher
ricevere receive
ricevimento *m* receipt *(receiving)*
ricevuta *f* receipt *(piece of paper)*
ricevuta in duplicato duplicate (of a) receipt
richiedere request (v)
richiesta *f* inquiry, request; demand
richiesta stagionale seasonal demand
richiesta, su on request
richieste *fpl* requirements
riciclare launder *(money)*
ricollocare reappoint
riconoscere un sindacato recognize a union
ricorrere a consulenza legale take legal advice
ricorrere in appello appeal (v) *(against a decision)*
ricorso *m* appeal *(against a decision)*
ricuperare recover *(get sth. back)*
ricuperare salvage (v)
ricuperare un debito collect a debt
ricupero *m* recovery *(getting sth. back)*; salvage
ricupero di crediti debt collection
ridurre reduce, knock down *(price)*
ridurre il valore write down *(assets)*
ridurre le spese cut down on expenses
ridurre proporzionalmente scale down
ridurre un prezzo reduce a price
riduzione *f* **delle spese** retrenchment
riferimento a, fare refer *(to item)*
riferire report (v)
riferirsi refer *(to item)*
rifinanziamento *m* **(di un prestito)** restructuring of a loan
rifiutare refuse, reject, turn down
rifiuto *m* refusal
rifornire restock *(goods)*
rifugio *m* **fiscale** tax haven
riguardante regarding
riguardare apply to *(affect)*
riguardo per, senza regardless of
rilasciare release *(make public)*
rilevamento *m* takeover
rimandare una lettera al mittente return a letter to sender
rimanenze *f* **iniziali** opening stock
rimanere indietro fall behind
rimborsabile repayable
rimborsare pay back, refund
rimborso *m* refund
rimessa *f* remittance
rimunerativo (-a) profitable
ringraziamento *m* vote of thanks

rinnovare un contratto d'affitto renew a lease
rinnovare una cambiale renew a bill of exchange
rinnovo *m* renewal
rinunciare waive
rinunciare ad un'azione abandon an action
rinviare return, send back; postpone
rinvio *m* return *(sending back)*; postponement
rinvio di pagamento deferment of payment
riordinare reorder (v)
riordinazione *f* reorder
riorganizzare reorganize
riorganizzazione *f* reorganization
ripagare repay; fix *(mend)*
ripartire un rischio spread a risk
ripartizione *f* breakdown *(items on list)*
ripetere un ordine repeat an order
riportare a nuovo carry forward
riprendere le negoziazioni resume negotiations
riprendersi recover *(get better)*
ripresa *f* recovery *(getting better)*
riprodurre reproduce, copy
risarcimento *m* **di danni** compensation for damage
risarcire make good *(a defect, loss)*
risarcire qu. per una perdita indemnify so. for a loss
riscattare surrender *(insurance)*
riscatto (di un prestito) redemption (of a loan)
riscatto *m* surrender *(of insurance policy)*
rischiare risk (v) *(money)*
rischio finanziario exposure, financial risk
rischioso (-a) risky
riscossione *f* **delle imposte** tax collection
riservare (un tavolo) reserve (a table)
riservato (-a) confidential
riserve *fpl* **occulte** hidden reserves
risorse *f* resources
risorse finanziarie financial resources
risorse naturali natural resources
risparmiare save (v)
rispettare una scadenza meet a deadline
rispondere answer, reply (v)
rispondere a qu., che deve responsible to so.
rispondere a qu., dover report to so.
risposta *f* answer, reply
ristrutturare restructure
risultati *mpl* results
ritaglio *m* swatch
ritardare delay (v)
ritardo *m* delay, hold-up
ritardo, in late (adv)
ritenuta *f* **d'acconto** withholding tax
ritirare withdraw *(an offer)*
ritiro *m* collection *(of goods)*
ritorno *m* return *(going back)*
riunione *f* meeting
riunione del consiglio di amministrazione board meeting
riuscire succeed *(do well)*
riuscire a manage to
rivalutazione *f* appreciation *(in value)*
rivendicare claim *(insurance)*
rivendita *f* resale
rivenditore (-trice) stockist
rivista *f* magazine
rompersi break down *(of machine)*
RS (ricerca e sviluppo) R&D (research and development)

S

S. E. & O (salvo errori e omissioni) e. & o.e. (errors and omissions excepted)
saggio *m* sample *(part)*
sala *f* **riunioni** conference room
sala transiti transit lounge
salario *m* salary, pay, wage
saldare un conto settle an account
saldi *mpl* sale, sales *(at a low price)*
saldi per inventario stocktaking sale
saldo *m* balance; sale *(at a low price)*
saldo a metà prezzo half-price sale
saldo da riportare balance brought down/forward
saldo di cassa cash balance
saldo dovuto balance due to us
saldo in banca bank balance
saldo riportato balance carried down/forward
salvaguadare save, back up *(computer file)*
salvaguardia *f* safeguard

salvare salvage
salvo errori e omssioni errors and omissions excepted
salvo vista e verifica on approval
saturazione *m* glut
sbarrare un assegno cross a cheque/check
sborsare pay out
scadenza *f* expiry
scadere fall due, expire
scaduto (-a) overdue
scaffalatura *f* shelving *(shelves)*
scaffale *m* shelf
scaglionare stagger
scala *f* scale
scala temporale time scale
scala ridotta, in small-scale
scambiare con exchange, swap (v) *(one thing for another)*
scambio *m* swap, barter
scappatoia *f* **fiscale** tax shelter
scaricare unload *(goods)*
scaricare della merce in un porto land goods at a port
scarsità *f* shortage
scarto *m* reject
scatola *f* **di cartone** cardboard box
scegliere choose
scelta *f* choice *(items to choose from)*
scheda *m* filing card
schedario *m* card index; filing cabinet
schema *m* **del ciclo** flow chart
sciolto (-a) loose
scioperante *m/f* striker
scioperare strike (v)
sciopero *m* strike
sconti *mpl* **al rivenditore** trade terms
sconto *m* discount
sconto ai rivenditori trade discount
sconto all'ingrosso wholesale discount
sconto cassa cash discount
sconto del valore attuale discounted cash flow
sconto di base basic discount
sconto per pagamento in contanti cash discount
sconto sul quantitativo quantity/volume discount
sconto di, fare uno deduct, take off
scoperto *m* overdraft
scopo *m* aim
scopo di lucro, senza non profit-making
scorrettamente incorrectly
scorretto (-a) incorrect
scorte *fpl* stock *(of goods)*
scritto (-a) a mano handwritten
scrittura *f* **contabile** entry *(writing)*
scrivania *f* desk
scuola *f* **per segretarie d'azienda** secretarial college
secondo under *(according to)*
secondo (-a) second (adj)
seconda mano, di secondhand
sede *f* head office
sede centrale main office, headquarters
sede legale registered office
segnale *m* **di linea occupata** engaged tone
segretario (-a) secretary
segretario (-a) personale personal assistant
segretario (-a) temporaneo (-a) temp
segretaria *f* **telefonica** answering machine
segreto (-a) secret (adj)
seguito a, in further to
semestre *m* half-year
sequestrare seize
sequestro *m* seizure
serratura *f* lock
servire un cliente serve a customer
servizi *mpl* facilities
servizi di elaborazione elettronica computer services
servizio *m* service
servizio di marketing marketing department
servizio in camera room service
servizio pacchi postali parcel post
servizio scadente poor service
servizio segreteria telefonica answering service
servizio sollecito prompt service
settimana, alla per week
settimanale weekly
settore *m* sector, branch
sezione *f* department *(in office)*
sicurezza *f* safety
sicurezza del posto di lavoro job security
sicurezza dell'impiego security of employment

sicurezza di possesso security of tenure
sigillare seal, attach a seal
siglare initial (v)
sindacalista *m/f* trade unionist
sindacato *m* trade union
sinistro (-a) left *(not right)*
sistema *m* **di acquisti a rate** hire purchase
sistema elettronico di elaborazione computer system
situazione *f* situation
situazione permettente di trattare bargaining position
smentita *f* disclaimer
società *f* company
società controllante holding company; parent company
società di capitali a responsabilità limitata limited liability company (Ltd)
Società di capitali a sottoscrizione pubblica (SpA) Public Limited Company (Plc)
società di factoring factor *(company)*
società di mezza misura middle-sized company
società sorella sister company
socio (-a) associate, partner (n)
socio accomandante sleeping partner
soddisfacente acceptable
soddisfare satisfy *(customer)*
soddisfare una richiesta satisfy/meet a demand
soddisfazione *f* **dei clienti** customer satisfaction
soggetto (-a) a subject to
soggetto (-a) a condizioni conditional on
soldi *mpl* money
soldi in anticipo money up front
soldi, fare make money
sollecitare un ordine solicit orders
sollecito *m* follow up
solo (-a) sole
solvente solvent (adj)
solvibilità *f* solvency
somma *f* sum *(of money)*
sondaggio *m* check; sampling
sondaggio d'opinione opinion poll
soprappiù *m* surplus
sorpassare exceed
sorvegliare supervise
sospendere suspend; close down
sospendere le trattative break off negotiations
sospensione *m* **dei pagamenti** suspension of payments
sostenere back up, support
sostenere spese incur costs
sostituto (-a) deputy
sostituzione *f* replacement *(item)*
sotto contratto under contract
sotto nuova gestione under new management
sottoporre refer *(pass to so.)*
sottoprodotto *m* spinoff
sottoscritto (-a) undersigned (n)
sottoscrivere una polizza take out a policy
sottrarsi al pagamento delle tasse evade tax
sovraccarico *m* **di scorte** overstocks
sovrapprezzo *m* surcharge
sovvenzione *f* subsidy
spartire share, divide among
spazio *m* space, room
spazio pubblicitario advertising space
specifica *f* specification
spedire dispatch, send; transport, ship
spedizione *f* consignment, dispatch, sending
spedizione marittima shipping
spedizione per espresso express delivery
spedizioniere *m* **marittimo** shipper
spendere spend *(money)*
spendere oltre il proprio budget overspend one's budget
spesa *f* expense, cost
spesa compresa inclusive charge
spesa non autorizzata unauthorized expenditure
spesa postale postage
spese *fpl* costs, expenditure, outgoings
spese bancarie bank charges
spese conto capitali capital expenditure
spese d'amministrazione administrative expenses
spese d'ammissione admission charges

spese d'entrata admission charges
spese d'esercizio operating expenses; running costs/expenses
spese di avviamento start-up costs
spese di magazzinagio storage cost
spese di manutenzione handling charges
spese di scarico landing charges
spese di trasporto freight costs
spese generali overhead costs, running costs, overheads
spese generali di produzione manufacturing overheads
spese impreviste incidental expenses
spese postali e imballo postage and packing (p & p)
spese supplementari additional charges, extras
spese trasporto merci via aerea air freight charges, rates
spiccioli *m* loose change, cash
spionaggio *m* **industriale** industrial espionage
sponsorizzare sponsor (v)
sponsorizzazione *f* sponsorship
sportello *m* **di cassa** cash desk
spot *m* (TV) commercial
sprecare waste *(use too much)*
spreco *m* waste, wastage
stabilire establish; arrange *(meeting)*
stabilire il prezzo fix a price
stabilizzarsi level off, level out
stagione *f* season *(time of year)*
stagione, fuori off-season
stagnante slack (adj)
stampante *f* printer *(machine)*
stampante a matrice dot-matrix printer
stampare print out
stampato *m* printout
standard standard, normal, stock
standista *m/f* exhibitor
stanziamento *m* **promozionale** advertising/promotional budget
stare al passo con la richiesta keep up with the demand
stato *m* state *(condition)*
stato giuridico legal status
stazione *f* **ferroviaria** rail station
sterlina *f* (pound) sterling
stima *f* estimate, valuation
stima, fare una nuova reassess
stimare estimate
stipendiato (-a) salaried
stipendio *m* salary
stipendio iniziale starting salary
stipendio interessante attractive salary
stipendio lordo gross salary
stipulare stipulate
stipulare un contratto draw up a contract/an agreement
stiva *f* hold *(on ship)*
stornare una registrazione contra an entry
strada *f* road
straordinario (-a) extraordinary, exceptional
strategia *f* **commerciale** business strategy
strozzatura *f* bottleneck
strumento *m* implement, tool; instrument *(document)*
strumento negoziabile negotiable instrument
strumento non negoziabile non-negotiable instrument
studio *m* study, survey, examination
studio della fattibilità feasibility report
subaffittare sublet, sublease
subaffitto *m* sublease
subappaltatore (-trice) subcontractor
subappalto *m* subcontract
successo, avere succeed, be successful
successo, che non ha unsuccessful
successo, di successful
suono *m* **di linea libera** dialling tone
superare exceed
superficie *f* **di pavimento** floor space
supervisione, di supervisory
supervisore *m* supervisor
supplementare supplementary (adj)
sussidiare subsidize
sussidiario (-a) subsidiary (adj)
sussidio *m* subsidy
svalutare devalue, depreciate, lose value
svalutazione *f* devaluation, loss of value, depreciation; write-off
svendere sell off
svendere delle merci sul mercato dump goods on a market

svendite *fpl* **di fine stagione** end of season sale
sviluppo *m* **economico** economic development
svincolo *m* **doganale** customs clearance
svolgere esercizio d'impresa carry on a business

T

tabella *f* **fissa dei prezzi** fixed scale of charges
tabulato *m* computer printout
taccheggiare shoplifting
taccheggiatore (-trice) shoplifter
taglia *f* size
taglia forte, di outsize
tagliare cut
tagliare i prezzi slash prices
taglio *m* cut
tangente *f* bribe
tardi late (adv)
tariffa *f* tariff, scale of charges; rate, price; fare
tariffa en vigore going rate
tariffa ridotta cheap rate
tariffe *fpl* **delle inserzioni pubblicitarie** advertising rates
tassa *f* tax (v)
tassa di base basic tax
tassa di registrazione registration fee
tassa esclusa exclusive of tax
tassare tax (v)
tassazione *f* taxation
tasso *m* rate, price
tasso d'inflazione rate of inflation
tasso d'interesse interest rate
tasso di cambio exchange rate, rate of exchange
tasso di cambio sfavorevole unfavourable/unfavorable exchange rate
tasso fisso di cambio fixed exchange rate
tasso fluttuante di cambio floating exchange rates
tasso ridotto reduced rate
tasso ufficiale di sconto bank base rate
tastiera *f* **numerica** numeric keypad
tastierista *m/f* keyboarder
tasto *m* key *(on keyboard)*
tasto delle maiuscole shift key
tasto di comando control key
telefonata *f* telephone call
telefonata a carico del ricevente reverse charge call, transferred charge call, collect call
telefonata in arrivo incoming call
telefonata urbana local call
telefono *m* **a gettoni** pay phone
telefono a schede card phone
telefono per conferenze conference phone
Telemat *m* card phone
televisione *f* **a circuito chiuso** closed circuit TV
tempo, per molto long, for a long time
tendenza *f* tendency, trend
tendenza di mercato market trends
tenere hold; stock *(goods)*
tenere in efficienza maintain *(keep going)*
tenere una seduta hold a meeting/ discussion
terminal *m* **per container** container terminal
terminare terminate, expire
termine *m* termination, expiration, end; date
termine *m* **ultimo** deadline, closing date
termine, a breve short-term
termine, a lungo long-term
termine, a medio medium-term
terra *f*, **terreno** *m* land
territorio *m* territory *(of salesman)*
terza persona *f* third party
tessera *f* ticket, season ticket
tessera prelievo contanti cash card
testimone *m/f* witness
tetto *m* **dei prezzi** price ceiling
tirare sul prezzo bargain (v)
tirocinante *m/f* trainee
titoli *mpl* securities
titoli di stato government bonds
titolo *m* share
togliere l'embargo *m* lift an embargo
togliere la seduta close a meeting
tonnellaggio *m* tonnage
tonnellata *f* ton
totale *m* **corrente** running total
totale generale grand total
totale parziale subtotal
tradurre translate

traduttore (-trice) translator
traduzione *f* translation
traente *m* drawer *(person)*
trafficare trade
transazione a pronti spot purchase
transito *m* transit
trarre vantaggio da benefit from, capitalize on
trasferimento *m* **di capitali** transfer of funds
trasportare transport, ship
trasportare merci via aerea airfreight
trasportatore *m* carrier, haulage company
trasporto *m* transport, carriage, freight
trasporto marittimo shipment
trasporto merci via aerea air freight
trasporto su strada road transport
tratta *f* draft *(money)*
tratta a vista sight draft
trattare process *(deal with)*
trattario *m* drawee
trattenere hold up *(delay)*
tredicesimo *m* Christmas bonus
tribunale *m* tribunal; law court
Tribunale Arbitrale arbitration board, arbitration tribunal
tribunale del lavoro industrial tribunal
trimestrale quarterly (adj)
trimestre quarter *(three months)*
triplice copia, in in triplicate
turno *m* shift *(team of workers)*
tutte le spese pagate all expenses paid

U

UE (Unione Europea) European Union (EU)
uffici *mpl* **in affitto** offices to let
ufficiale *m* **di dogana** customs official
ufficio *m* office; department
ufficio acquisti buying department
ufficio assistenza service department
ufficio assistenza ai clienti customer service department
ufficio cambio bureau de change
ufficio indennità claims department
ufficio reclami complaints department
ufficio senza divisioni open-plan office
ufficio vendite sales department
ufficioso (-a) unofficial
unico (-a) sole
unico proprietario sole owner
uniforme uniform, across-the-board
Unione *m* **Europea (UE)** European Union (EU)
unire join
unità *f* unit
unità a dischi magnetici disk drive
uomo *m* **d'affari** businessman
usare use
usato (-a) used, secondhand
uso *m* use
usuale usual, normal, standard
usurpare un brevetto infringe a patent
usurpazione *f* **di brevetto** infringement of patent
utenti *m* **finali** end users
utile (adj) useful
utile *m* profit
utile al lordo delle imposte profit before tax, pretax profit
utile al netto delle imposte profit after tax, after-tax profit
utile d'esercizio operating profit, trading profit
utile lordo gross profit
utile netto clear profit, net profit
utili *mpl* **ipotetici** paper profits
utili societari corporate profits
utilizzazione *f* utilization

V

vaglia *f* money order
vaglia postale postal order
valere be worth
valido (-a), essere be in force
valore *m* value
valore contabile book value
valore di riscatto surrender value
valore di sostituzione replacement value
valore dichiarato declared value
valore nominale par value; face value, nominal value
valore patrimoniale asset value
valore patrimoniale netto net assets, net worth

valore totale della fattura total invoice value
valuta *f* currency
valuta debole soft currency
valuta estera foreign currency, foreign exchange
valuta solida hard currency
valutare value; estimate
valutare i costi evaluate costs
valutazione *f* valuation; estimate, calculation
valutazione approssimativa rough estimate
variazioni *f* **stagionali** seasonal variations
vario (-a) miscellaneous
vecchio (-a) old
veicolo *m* **per merci pesanti** heavy goods vehicle
vendere sell, market
vendere a minor prezzo di un concorrente undercut a rival
vendere a termine sell forward
vendere al dettaglio retail *(goods)*
vendere all'asta auction
vendere sotto costo discount
vendersi a retail at, sell for *(a price)*
vendita *f* sale, selling
vendita a domicilio house-to-house selling
vendita coatta forced sale
vendita (di merce) sotto costo distress sale
vendita diretta tramite corrispondenza direct mail
vendita per contanti cash sale
vendita porta a porta door-to-door selling
vendita sotto costo dumping
vendita, in for sale, on sale
vendite *fpl* sales
vendite basse low sales
vendite interne domestic sales
vendite nazionali home sales
vendite presunte estimated sales
vendite previste projected sales
vendite sul mercato interno home sales
venditore (-trice/-a) salesman; vendor
venditori *mpl* sales people
venduto (-a), essere be sold, change hands
venire a un compromesso compromise (v)
verbale *m* **(di assemblea)** minutes *(of meeting)*
verbale, mettere a minute (v)
verbalizzare minute (v)
verifica *f* verification; control *(check)*
verificare verify
verificare i conti audit the accounts
versamento *m* **d'acconto** down payment
versare soldi deposit (v)
vertenza *f* **di lavoro** labour/labor disputes
veto a una decisione, porre il veto (v) a decision
vetrina *f* shop window
vice-amministratore (-trice) delegato (-a) deputy managing director
vicedirettore (-trice) assistant manager
vie *f* **legali** legal proceedings
vietare ban
vigilanza *f* supervision
vincere un contratto win a contract
violare la legge break the law
virgola *f* **decimale** decimal point
visita *f* **a freddo** cold call
visto *m* visa
visto consolare di transito transit visa
visto consolare multiplo multiple entry visa
visto d'ingresso entry visa
volo *m* flight
volo a lungo raggio long-haul flight
volo di coincidenza connecting flight
volo di linea scheduled flight
volume *m* amount, quantity, volume
volume d'affari sales figures, turnover
volume degli scambi commerciali volume of trade/business
voto *m* **decisivo** casting vote
voto per delega proxy vote
vuoto (-a) empty (adj)

W, X, Y, Z

zona *f* **di libero scambio** free trade zone

SWITZERLAND
AUSTRIA
HUNG
VALLE D'AOSTA
ALTO
ADIGE
Trento
FRIULI-
VENEZIA
GIULIA
Aosta
SLOVENIA
FRANCE
Milano
Udine
Torino
LOMBARDIA
VENETO
Trieste
Venezia
PIEMONTE
CROATIA
EMILIA-ROMAGNA
Genova
LIGURIA
Bologna
Firenze
Ancona
TOSCANA
MARCHE
Perugia
UMBRIA
Corsica
Pescara
ROMA
ADRIATIC
ABRUZZI
LAZIO
MOLISE
Campobasso
CAMPANIA
Bar
PUGLIA
SARDEGNA
Napoli
Potenza
BASILICATA
Cagliari
MEDITERRANEAN
CALABRIA
Catanzaro
Palermo
Reggio Cal.
SICILIA
Catania
ALGERIA
TUNISIA